Charities, Trading and the Law

Second Edition

Stephen Lloyd
Senior Partner & Head of Charity and Social Enterprise,
Bates Wells & Braithwaite

Alice Faure Walker
Consultant, Bates Wells & Braithwaite

Bill Lewis, Lawrence Simanowitz, Mairead O'Reilly, Alana Lowe-Petraske
Bates Wells & Braithwaite

JORDANS

Published by
Jordan Publishing Limited
21 St Thomas Street
Bristol BS1 6JS

British Library Cataloguing-in-Publication Data

A catalogue record for this book is available from the British Library.

ISBN 978 1 84661 106 3

Typeset by Letterpart Ltd, Reigate, Surrey

Printed in Great Britain by CPI Antony Rowe, Chippenham, Wiltshire

Charities, Trading and the Law

Second Edition

PREFACE

When I wrote the first edition of this book in 1994, charities had only recently begun to seek to diversify their income sources by setting up separate trading companies. Charities had been trading in fulfilment of their primary purposes, of course, for generations. By now, 15 years later, the trend that had begun in the 1980s is very marked. More than 50% of charities' income in England and Wales now comes through the sale of goods and the provision of services – in many cases through operating contracts with the state, local government or the health service.

The law that affects trading in this period has changed very considerably as well. The Companies Acts have been overhauled; the tax laws are constantly being refined – but remain remarkably benign; issues of state aid and public procurement were much less prevalent in 1994 than they are now – many charities have to face these issues in engaging with the state; and while in 1994 the internet had hardly got under way, trading on the internet is a major activity which charities, of course, engage in as well. The internet has also had a major impact for charities on the whole question of brands, and registering their brands through trade marking: here, too, there have been changes, as prior to 1994 it was very difficult for charities to register trade marks. There is also much more regulation of trading generally. However, charities now have access to a great deal more guidance on trading – we refer throughout this book to guidance from the Charity Commission and HMRC, which is accessible to all via the internet.

When we started rewriting this book, the implosion of the world's financial system had not started. Its impact will undoubtedly be felt for years to come and charities will be greatly affected by it. In some areas charities may find that a benefit. The state is having to pump prime the economy and there will no doubt be large numbers of public work schemes set in train in order to help alleviate unemployment, which charities will bid to run. Charities that contract with the state already will, with luck, be able to continue to do so – depending on the state of the nation's finances. But those charities that depend on public fundraising for their income will almost certainly be grievously hit. They will have to try and diversify their income sources, and trading may be one way for them to do so, if they have something that is worth selling and if people want to buy it.

However, there may be one other possible silver lining for charities in the black cloud that currently envelops western capitalism. The values that charities stand for: of justice, of community, of selflessness, may be seen now as having greater relevance. Charities have been at the forefront of trying to ensure that trading is done ethically – for example, the Fairtrade Foundation. Charities have also been encouraging people to think about how their money is invested and whether that investment allies with the investor's personal beliefs. Hence, the whole development of ethical investment. It is striking that the Co-operative Bank is one of the few British banking institutions that has emerged the stronger from the tumult of the last 18 months. Its business and investment strategies must now be commanding wider respect.

I would like to thank all my colleagues who helped on the rewriting of this book, principally Bill Lewis, Lawrence Simanowitz, Mairead O'Reilly and Alana Lowe-Petraske, but also Malcolm Robson, Martin Gunson, Julian Blake, Christine Rigby, Louise McCartney, Rupert Earle, Sean Egan, Peter Bohm and Augustus Della-Porta. And as well as all of those, I thank my co-author Alice Faure Walker, who has done the vast bulk of the rewrite in her inimitable careful, considered and wonderful way. Writing a book today is not easy, because of the constant flow of new information through the internet. It also means there is a huge amount of information to absorb and process. Alice has done that and I am hugely grateful to her for it.

We also owe a debt of thanks to those outside BWB who have helped with this book. First, to Hilary Blume, of the Charities Advisory Trust, who inspired the first edition of this book in 1994, and who published it, together with the Directory of Social Change. We would also like to thank Lekha Klouda of the Association of Charity Shops, Dr Liz Philpots of the Association of Medical Research Charities, Greyham Dawes of Horwath Clark Whitehill and Mike Parkinson of Oxfam, who have assisted with various specific queries. Alice is particularly grateful to the charitable organisations in Harrogate and North Yorkshire whom she has pestered for information about their trading practices! We would also like to pay tribute to the extraordinarily varied and inspiring work done by charities throughout England and Wales to raise funds for their beneficiaries through trading in good times and bad.

Finally, this book deals with the law in England and Wales. We should emphasise that it constitutes general guidance only and that legal advice should be taken on specific issues, and that any errors are our own.

Stephen Lloyd
January 2009

CONTENTS

Chapter 1

INTRODUCTION

CAN CHARITIES TRADE?

1.1   There is a popular misconception that charities cannot trade, that they are debarred by law from trading. This is wrong. Provided they operate within the rules described in this book, charities are able to carry on a trade.

1.2   And they do. Reflect on the many ways in which charities (including their associated trading companies) actually do sell goods or supply services: organising coffee mornings; selling new and donated goods in 'charity shops'; the sale of tickets by the Royal Opera House or a fringe theatre group; the provision of education by private schools; the provision of healthcare by clinics and hospitals; selling educational books; running conferences; licensing charity logos to 'affinity' credit card companies; running a children's home or residential care home under contract to a local authority.

1.3   This is just a sample of the very many ways in which charities do trade. The range of trading activity is huge and growing. NCVO's *The UK Civil Society Almanac 2008* reported that for the first time in 2005/06 income from the sale of goods and services by the voluntary and community sector made up over half of the sector's incoming resources, accounting for 50.3% of total income, up by 10% from five years previously.

1.4   Several factors have influenced the nature and level of trading activity carried out by charities in recent years. Pressure on resources has encouraged charities to diversify their income streams to become less reliant on donations and grant funding. For some, this has meant ever more imaginative ways of fundraising, through events, for example, and partnerships with commercial organisations. Others have become involved in what is commonly known as 'social enterprise' activity – charging for the services they provide to their beneficiaries (albeit at a subsidised rate in many cases) – instead of offering them for free.

1.5   And the radical changes in the roles of central and local government and other statutory agencies during the past two decades have elevated charities into a third force, to stand alongside government and the private sector as a deliverer of health, welfare, housing and caring services. The 2006 Department of Health white paper 'Our Health, Our Care, Our Say', for example, encourages Primary Care Trusts to become 'commissioners' rather than 'providers' of primary care services, explicitly citing 'third sector' organisations, such as charities, as possible future providers of these services.

1.6   This form of arrangement between the voluntary sector 'providers' and the statutory sector 'purchasers' has been termed the 'Contract Culture'. According to the NCVO *UK Civil Society Almanac 2008*, in 2005/06, over 35% of the voluntary and community sector's income originated from the public sector, with over 60% of that comprising contract, rather than grant, funding.

SOCIAL ENTERPRISE

1.7   In recent years the social enterprise movement has become increasingly prominent, with support across the political spectrum. Charities are major players in the field of social enterprise: indeed, in many ways the expression 'social enterprise' is simply a relatively new term for what some charities have been doing for years, namely promoting their social purposes through a sustainable business model.

1.8   There is no legal definition of 'social enterprise', and debate over a precise meaning continues at many levels. In 2002 the Department of Trade and Industry put forward the following definition, which is still commonly used:

> 'A social enterprise is a business with primarily social objectives whose surpluses are principally reinvested for that purpose in the business or in the community, rather than being driven by the need to maximise profit for shareholders and owners.'

Charity trading, particularly trading which directly furthers the charity's purposes (called primary purpose trading), falls squarely within this definition. Some might argue that all trading by charities is social enterprise, as the profits of the activity must ultimately be spent for charitable purposes.

1.9   So all charities which trade may well be regarded as social enterprises: although this may come as a surprise to charities which have been carrying out social enterprise activity for years without calling it that! It has been estimated that over 60% of social enterprises are charities. A significant minority of social enterprises are not charities: businesses may operate along social and not-for-profit lines without necessarily being charitable.

1.10   Social enterprises do not qualify for any automatic special legal or tax treatment: the tax breaks associated with primary purpose trading by a *charitable* social enterprise, for example, stem from the charity's charitable status, and the nature of the trade. Increasingly, however, a range of financial and business support is available to organisations carrying out social enterprise activity, and these may be of interest to charities. (See, for example, information provided by the Social Enterprise Coalition (www.socialenterprise.org.uk) and the Office of the Third Sector (www.cabinetoffice.gov.uk/third_sector).) There is also a large degree of political support for social enterprise.

THE CHALLENGES OF TRADING

1.11 Charities do not just face the usual problems associated with trading: problems of obtaining finance, of risk, of management, of profitability and of cash flow (although, of course, they may encounter all of these). Charities wishing to trade encounter a number of particular issues which stem from their charitable status.

1.12 Before embarking on any form of trading activity, charities should ask themselves the following questions:

(1) Is this trading? In many cases the answer will be obvious: trading essentially involves buying and selling goods or services. But in some cases it is not so easy to tell, and a body of case law has built up around the so-called 'badges of trade'. Defining the nature of the activity is less likely to be an issue where the 'trade' involves activities which directly further the charity's objectives, as we see in Chapter 3. But where the principal focus of the activity is raising money, it may be necessary to explore whether the activity really is trading: this is explored in detail at **5.5–5.27**.

(2) Do we have constitutional capacity to carry out the trading activity? If not, should we change our constitution? This is discussed at **2.5–2.19**.

(3) Does charity law permit us to carry out this type of activity? What is the Charity Commission's approach? At the time of writing, the Commission recommends that so-called 'non-primary purpose trading', which does not of itself further the charity's objectives, should only be carried out by charities where it 'involves no significant risk to the assets of the charity' (Charity Commission publication CC35 'Trustees, trading and tax', para C8). We explore this in more detail at **2.20–2.33**.

(4) What are the tax implications of this activity? How can we avoid any potential tax? Although charities enjoy significant exemptions from UK tax, there is – contrary to popular belief – no blanket tax exemption for charities. The profits of charitable trading activity may well be subject to tax: either income or corporation tax, depending on the charity's legal form. There are exemptions for trading which furthers the charity's main purposes, certain fundraising events and small scale-trading which falls within defined limits. But where these exemptions do not apply, the charity may be facing a tax bill. More often than not this comes as a shock.

    Tax can be avoided if the trading activity is carried out via a trading subsidiary. Although the trading company will, in principle, pay tax on its profits, to the extent that those profits are paid up to its parent charity under the gift aid scheme, there will be no profits to tax. If charity trustees carry out taxable trading directly through the charity, rather than avoiding tax by using a trading subsidiary, they may be in breach of their duties under charity law to maximise the charity's resources, and could therefore be made personally liable to reimburse the charity for the tax. We deal with tax in detail at **2.35–2.58** and trading companies in Chapter 7.

(5)   What about VAT? It is often thought that charities do not pay VAT – this could not be further from the truth. In most cases where a charity (or its trading subsidiary) trades, it is also making a taxable supply for VAT purposes. And, unhelpfully, the direct tax and VAT rules can apply differently in different circumstances: many a charity has adopted a practice to avoid an income tax problem only to find that this has created a VAT problem! However, with careful structuring VAT can be minimised and sometimes quite legally avoided. Charities need to be aware of the rules so that they can structure their trading activities in a way which makes sense from a VAT perspective. While VAT invariably requires specific advice, we discuss it where relevant throughout this book.

(6)   Should we establish a separate trading company? As we see throughout this book, many of the problems associated with trading can be dealt with by running a trading activity through a separate company which is owned by the charity. But this can give rise to headaches of its own.

1.13   As this book seeks to show, the field of charities and trading is littered with traps for the unwary. Many of these traps spring from the need to separate out for-profit trading activities which do not of themselves further the primary purposes of the charity and run them via a trading company. This then throws up problems, such as: how to finance the trading company; inter-company charges; VAT; profit shedding to create a tax-free income for the charity; and rate relief on the premises occupied by the trading company.

1.14   If all for-profit trading activities undertaken by a charity could be treated in the same way as primary purpose trading, then most of these problems would drop away and there would be little need for this book! Charities would be liberated from the need to create complex and costly structures. In its 2002 report on charities and the not-for-profit sector, *Private Action, Public Benefit*, the Cabinet Office highlighted the difficulties with the current system and recommended radical changes to the law. Charities, the report suggested, should be able to undertake as much trading as they wished, without adverse tax or charity law consequences, without setting up a separate trading company. Instead, charity trustees would have to comply with a specific statutory duty of care when undertaking trading.

1.15   The recommendation was one of the few in the report which was not accepted by the Government. The Home Office's 2003 response to the report concluded that more flexibility for charities in this regard would give them an unfair advantage over the private sector:

'Conducting trading activities within the tax exempt structure of charities would offend the principle of a level playing field with private sector businesses. At present, companies owned by charities are in the same position as any other company. It is a matter of choice whether or not profits are passed to shareholders within the Gift Aid arrangements. In addition, there is a statutory exemption from tax for small trades carried on by charities and a concession providing exemption from tax for minor trading activities for charitable purposes, such as bazaars and jumble sales. These relieve smaller charities of any administrative burden in conducting modest trading activity.'

1.16 The 2002 Cabinet Office review was the first major overhaul of charity law for several hundred years. It is likely, therefore, that although the current system is, in the words of the Cabinet Office, 'administratively complex, expensive for individual charities, and can inhibit them from diversifying their income streams', it is something which charities will have to continue to grapple with for some time to come.

HOW TO USE THIS BOOK

1.17 This book is roughly divided into two parts. Chapters 2 to 7 deal with the legal issues which affect charities involved in trading precisely because they are charities. Chapter 2 highlights the preliminary issues which charities carrying out trading activity must be aware of, and provides an outline of the tax and VAT implications of the various types of trading activity. Chapters 3 to 6 cover specific types of trading activity: primary purpose trading, charity sales activity (including charity shops), trading aimed purely at raising funds, and income from charity property.

1.18 Chapter 7 explains why, when and how to establish and run a separate trading company.

1.19 Chapters 8 to 11 cover issues which are of more general concern to anyone involved in trading: contracts and the regulation of trading, intellectual property, insurance and insolvency.

Chapter 2

CHARITY TRADING – THE BASICS

2.1   *This chapter explains the legal framework which applies to charity trading. We explain the crucial difference between primary purpose and non-primary purpose trading. What are the first questions which a charity wishing to trade must ask itself? In particular, does the charity have constitutional capacity to trade, and what might the Charity Commission's attitude be? We outline the tax rules, and give full details of the tax exemption for small-scale trading by charities. We also highlight the key VAT rules likely to affect charity trading.*

PRIMARY PURPOSE AND NON-PRIMARY PURPOSE TRADING

2.2   There is a key distinction between two types of trading carried out by charities: primary purpose trading and non-primary purpose trading. This distinction affects many aspects of the charity trading rules, including constitutional capacity, the Charity Commission's approach, and tax.

2.3   Primary purpose trading is trading which a charity carries out in fulfilment of its main or primary purpose, ie in fulfilment of its charitable objects. This includes educational charities charging for their courses or publications, community groups charging a small fee to access their activities, and heritage properties charging visitors an entrance fee. Broadly speaking, charities have considerable freedom to carry out primary purpose trading. They need constitutional power to carry out the activity. They need to be alert to the VAT implications of the trading activity and, particularly, the rules on public benefit. All of these are explored in detail in Chapter 3. But tax and charity law are unlikely to throw up significant problems.

2.4   Non-primary purpose trading is trading which is intended simply to raise funds for the charity. The educational charity which buys in a stack of ready-made Christmas cards and sells them at a profit is invariably carrying out non-primary purpose trading. The activity of selling Christmas cards does not (in most cases) have a direct educational impact on the charity's beneficiaries. Many forms of 'pure' fundraising activity carried out by charities, such as fundraising events, and sponsorship deals with commercial organisations, fall into the category of non-primary purpose trading. Non-primary purpose trading throws up much greater challenges for charities, from both a charity law and a tax perspective. These are explored in detail in Chapters 4 and 5.

IS THERE POWER TO TRADE?

2.5   If a charity is to carry on a trade itself, it must have the necessary constitutional capacity – what lawyers (ever dependent on Latin terminology) call 'vires'. This means that the charity's constitution will need to contain an express or implied power to carry out the trading activity in question.

Objects and powers

2.6   A charity's constitution typically contains both objects and powers. A charity's *objects* are the purposes which it is set up to achieve. The objects of the charity must be exclusively charitable: that is what makes it a charity. The objects which the law recognises as charitable are set out in s 2(2) of the Charities Act 2006. They include 12 specific charitable purposes, and a general 'sweep-up' category of other purposes which the law regards as charitable.

2.7   The *powers* are the tools which the charity can use to achieve its objects. The powers of a charity must always be exercised in furtherance of its objects.

2.8   Thus, the *object* of an educational charity might be, for example, 'to advance the education of the public'.

2.9   It may have the following *powers*:

(a)   'to run lectures and educational programmes and to charge fees at such levels as the trustees shall from time to time think appropriate';

(b)   'to publish and distribute books, pamphlets, reports, leaflets, journals, films, tapes and instructional matter';

(c)   'to trade in the course of carrying out the objects of the charity and carry on any other trade (provided it is not substantial permanent trading activity)'.

This charity clearly has power to engage in primary purpose trading. Under (a) it may run educational courses for which it charges a fee. Under (b) it may carry out publishing activity, and it is clear from (c) that it has power to charge for those publications, provided such trading activity furthers its educational objects.

2.10   If this charity wishes to carry out non-primary purpose trading, for example selling Christmas cards or holding a fundraising ball, it will need to rely on the power to 'carry on any other trade' in the second part of (c), although thanks to the qualification at the end of (c) this cannot be substantial permanent trading.

2.11 Note that the constitution may include a power to trade provided that the trade does not give rise to taxable profits: this will limit the charity to trading activity which qualifies for the exemptions from tax described at **2.36–2.50** below.

2.12 The constitution may also include a general sweep-up power to 'do all such other lawful things as shall further the charity's objects'. It may be possible to rely on a power of this kind if there are no specific powers to carry out the trading activity in question.

2.13 If there are no appropriate powers, the charity's constitution will normally need to be changed.

Changing the constitution

2.14 The mechanism for changing the powers in the charity's constitution will vary according to its legal form.

2.15 If the charity is a company, its constitution is changed by passing a special resolution, which is, broadly speaking, a resolution passed with the consent of 75% of the members present (in person or by proxy) at a meeting of which 14 days' notice has been given, or by written resolution of 75% of the members. If, as is sometimes the case with older charities, the charity's powers appear within its objects clause, prior written consent from the Charity Commission will be necessary under s 64 of the Charities Act 1993 (which requires such consent whenever the objects clause is changed). It is important to get consent where necessary, as failure to do so will invalidate the resolution. The Commission's consent should not be required, however, if the powers appear in a separate clause.

2.16 If the charity is *not* a company, the provisions for amending its constitution should be set out in a clause in the constitution, and in the absence of such a power the charity may be able to rely on the statutory power in s 74D of the Charities Act 1993 for trustees of unincorporated charities to alter their administrative powers.

The consequences of trading without appropriate powers

2.17 The consequences for the trustees of carrying on an activity which is outside their powers – known as 'ultra vires' – are serious. If the charity suffers any loss as a result of the activity, the trustees will potentially be personally liable to repay that loss to the charity out of their own pockets. The position is the same whether the charity is a limited liability company, incorporated by Royal Charter, a charitable incorporated organisation, a trust, or an unincorporated association.

2.18 If the charity makes a profit from the ultra vires activity, the trustees may also be at risk. If the profits are taxable, which may well be the case (see

2.35–2.58), and it is decided that the trustees should have carried out the activity via a separate trading subsidiary in order to avoid the tax, the trustees could be made personally liable to meet the tax bill out of their own pockets.

2.19 As an alternative to changing the constitution, the trustees could consider setting up a non-charitable trading subsidiary to undertake the trading activity, although, as explained in Chapter 7, which deals with trading companies in detail, it will also need power to set up a subsidiary company!

DOES CHARITY LAW ALLOW THE ACTIVITY?

2.20 Some types of trading cannot be carried out by charities as a matter of charity law, regardless of what the constitution says. Here, the distinction between primary purpose and non-primary purpose trading, explained at **2.2–2.4** above, is again key.

2.21 The Charity Commission's position at the time of writing is that charities may carry out trading activity provided that it is:

- primary purpose trading, or ancillary trading – the Commission describes this as trading which contributes directly or indirectly towards the objects of the charity: both are dealt with in detail in Chapter 3; or

- non-primary purpose trading that does not involve significant risk to the resources of the charity.

In all other cases, charities should establish a trading company for the purposes of conducting their trading activity.

2.22 This view is set out in the Charity Commission's publication CC35 'Trustees, trading and tax' (see www.charity-commission.gov.uk). References in this book are to the version of CC35 published in April 2007, which is current at the time of writing.

2.23 This means that as far as the Charity Commission is concerned charities can carry out primary purpose trading directly. As a matter of charity law they do not need to set up a trading subsidiary, although they may wish to do so for other reasons (see **7.8–7.37**). An educational charity which charges fees to students should have nothing to fear from the Charity Commission, provided it has regard to the public benefit rules (see **3.88–3.102**). Nor should a charity relieving poverty in the developing world which sells items made by its beneficiaries.

2.24 Any other trading which does not involve significant risk to the assets of the charity may also be carried out directly by the charity itself. The Commission acknowledges that running lotteries (see **5.193–5.201**) and undertaking small-scale trading which falls within the relevant tax exemption for small trading operations (see **2.41–2.50**) will generally not involve significant risk to the assets of the charity.

2.25 But where the charity wishes to carry out non-primary purpose trading activity which does involve significant risk, a trading subsidiary must be used. This will be the case *even if* the trading activity is not subject to tax, for instance because it qualifies for the tax exemption for fundraising events (see **5.36–5.54**).

2.26 The Commission's guidance goes on to explain that 'significant risk' is the risk that the turnover from the trading activity is insufficient to meet the costs of carrying on the trade, and the difference has to be financed out of the assets of the charity. The Commission states that whether or not the risk is significant will depend on a number of factors, including:

- the size of the charity;

- the nature of the business;

- the expected outgoings;

- turnover projections; and

- the sensitivity of business profitability to the ups and downs of the market.

2.27 This position represents a change of focus by the Charity Commission. Its previous version of CC35, called simply 'Charities and Trading' (dated July 2001), highlighted the size of the trading activity as being the relevant factor, rather than the risks involved. The guidance stated (para 8):

> 'Charity law does not permit charities to carry out non-primary purpose trading themselves *on a substantial basis* in order to raise additional funds' (emphasis added).

It went on to say (para 17):

> 'If a charity exercises a fund-raising trade which is expected to have a *significant turnover*, we strongly advise that the activity should be carried out through a subsidiary trading company' (emphasis added).

2.28 In most cases, this change of approach will not make much difference: large-scale trading is generally more likely to be risky than a smaller enterprise with a less significant turnover. However, the authors do have some concerns about the Commission's revised analysis.

2.29 Say, for example, that a charity wishes to carry out a new type of fundraising activity, which involves non-primary purpose trading. It has little or no way of gauging how successful the activity might be, so it wishes, perfectly reasonably, to carry out a pilot, or a trial run. The layout and overall financial risk of carrying out a trial run might not be great, but the turnover from the trial might well be insufficient to meet the accompanying costs. As mentioned at **2.26**, the Charity Commission regards 'significant risk' as the risk that the turnover from the trading activity is insufficient to meet the costs of carrying on the trade, so the difference has to be financed out of the assets of the charity. In this example, the charity has no way of telling whether the trial run represents a 'significant risk'. It is for precisely that reason that it wishes to carry out a trial run before it rolls out the proposed activity on a large scale! The Charity Commission's guidance suggests that, in the circumstances, the charity would need to use a trading subsidiary for the trial run.

2.30 This approach seems heavy-handed: a concern raised by the authors in correspondence with the Charity Commission. The Commission's response suggests that the definition of 'significant risk' referred to at **2.26** above is not an absolute test, and that the trustees must look at the list of factors mentioned there, in order to reach a view on whether the threatened level of loss is significant in the context of the charity's business as a whole. The Commission's view was that a trial run of a fundraising event in the circumstances described above could be run by the charity itself, provided the threatened level of loss was not significant.

2.31 A further query is whether, if the level of trading represents a significant risk, the charity must set up a trading subsidiary even if the costs of doing so are greater than the sums involved in the trading operation. The Commission has expressed the view, in correspondence with the authors, that a trading subsidiary would be required in these circumstances. Again, in the authors' view this approach seems questionable. (The Charity Commission does concede that where the primary motive for establishing a trading subsidiary is tax, the tax benefits may be insufficient to justify the additional costs of establishing a trading company. However, the Commission does not appear to make the same concession for the case where the primary motive for establishing a trading company is risk (eg where the trading activity qualifies for a tax exemption, such as the exemption for fundraising events, but is risky!).)

2.32 Having said that, it would be a brave charity that disregarded official guidance from the Charity Commission. Charities proposing to carry out trading activity directly, rather than via a trading subsidiary, in circumstances which appear to conflict with the published guidance would be well advised to seek professional advice, or formal advice from the Charity Commission on the proposals under s 29 of the Charities Act 1993.

2.33 Where charity trustees trade in breach of the constraints imposed by charity law, they are acting in breach of trust. If the charity suffers loss as a result of the activity, the trustees will potentially be personally liable to repay that loss to the charity out of their own pockets. This will be the case regardless of the legal form of the charity.

2.34 The flowchart below illustrates the preliminary questions a charity considering embarking on any form of trading activity should ask.

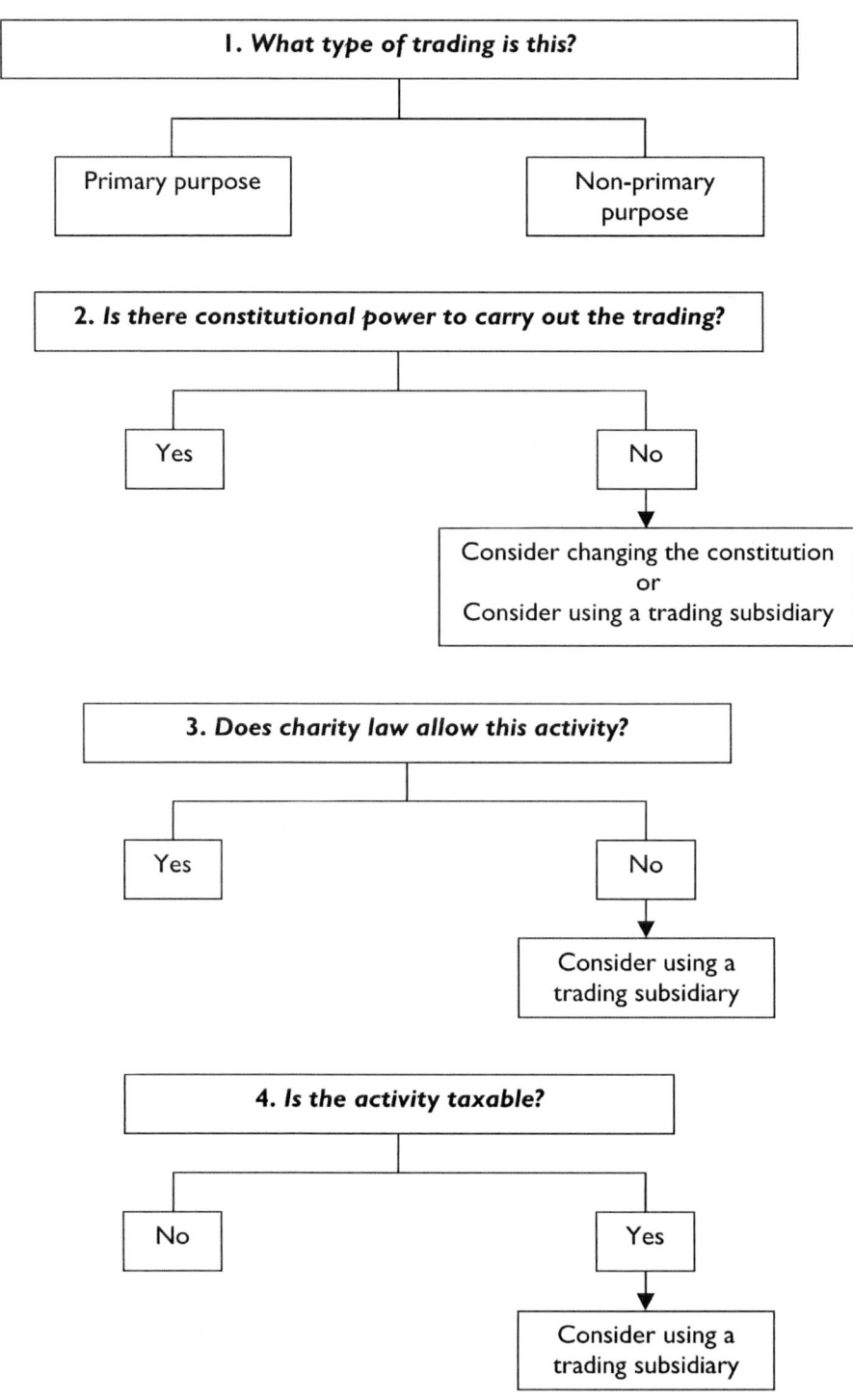

TAX

2.35 The basic rule is that where a trade is carried on by a charity the profits are taxable, unless an exemption applies. HMRC must consider the activity to be a trade. In most cases this will be obvious, but the courts have developed nine 'badges' of trade over the years, which will help to determine whether the activity is regarded as a trade. These are explored at **5.11–5.22**. The exemptions from tax are outlined below.

Exemptions

Primary purpose trading

2.36 There is an exemption from tax where the trade is exercised in the course of the actual carrying out of a primary purpose of the charity, or where the work in connection with the trade is mainly carried out by beneficiaries of the charity. This would apply, for instance, to the sale of Christian publications by a Christian charity. It would also apply to the sale of goods made by partially sighted people in a workshop run by a charity for the partially sighted. The exemption is explored in more detail in Chapter 3.

Ancillary trading

2.37 Ancillary trading is trading which is in some way complementary to a charity's primary purposes, although it does not directly further a primary purpose. An example is a charitable art gallery providing a café for its visitors. HMRC accepts that ancillary trading falls within the statutory exemption which applies to primary purpose trading. Ancillary trading is discussed in more detail in Chapter 3.

Fundraising events

2.38 There is a specific exemption from tax, awarded by extra-statutory concession, for certain types of fundraising events. This is examined in detail in Chapter 5.

Donated goods

2.39 As explained in more detail in Chapter 4, HMRC does not regard the sale of donated goods as trading. It is simply a case of converting a donation received in kind (eg second-hand clothes or books) into cash. The profits of this type of activity are therefore not taxable.

Annual payments

2.40 Certain payments made on an annual basis, such as those payable to a charity for the use of its name and logo, where no other additional services are rendered, fall within the scope of a special exemption. See **5.96** and **7.199** for more detail.

Small-scale trading

2.41 Where a charity's trading activity falls within certain defined limits, it will fall within a small trades exemption and will not be liable for tax.

2.42 This exemption is extremely useful. It means that charities can carry out a small amount of trading activity – whether as a stand-alone activity such as a small Christmas card operation, or as part of a primary purpose trade, such as a museum shop selling pens and tea towels as well as material linked to its primary purpose – without any risk of incurring a tax liability.

2.43 The limits of the exemption are set out in s 46 of the Finance Act 2000 in relation to corporation tax and ss 526 and 528 of the Income Taxes Act 2007 in relation to income tax. The total turnover from all of the charity's non-exempt trading activity (with the exception of some rare and unusual sources of income which will not generally be relevant, such as gains from contracts for life assurance) must not exceed the annual turnover limit.

2.44 The annual turnover limit is:

- £5,000; or

- if the annual turnover is more than £5,000, 25% of the charity's total incoming resources, up to a maximum of £50,000.

A charity's 'total incoming resources' means the charity's total receipts from all sources, including grants, donations, investment income and trading receipts.

2.45 The limits will be applied to the charity's 12-month accounting period and will be reduced pro rata if the accounting period is less than a year. These limits mean that larger charities, with a total annual turnover of more than £200,000, cannot undertake more than £50,000 of taxable trading activity in any financial period. The following example illustrates how the limits affect smaller charities:

A charity has two sources of income – donations and the sale of Christmas cards. The sale of Christmas cards is not primary purpose trading, nor does it fall within the fundraising event exemption.

Income for 2005/2006
- Income from donations in the financial year £10,000

-           Income from Christmas cards in the   £3,000
  financial year

The small-scale exemption will apply because the trading income is less than £5,000.

Income for 2006/2007

-           Income from donations   £22,000
-           Income from Christmas cards   £6,000

The charity's total incoming resources are £22,000 plus £6,000 = £28,000.

25% of the total incoming resources is £7,000. The small-scale exemption will apply because the trading income is less than 25% of the total incoming resources, and falls under the £50,000 cap.

Income for 2007/2008

-           Income from donations   £15,000
-           Income from Christmas cards   £6,000

The charity's total incoming resources are £15,000 plus £6,000 = £21,000.

25% of the total incoming resources is £5,250. The small-scale exemption will not apply because the trading income exceeds 25% of the charity's total incoming resources. All the profits from the Christmas card activity will be subject to tax.

2.46 However, the exemption can also apply if, at the start of the relevant accounting period, the charity had a reasonable expectation that the charity's non-exempt trading income would not exceed the annual turnover limit. Thus, using the example above, if at the start of the 2007/2008 accounting period the charity trustees expected the turnover from the Christmas card sales to be less than £6,000 or, which is more likely in this case, expected that its total incoming resources would be more than £21,000, they may be able to argue that the exemption should apply.

2.47 HMRC will consider any evidence that the charity has to show that it had a reasonable expectation that the annual turnover limit would not be exceeded. Budgets, business plans and forecasts, and minutes from trustee meetings will all be helpful. Past performance will also be relevant: the trustees may be able to show that the income from the trading activity was much greater than might be predicted from previous years' results, or that the total incoming resources were lower than expected following the sudden withdrawal of a grant.

2.48 Note, however, that HMRC advises that if a charity expects to be regularly trading around the exemption limits, it may be better to consider using a trading subsidiary (see Chapter 7). Note in particular:

- For the purposes of applying these limits, it is *turnover* rather than profit which is important. It does not matter that the trading activity is making minimal profits – although clearly if this is the case the level of tax payable will be low. However, if the profits are minimal, the trustees may clearly wish to reassess whether it is appropriate for the charity to be involved in an activity which makes very little money (see **2.55**).

- Once the limits are exceeded, *all* the profits of the non-exempt trading activity (and other miscellaneous income) are taxed – there is no pro rata adjustment. However, if the limits are exceeded by only a minimal amount it will clearly be easier to seek to persuade HMRC that the charity had a reasonable expectation that they would not be exceeded.

- In applying the limits, income from trading activity which is exempt from tax for some other reason (eg primary purpose trading or trading falling within the fundraising event exemption) will be relevant in assessing total incoming resources, but not the level of taxable trading. For example:

    A charity's annual income from several sources is:
    - £30,000 from donations;
    - £25,000 from fundraising events falling within the fundraising event exemption;
    - £20,000 from primary purpose trading;
    - £15,000 from non-exempt trading.

    The total incoming resources for the charity are £30,000 plus £25,000 plus £20,000 plus £15,000 = £90,000. 25% of £90,000 is £22,500. The non-exempt trading activity falls within the limits, so the small-scale exemption will apply.

2.49 In order for the exemption to apply, the profits from the trading activity must be used solely for the purposes of the charity, but this is highly likely to be the case. There is no comparable small-scale exemption for VAT, so the usual rules will apply (see **2.60–2.68**).

2.50 The Charity Commission's view is that carrying on a trade which is within these limits is unlikely to be in breach of charity law (see **2.24**), as any risk to the charity's resources from the trading is likely to be small. However, the charity should ensure that the trading is permitted by its governing document (see **2.5–2.19**).

2.51 The 'Taxation' flowchart below highlights the tax implications of trading.

Taxation

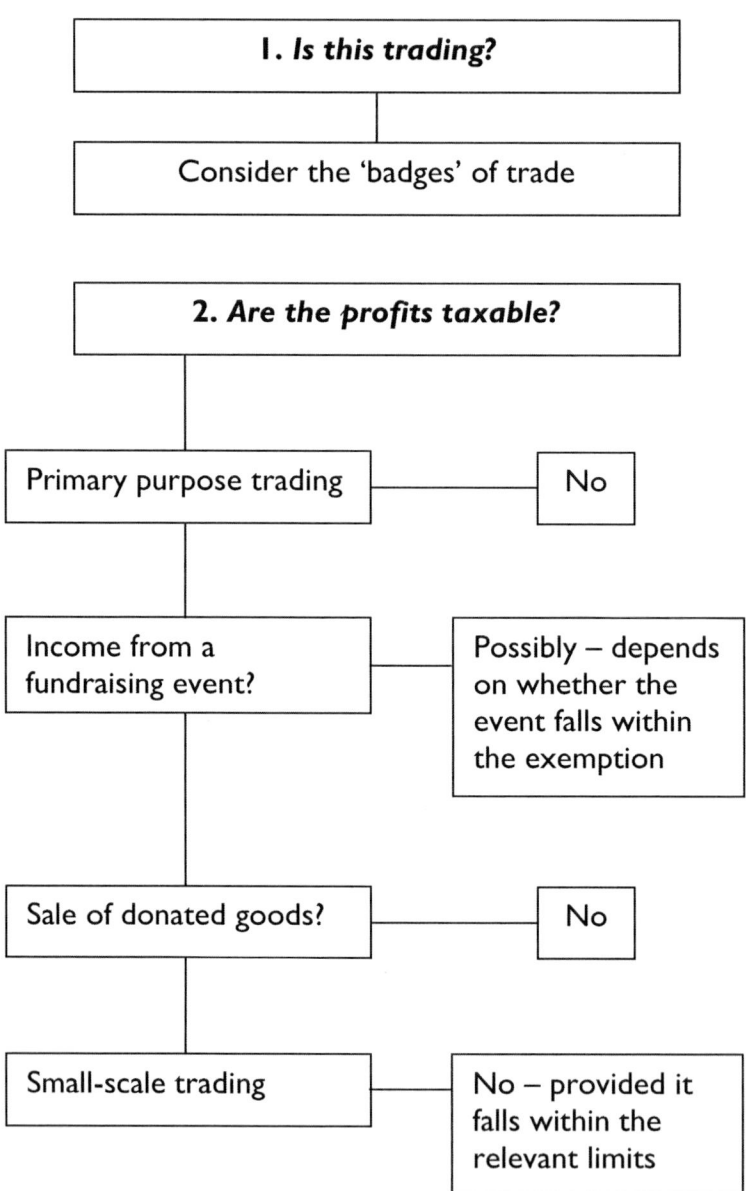

1. *Is this trading?*		
Consider the 'badges' of trade		
2. Are the *profits* taxable?		
Primary purpose trading		No
Income from a fundraising event?		Possibly – depends on whether the event falls within the exemption
Sale of donated goods?		No
Small-scale trading		No – provided it falls within the relevant limits

What profit?

2.52 If a charity undertakes trading activities and makes profits which are not exempt from tax under the rules described above, they will be subject to tax. The next step for the charity is to work out what the actual taxable profits are. In assessing the profits of the trade, a charity should make sure that all proper costs and expenses attributable to the trading activity are offset against the profits generated. It should take proper professional advice on this. The allocation of costs will be particularly challenging where a charity is carrying out mixed trading activity, and separate accounting records will be required.

2.53 Where charities receive goods or services in the course of their trading activity at less than cost price – or for free – it may be possible to deduct a notional cost or market price when calculating the profits. They should be calculated on a reasonable basis. For example, if the profits are partly attributable to voluntary labour, the notional costs of the volunteers' time may be taken into account as a business expense in computing the tax due on the trading activity.

2.54 Complex questions may arise about the attribution of fixed overheads.

2.55 Once the costs of the trade are fully accounted for, the charity may find that there is no, or only a small, taxable profit. If this is the case, the trustees will need to think carefully about whether the charity should be undertaking the activity. In most cases a charity should not be carrying out unprofitable trading, unless it is primary purpose trading which advances the charity's objects. Are there any fringe benefits to the activity, such as publicity for the charity, which outweigh the fact that it makes a loss? See, for example, the discussion of Christmas card sales at **4.76**.

How much tax?

2.56 To the extent that the charity has made a profit which is not subject to any exemptions, HMRC will seek to charge tax. Where a charity has a tax liability, it is under an obligation to notify HMRC, even if it has not been sent a tax return. HMRC usually has six years in which to make a tax assessment. To reopen years outside the normal time limit, HMRC has to show fraudulent or negligent conduct, in which case it can make assessments going back up to 20 years.

2.57 The type and level of tax payable will depend on the legal structure of the charity:

• Charitable trusts pay income tax, at a rate of 40%.

• Charitable unincorporated associations, charitable companies and Royal Charter bodies all pay corporation tax. The rates of corporation tax for 2008/2009 are 21% for companies with taxable profits under £300,000 and 28% for companies with profits of over £1.5 million, with a sliding scale for companies falling between those limits.

Where a charity has made a tax return to HMRC, it should set aside a sufficient reserve to meet the tax which it estimates will be payable pursuant to the tax return.

2.58   If a charity does incur a tax liability as a result of its trading activity, it is more than likely that this will have been a mistake. Use of a trading subsidiary can limit, and even eliminate, tax which would otherwise be payable on non-charitable trading. Charity trustees are under a duty to safeguard their charity's resources, and to take appropriate professional advice. Where charity trustees find their charity on the receiving end of a significant tax bill, they may also find themselves vulnerable to a claim against them personally for breach of trust. The charity may well have a claim against the trustees for the tax incurred, on the basis that if the trustees had acted properly there would have been no tax to pay. In these circumstances the liability of the trustees will not be affected by the legal form of the charity. In contrast, while the Charity Commission's guidance on trading concedes that a trading subsidiary may not be appropriate in all cases, given the additional management costs involved, it would be rare for trustees to be criticised for using a trading subsidiary as a means of avoiding tax.

USE OF A TRADING SUBSIDIARY

2.59   The charity law and tax implications of trading can generally be avoided if a trading subsidiary is used. In simple terms, the charity sets up and funds a trading company in which it owns all the shares. The trading company carries out the trading activity outside the constraints of charity law, as it is not itself a charitable entity. Although the trading company benefits from no direct tax exemptions, the trading company's profits are paid to the parent charity under the gift aid scheme, so the trading company will, in fact, pay no tax. The trading activity has effectively been carried out tax free. However, running a trading company has its own complications. Trading companies are dealt with in detail in Chapter 7.

VAT

2.60   While a raft of tax exemptions and concessions may apply to ensure that no tax is paid on trading activity carried out by a charity, the situation as far as VAT is concerned is very different. There is no general exemption from VAT for charities which undertake trading activities. The trading activities of many charities will fall within the definition of business supplies for VAT, even though charities do not pursue a 'profit motive'.

2.61   The basics of VAT are:

(1)   A transaction is within the scope of UK VAT if all the following conditions are met:
  • it is a supply of goods and services;
  • it takes place in the UK;
  • it is made by a taxable person (ie an individual or organisation which is or is required to register for VAT);

- it is made in the course or furtherance of any business carried on by that person.

(2) A charity (like any other organisation or individual) is required to register for VAT if it makes taxable supplies of more than the VAT registration threshold in any year (£67,000 for 2008/2009). A charity whose income from taxable supplies is below the threshold can register voluntarily, but a charity that makes no taxable supplies cannot register.

(3) A 'taxable supply' is defined as 'a supply of goods or services made in the United Kingdom, other than an exempt supply'. Exempt supplies are considered in more detail below. Trading will generally consist of the supply of goods and services, which is why charities engaging in trading need to be aware of the VAT implications.

(4) 'Business' has a wide meaning. A charity may be regarded as carrying on a business activity for VAT purposes even though the activity may be performed for the benefit of the community, which will generally be the case with primary purpose trading. It is therefore important for a charity to determine whether any particular activity is a 'business' or a 'non-business' activity. This distinction is not always easy to draw, particularly as recent VAT case law (see, for example, the nursery and crèche cases in Chapter 3) suggests that the definition of 'business activity' is not as wide as HMRC believe. Charities may therefore need to take detailed advice.

(5) Where a charity is registered for VAT, it must charge and account to HMRC for output VAT at the standard rate of 15% (or 17.5% from 1 January 2010) on the taxable supplies of goods and services that it makes (unless the rate of VAT on that supply is zero). The output tax charged, less any recoverable input tax (see **2.61**(6) below), must be paid to HMRC.

(6) Charities have to pay VAT on goods and services which they purchase, just like anyone else. VAT paid on purchases is called 'input tax'. Input VAT is not recoverable if the charity is not registered for VAT. If the charity is registered for VAT it will be able to recover input tax on purchases made in connection with taxable supplies, but this will not extend to input tax paid on a purchase in connection with an exempt supply by the charity or a non-business activity such as pure fundraising. In some circumstances input tax may be only partially recoverable.

(7) Most charities are not able to recover all of the input tax they pay, either because they are not registered for VAT, or because of the type of services they supply, or because part of their work is paid for by grants and donations. It is estimated that irrecoverable VAT costs the charity sector between £400 and £500 million a year.

(8)   Note that VAT is a tax on turnover, not profit, so even trading which does not make a profit will need to be considered for VAT purposes. For example, if a community centre charges a nominal fee for admission to some of its activities, which does not cover its costs, so does not even begin to make a profit, the fee will nonetheless need to be considered from a VAT perspective.

Exempt supplies

2.62   There are a number of exemptions from VAT which are significant for charities. The list of exempt activities is detailed, and covers supplies such as:

- Land.

- Insurance.

- Postal services.

- Betting, gaming and lotteries.

- Finance.

- Education.

- Health and welfare.

- Burial and cremation.

- Trade unions and professional bodies.

- Sports competitions.

- Works of art.

- Fundraising events.

- Cultural services.

2.63   If a supply is exempt from VAT, certain consequences follow:

(1)   No VAT is charged on such supplies.

(2)   Any input VAT incurred in making an exempt supply is not recoverable.

(3)   Exempt supplies are ignored for the purpose of calculating whether or not a trader is making 'taxable supplies', and turnover from exempt supplies does not count towards the VAT registration threshold.

Hence, if a charity is trading but only making exempt supplies, it will not be able to register for VAT, whatever its turnover.

2.64 The type of exempt supplies which are most likely to be provided by charities are rental or property, cultural services, healthcare, ambulance services, welfare, education, research and vocational training, and fundraising. These are considered in more detail in Chapters 3 and 5.

Zero rating

2.65 Zero-rated supplies enjoy special treatment. They are taxable supplies, but the rate of VAT charged on them is 0%. This means that where a charity makes zero-rated supplies, those supplies will be taken into account in determining whether its taxable supplies have reached the compulsory VAT registration threshold. But the charity will not need to charge output tax on the supplies, even though it can claim back input tax on purchases made in connection with the zero-rated supplies, if it is registered for VAT. To make zero-rated supplies is therefore the most favourable position for VAT purposes.

2.66 The key areas of zero-rated supplies for charities undertaking trading activities are:

- The supply of books, booklets, brochures, pamphlets and leaflets, newspapers, journals and periodicals, children's picture books and painting books, music, maps, charts and topographical plans.

- The supply of talking books for the blind and handicapped, and wireless sets for the blind.

- The sale of donated goods (see Chapter 4).

- The export of any goods by a charity to a place outside the European Community.

- The sale, adaptation, and repair of goods designed or adapted for use by disabled people.

Sales of donated goods by a trading company are also zero rated for VAT, provided the trading company has agreed in writing to give all its profits to the parent charity (see **4.36–4.37**). The trading company may decide to retain some of its profits so as to provide working capital and to reduce its dependence on loans from the parent charity (see Chapter 7). That may well be very sensible as regards charity law, but it would have serious VAT effects. Since not all the profits of the trading company are gifted to the charity, the trading company will lose its advantageous zero-rated status and would have to charge VAT on sales, thus affecting either the prices it charges or its profit margins, or both. (See also **4.42**.)

Failure to register for VAT

2.67 A person who is making taxable supplies must register for VAT if those supplies exceed the compulsory registration threshold in any year (£67,000 for 2008/2009). Registration in such circumstances is compulsory. There is no choice. Failure to register without reasonable excuse may result in far greater liabilities than, for example, in the case of failure to pay income tax on the due date. Failure to register is a criminal offence. The penalty is the greater of £50 and 'the specified percentage of relevant tax'. Relevant tax is the VAT which should have been paid to HMRC, calculated from the date from which the trader should have registered to the date of discovery. The specified percentage is 5% (where the period of delay is 9 months or less), 10% (where the period of delay is between 9 and 18 months) and 15% in any other case. Of course, the organisation also has to pay the arrears of VAT. This can build up a considerable liability. The excuse 'we didn't realise we had to' is not acceptable.

2.68 Note that VAT is a remarkably specialised area, where the devil really does lie in the detail. Charities carrying out trading should take specialist advice on their VAT position. Failure to comply with the rules can have very unattractive consequences, as HMRC are not known for their benevolence with defaulters.

RATE RELIEF

2.69 Charities qualify for certain reliefs from business rates on their premises. Under s 43(5) of the Local Government Finance Act 1988:

(1)   where the ratepayer is a charity (or the trustees for a charity), and

(2)   the property is wholly or mainly used for charitable purposes,

the charity will be granted 80% mandatory relief from non-domestic rates.

2.70 Section 47 of the Local Government Finance Act 1988 also allows local authorities to grant additional discretionary relief of up to 20% in circumstances where the mandatory relief for charities would apply. An application must be made to the local authority and practice varies throughout the country. A charity's entitlement to rate relief may be affected by its trading activity. Charities which carry out primary purpose trading (see **3.72–3.73**) or which sell donated goods (see Chapter 4) on their premises will be treated as carrying out charitable activity and should therefore continue to qualify for relief.

2.71 Non-primary purpose trading activity (see **4.20**, for example) and the sale of donated goods on behalf of a charity's supporters (see **4.43–4.57**) will not be regarded as charitable trading activity. Occupation of property by a trading subsidiary (see **7.41–7.43**) will not qualify for the relief, since the ratepayer in this case is not a charity.

2.72 If the level of non-charitable activity by the charity, or the level of occupation by a trading subsidiary which shares premises with its parent charity, means that the property is no longer wholly or mainly used for charitable purposes, the entitlement to rate relief may be lost. There is no definitive guidance on what is meant by 'mainly', although 'mainly' has been defined in another context as 'probably ... more than half'. In practice this probably means more than half of the floor space or turnover. This issue will be particularly acute where charities and trading subsidiaries share premises (see **4.67** and **7.206–7.209**), or where a range of trading activities is carried out by a charity shop (see **4.61–4.64**).

2.73 These reliefs apply in England and Wales, but the rules are different in Northern Ireland and in Scotland. However, in Scotland there is mandatory 80% rate relief for charities, with an additional discretionary 20% relief. In Northern Ireland there is a full exemption for charities.

THE CHARITY SORP

2.74 The Statement of Recommended Practice (known as 'SORP') is the code of best practice for charity accounts. It was last revised in 2005. Although it is a statement of recommended practice, in some cases charities are obliged by statute to comply with SORP, and in practice all charities, especially larger charities, are expected to comply. SORP will dictate how trading income should be treated in a charity's accounts. For instance, income from primary purpose trading will fall under the heading of 'incoming resources from charitable activities' in the Statement of Financial Activity in a charity's accounts. Income from non-primary purpose trading will fall under 'activities for generating funds'.

CHARITIES ACT 1993

2.75 Under s 5 of the Charities Act 1993, a registered charity with a gross income in its last financial year of more than £10,000 must state in legible characters the fact that it is a registered charity on various documents specified in s 5(2), namely:

(a) notices, advertisements and other documents issued by or on behalf of the charity and soliciting money or other property for the benefit of the charity;

(b) bills of exchange, promissory notes, endorsements, cheques and orders for money or goods purporting to be signed on behalf of the charity; and

(c)   bills, invoices, receipts and letters of credit.

This means that a charity carrying on trading activity must ensure in particular that its cheques, purchase order forms, invoices and receipts – including till receipts – contain the magic words 'a registered charity'. Breach of s 5 is a criminal offence. In the case of bills of exchange, cheques, etc, the offence is committed by the person who signs the relevant document. In the case of bills, invoices, etc, it is committed by the person who issues or authorises the issue of a document which breaches the statutory requirement. Thus, if a fair trade charity sells fair trade goods by way of primary purpose trade, if the receipt breaches s 5, both the trustees of the charity (who as the persons having the general control and management of the charity must be deemed in law to have authorised the issue of the receipt) and the employee who issues the receipt could be charged with an offence.

2.76 In the case of a registered charity which sells publications, it could be argued that each publication which bears a price 'solicits money for the charity'. A book is clearly a document and, hence, all such publications should bear the words 'a registered charity'.

2.77 The maximum fine for breach of s 5 is £1,000, but at the time of writing the authors are not aware that anyone has been prosecuted under this section.

Chapter 3

PRIMARY PURPOSE TRADING

3.1   *In this chapter we look at what primary purpose trading is, and give a number of examples. We look at the VAT implications of the more common primary purpose trades. We explore particular issues which might be faced by charities which charge for admission to their premises, and charities carrying out research. We look at the implications of the Charity Commission's public benefit guidance for charities which charge for their services, and highlight areas which charities involved in public service delivery should watch out for. We also cover trading which is ancillary to primary purpose trading, and the implications of carrying out mixed trading which combines primary purpose and non-primary purpose activity.*

INTRODUCTION

3.2   Primary purpose trading is trading which a charity carries out in fulfilment of its main or primary purpose. Much of the trading which charities carry out today is primary purpose trading.

3.3   For instance, a charity is established to run a hospital. Its legal object is the advancement of health. The hospital charges its patients for the supply of medical treatment. This is trading, as the charity is selling its services. However, the trading is carried out in fulfilment of the charity's main purpose, so it is primary purpose trading. Similarly, educational charities which run private schools charge for providing educational services to the pupils: this too is trading, but it is primary purpose trading, as it is carried out in order to advance education. Note that fee-charging charities, such as private schools and hospitals, need to be able to demonstrate that they are established for the public benefit: there is otherwise a risk that they will not qualify for charitable status at all. This is explored in more detail at **3.88–3.102**.

3.4   A further example of primary purpose trading is a charity which carries out public service delivery. Many charities now provide services to the public sector under contract. They include charities which run care homes and sheltered accommodation, education, leisure services and advice services. Where the charity is paid under a contract to deliver the services, this is trading. The charity is providing services to the public authority, such as the local authority or Primary Care Trust, and it is being paid to do so.

3.5   Charities which carry out public service delivery are sometimes surprised to learn that they are trading. But very often they are. The exception is where they have been awarded a grant to deliver the services, as opposed to carrying out the services under a contract, although it is not always easy to tell the difference. This issue, and other pitfalls that charities delivering public services need to be aware of, are explored in more detail at **3.103–3.134**.

3.6   The beauty of primary purpose trading is that charities are perfectly free to carry it out. Provided there is power in the constitution – which there should be – there are no charity law restrictions on primary purpose trading, and it is highly likely that the charity will not have to pay any tax at all on the trading activity, although it may be subject to VAT. The rules are explored in more detail in this chapter.

EXAMPLES OF PRIMARY PURPOSE TRADING

3.7   The following sections illustrate the range of trading activities which charities undertake in the course of fulfilling their primary purposes. This is not a comprehensive list, but it aims to show the wide variety of ways in which charities trade. It is based on the statutory list of charitable purposes in s 2 of the Charities Act 2006, which came into force in April 2008.

The prevention or relief of poverty

3.8   *Workshops for the poor*: a charity established in the United Kingdom, such as Oxfam, sells goods made by the poor in a workshop in India run by the charity.

3.9   *Debt advice*: a charity which provides debt advice services, such as Citizens Advice, sells information and resource packs to other organisations delivering similar services.

The advancement of education

3.10   *University presses*: universities have charitable status (although many are exempt from the requirement to register with the Charity Commission). A number of universities have their own publishing arms, which carry on the trade of commissioning, publishing and selling books so as to advance education (e g Oxford University Press and Cambridge University Press). There has been controversy about the ability of university presses to make significant profits, tax free. But while the presses are simply fulfilling the universities' purposes of advancing education, their work is primary purpose trading.

3.11   *Universities and charitable private schools*: universities, private schools and certain other charitable educational institutions carry on a primary purpose trade by virtue of providing educational places in return for fees. Sometimes these fees are wholly or partly paid by a local educational authority (university fees or an assisted places scheme). Sometimes the institution will offer bursaries to students who cannot afford to meet the full fees. These charities need to be particularly alert to the public benefit rules described at **3.88–3.102** below.

The advancement of religion

3.12 *Retreat centres*: many religious charities run retreat centres which charge fees for courses, meals and accommodation. The centres are fulfilling the charities' religious objectives.

3.13 *Religious publications*: charities carry out the commissioning, publication and sale of printed matter, such as prayer books and religious literature, or of CDs and DVDs of services and religious music. The Society for Promoting Christian Knowledge, for instance, which is a registered charity, sells a range of Christian publications.

The advancement of health or the saving of lives

3.14 *Fee charging and the sale of goods*: charitable hospitals, such as the London Clinic, nursing homes and family planning clinics, such as those run by FPA, may charge for their services. The Red Cross sells wheelchairs and other independent living aids. The National Childbirth Trust sells products to help pregnant women and new mothers.

3.15 *Publications*: charities dedicated to improving health, such as Cancer Research UK, may charge for publications informing the public about healthcare issues.

The advancement of citizenship and community development

3.16 *Community centres*: a regeneration charity runs a community centre which is the venue for a café and courses open to members of the community. The café charges for food and drink, and a small charge is made for attendance at the courses.

3.17 *Support and advice services to charities*: a number of organisations charge for the provision of training, information and advice to other charities (eg the Charities Advisory Trust, the Directory of Social Change and the Institute of Fundraising).

The advancement of the arts, culture, heritage or science

3.18 *Museums and heritage sites*: many museums, galleries and heritage charities charge admission fees, eg the National Trust and some exhibitions at the Natural History Museum and Tate.

3.19 *Musical societies*: the Glasgow Musical Festival Association was established in 1926 to promote and conduct choirs and singing. It obtained an income from admission fees which were charged to people who attended its annual musical festival, where choirs and singers competed. In *IRC v Glasgow Musical Festival Association* (1926) SG 920, HMRC challenged the tax treatment of the profits derived from running the festival. The court held that the Association was trading in fulfilment of its primary purposes.

3.20 *Opera houses and theatres*: the Royal Opera House and the English National Opera are both charities which carry on a trade in fulfilment of their primary purposes by selling opera tickets, programmes and auxiliary catering. So, too, is that bastion of English society, Glyndebourne! The National Theatre and the Royal Shakespeare Company are educational charities which carry out primary purpose trading by selling theatre tickets.

The advancement of amateur sport

3.21 *Sports clubs*: many sports charities make a charge for the use of their facilities, and may charge a membership fee. Their challenge is to ensure that their facilities are sufficiently affordable as to be for the public benefit, as explained in more detail at **3.88–3.102**.

The advancement of human rights

3.22 *Legal assistance*: a charity dedicated to improving human rights in a particular region in Europe provides legal assistance to enable applicants to bring cases before the European Court of Human Rights under the European Convention on Human Rights. It makes a charge for these services, which successful applicants can generally reclaim from the court.

The advancement of environmental protection or improvement

3.23 *Public service delivery*: a recycling charity may charge local authorities for providing recycling services.

3.24 *Rights of admission*: environmental charities such as the Eden Trust charge for admission to their sites.

The relief of those in need by reason of youth, age, ill-health, disability, financial hardship or other disadvantage

3.25 *Youth organisations*: North Yorkshire Youth, a charity established to promote the development of young people, runs courses for young people at its outdoor centre in Yorkshire, for which it sometimes charges. The Youth Hostels Association charges for the accommodation it provides, in order to fulfil its objects of providing recreational facilities to the young.

3.26 *Holidays*: Vitalise is a national charity set up to promote the welfare of disabled people: it does this by a variety of means, including providing holidays for those with disabilities, for which a charge is made.

The advancement of animal welfare

3.27 *Sale of animals*: an animal rescue charity sells recovered pets to new homes.

Other charitable purposes

3.28 *The promotion of horticulture*: the Royal Horticultural Society charges for entry to its gardens.

3.29 *Prevention of crime*: a charity sells rape alarms to the public.

3.30 *Relief of unemployment*: a charity charges for arranging work placements which provide employment opportunities.

CONSTITUTIONAL AND CHARITY LAW ISSUES

Does the charity have power to trade?

3.31 As explained in Chapter 2, a charity will need constitutional power to carry out the trading activity in question. In the case of primary purpose trading a charity will need to demonstrate:

–   that the trading activity is in fulfilment of the formal legal objects of the charity, as set out in its constitution; and

–   that the constitution contains the necessary powers to carry out that form of trading activity.

For example, a charity set up to advance education may have power to publish books and other instructional material. Or the constitution may contain a specific power to trade in the course of carrying out the objects of the charity. In the absence of a specific power of this nature, it may be possible to rely on a general power in the constitution to 'do all such other lawful things as shall further the charity's objects'.

3.32 Note that it is the legal objects of the charity which are important. A charity carrying out a trade which does not directly further its own objects, but which furthers a purpose which is regarded as charitable in some other way, is not carrying out primary purpose trading. For example, a charitable museum, established to advance heritage, has spare rooms which it rents out to other organisations on a daily basis, providing tea, coffee and sandwiches. If the rooms are let to a relief of poverty charity for its trustees' annual awayday, this is unlikely to be primary purpose trading. The activity of renting out the rooms is not directly furthering the objects of the museum, even though it may be furthering the charitable objects of the relief of poverty and promoting the efficiency and effectiveness of charities. If, however, the museum rented its rooms to another museum, or heritage charity, it might well be carrying out primary purpose trading, as the activity of renting the rooms would, in some way, be advancing heritage.

Charity law

3.33   Charity law imposes no limits on primary purpose trading by charities. The Charity Commission is absolutely clear that charities may carry on primary purpose trading.

Work by the beneficiaries

3.34   Trading activity in which the work in connection with the trading is mainly carried out by the beneficiaries of the charity is generally regarded as primary purpose trading. In most cases such trading will, of itself, actually further the charity's purposes: indeed, it is hard to imagine a situation where this would not be the case. For example, a charity which supports those with physical and learning disabilities provides a range of commercial print finishing, packaging and mailing services to paying customers. The charity's beneficiaries make up the bulk of its workforce. The trading activity is of itself providing training and work experience to the beneficiaries on its staff, which fulfils the charity's objects. Similarly, a relief of poverty charity which sells goods made by its beneficiaries overseas (see **3.8**) is helping its beneficiaries through the employment opportunities it provides.

TAX

Exemption from tax

3.35   The usual rule is that profits from a trading activity are subject to tax, even if the trade is carried out by a charity. However, there is a very significant exception from this rule in the case of primary purpose trading.

3.36   Section 505(1)(e) of the Income and Corporation Taxes Act 1988 provides for:

> 'exemption from tax under Schedule D in respect of the profits of any trade carried on by a charitable company (whether in the United Kingdom or elsewhere), if the profits are applied solely to the purposes of the charitable company and either:
>
> (i)   the trade is exercised in the course of the actual carrying out of a primary purpose of the charitable company; or

(ii)   the work in connection with the trade is mainly carried out by beneficiaries of the charitable company'.

The reference to 'tax' is to corporation tax, which is otherwise payable by limited companies, other forms of corporation, unincorporated associations, and industrial and provident societies. There is a similar exemption, contained in ss 524 and 525 of the Income Tax Act 2007, which applies to the income of charitable trusts, which are otherwise subject to income tax.

UK charities only

3.37   The exemption only applies to the income of a charity established in the United Kingdom. It does not apply to income arising in the UK of a charity established abroad. This was decided by the House of Lords in *Camille and Henry Dreyfus Foundation, Inc v IRC* [1955] 3 All ER 97. The Foundation was incorporated under the laws of the state of New York, USA. It received substantial royalties from a company resident in the UK and was therefore liable to account for tax in the UK. However, the Foundation claimed that it was entitled to receive the royalties free from tax (under a similar exemption which applied to royalty income), as it was established for charitable purposes only. But the House of Lords ruled categorically that the exemption from tax was only available to a charity established in the United Kingdom.

3.38   This means that income derived from primary purpose trading in the UK by a charity established overseas, such as a French charity, would, at present, be taxable and would not qualify for an exemption. If, however, the French charity established a local UK charity to carry out its primary purpose trading work in the UK, the profits of that charity would be eligible for relief from taxation. Note that recent European Union court cases suggest that the government will soon be under pressure to review the law here to enable tax relief to be granted to overseas charities that operate in the UK. The European Court of Justice ruled in the *Stauffer case* in 2006 that differential treatment of tax for resident and non-resident charities was contrary to European principles of free movement of capital, and made a similar ruling in the 2009 *Persche* case (C-318/07).

The test

Option one: carrying out a primary purpose

3.39   The first limb of the test is that the trade must be exercised in the course of the actual carrying out of a primary purpose of the charity. Thus, the tax rules are similar to the charity law rules. The first step is to establish what the primary purposes of the charity are, by looking at its objects clause. If the trade is not in fulfilment of one of the charity's primary purposes as set out in the objects clause, the profits will be taxable. Hence, an educational charity set up to run a school will be exempt from income or corporation tax on profits derived from selling educational services. But if it sold Christmas cards bought in from another source, the profits from that activity would probably be taxable, because they would not have been derived from the 'actual carrying out of a primary purpose of the charity'.

3.40 For example, in *Grove v Young Men's Christian Association* (1903) 4 TC 613 the YMCA ran a restaurant on commercial lines which was open to the public. The trading activity (running a restaurant) was not in fulfilment of the charity's primary purpose, so the profits were taxable. A further example is the case of *British Legion, Peterhead Branch, Remembrance and Welcome Fund v IRC* (1953) 3 STC 84. The British Legion in this case was a branch of a charity registered under the War Charities Act 1940. Its objects were to perpetuate the memory of local men and women who fell in the war, to further the social and recreational welfare of survivors and to assist needy dependants. The branch raised money by running dances at the local drill hall every Saturday night for three years. The dances were not only open to survivors of the war. The hall was let at a nominal rent; the admission charge was 2s 6d, but was often added to by donations, and the dances were run by volunteers from the British Legion. If the dances had been run on normal commercial lines, the profits would have been greatly reduced by expenses. Tax assessments were raised on the profits from the dances. These assessments were upheld by the Special Commissioners, who found the branch was carrying on a trade in respect of which it was liable to tax. The fact that the profits were higher because voluntary labour had been used was *not* taken into account in assessing the taxable profits.

3.41 As under charity law, it is the objects of the charity in question that are relevant. If a charity with the sole object of advancing animal welfare sells publications designed to help children with maths, profits from this activity would be taxable, even though the activity itself does further another charitable purpose.

Option two: work by the beneficiaries

3.42 The second alternative afforded by the test is that the work in connection with the trade is mainly carried out by beneficiaries of the charity. 'Mainly' was defined by Lord Morton in *Fawcett Properties v Buckingham* [1960] 3 All ER 503 at 512 (a case involving agricultural tenancies) as being 'probably … more than half'. In other words, to fall within this exemption, not all the work in connection with the trade has to be carried out by beneficiaries, but only a majority of the work.

3.43 There are countless examples of situations where such work is carried out, including:

(a) The sale of goods produced by poor people in a developing country in a project organised by a charity to alleviate poverty and to train local people in relevant work skills.

(b)   The sale, in a centre established to educate people in the art of painting, of postcards produced by the students.

(c)   The provision of services or the sale of products by training schemes for unemployed young people, e g printing or data processing work.

(d)   The sale by a charity established to help people with disabilities of goods produced by its beneficiaries in a workshop.

3.44   Similarly, while the sale of Christmas cards by a charitable school would not necessarily fall within the first option afforded by the test, if the cards were designed and printed by the students, the second alternative may well apply. And although the profits from the restaurant in the *YMCA* case referred to above were not eligible for the exemption, the position might have been different if the restaurant had been staffed by the charity's beneficiaries.

The purposes of the charity

3.45   ICTA, s 505(1)(e) and its income tax equivalent in ITA 2007 require that if the exemption is to apply, the profits of the trade must be applied solely to the purposes of the charity. This means that the profits cannot be distributed to the members or trustees by way of dividends, bonuses, etc. It is more than likely that the charity's constitution will be drawn up in a way that prohibits distributions of this nature, so this requirement is unlikely to cause any real problems. Note that this restriction does not mean that a charity cannot pay its employees a surplus-related bonus – in theory it can do this and pay employees under any profit related pay arrangements.

3.46   The courts considered the question of an application of funds for charitable purposes in *IRC v Helen Slater Charitable Trust Ltd* [1982] Ch 49, when the Court of Appeal ruled that a transfer of money to another charity would represent an application of the funds for charitable purposes.

3.47   If the profits of a primary purpose trading activity were to be misapplied, the exemption from tax on the profits might be lost. This might include using the profits to fund activity outside the charity's objects, which would be a breach of trust, or to fund further trading activity which was not in fact permitted by the charity's constitution. HMRC could demand that the charity pay tax on the profits which had been so spent. And the charity trustees, having sanctioned the charity engaging in the 'ultra vires' activity, might be personally liable to reimburse the charity for the tax, since this would have resulted from their breach of trust.

VAT

3.48   We have seen that, provided the relatively straightforward strictures of ICTA, s 505(1)(e) and its income tax equivalent in ITA 2007 are complied with, charities which carry out primary purpose trading are unlikely to be troubled by direct tax. VAT is a different story. A charity which carries out primary purpose trading may well be making taxable supplies for VAT purposes. An outline of the VAT rules is given at **2.60–2.68**. Here we explore the VAT implications of some of the more common primary purpose trades.

Admission to cultural premises

3.49 A charity which makes an admission charge to visitors to its premises is making a taxable supply. However, admission charges by an 'eligible body' to a museum, art gallery, art exhibition or zoo, or to a theatrical, musical or choreographic performance of a cultural nature, are exempt from VAT. HMRC does not accept that a botanical garden qualifies as 'an art exhibition or zoo'. It will generally accept that a live performance of any form of stage play, dance or music is cultural.

3.50 In order to qualify as an eligible body, the organisation must fulfil the following conditions:

- It must be precluded from distributing, and must not distribute any profit it makes. Since charities are prohibited from distributing their profits, this condition should not cause any problems.

- It must apply any profits made from admission charges which are exempt from VAT under this rule to the continuance or improvement of the facilities made available by means of the taxable supplies. This will include the application of the profits to related cultural supplies. Again, this condition is unlikely to cause any problems for charities.

- It must be managed and administered on an essentially voluntary basis by persons who have no direct or indirect financial interest in its activities. This condition originally caused a flurry of litigation, with HMRC contending that the presence of salaried employees in a charity could prevent it from being managed and administered on a voluntary basis. Following the landmark *London Zoo* decision in the European Court of Justice (*C&E Commissioners v The Zoological Society of London* [2002] STC 521), HMRC accepts that where a charity is run by a body of trustees who are neither paid a commercial rate of pay, nor have any right to be paid at such a rate, the exemption will apply. This does not prohibit the payment of out of pocket expenses to trustees. Since then the law has expanded and it is now the case that a board of trustees can include a paid employee and the VAT exemption will apply. However, if the employee is paid at more than commercial rates or is entitled to a profit-related bonus, then that employee is deemed to have a financial interest and the terms for the VAT exemption will be broken.

3.51 Note that if no charge is made for admission, there is no taxable supply. Some charities suggest that visitors make a donation to the charity: provided this is a true donation it will be outside the scope of VAT. If, however, a benefit is offered 'in return for' a 'minimum donation', HMRC will treat the donation as a fee and apply the VAT rules accordingly. (See **4.79** and **5.33** for details of HMRC's approach to offering goods or entry to an event in return for a 'minimum donation'.) If the admission charge is for a fundraising event, the VAT exemption may apply: see Chapter 5 for more details. See **3.76–3.79** below for details of the special gift aid rules which apply to rights of admission.

Ambulance services

3.52 The supply of transport services for sick or injured persons is exempt from VAT, subject to the following conditions:

- The passengers being transported must be sick or injured.

- The transport must form part of a journey to or from a place of medical treatment.

- The vehicle in which the person is transported must be 'specially designed' for the purposes of providing such transport.

To qualify as 'specially designed', a vehicle must have the facility to secure a recumbent person on a stretcher or be fitted with a ramp or a lift, and clamps sufficient to enable a person in a wheelchair to be safely wheeled on, transported in, and wheeled off the vehicle. The term 'specially designed' is not restricted to road vehicles or to emergency vehicles.

Educational supplies

3.53 For the purposes of VAT, 'education' has a wider meaning than pure academic study. Although there is no definition in the legislation, HMRC regards education as meaning a course, class or lesson or instruction or study in any subject, whether or not that subject is normally taught in schools, colleges or universities, and regardless of when and where it takes place. Education includes lectures, educational seminars, conferences and symposia, holiday, sporting and recreational courses, and distance teaching and associated materials (provided the student is subject to assessment by the teaching institution).

3.54 Education is exempt from VAT if it is provided by an eligible body including:

(1) A school, university, sixth form college, tertiary college or other further education college or other centrally funded higher or further education institution (defined as such under the Education Acts), or the governing body of one of these institutions.

(2)   A non-profit making body that carries out duties of an essentially public nature similar to those carried out by a local authority or government department, such as Executive Agencies and Health Authorities.

(3)   A non-profit making body which:
   (a)   is precluded from distributing and does not distribute any profits it makes, and
   (b)   applies any profits made from exempt supplies of education, research or vocational training to the continuance or improvement of such supplies.

Charities can fulfil condition (a). In order to fulfil condition (b), if they are involved in several types of activity (eg advancing education and relieving poverty) they must ensure that any surplus from the educational activity is ploughed back into educational activities: if the surplus is used to relieve poverty the VAT exemption will be lost. A charity in such a situation must therefore monitor its income and expenditure closely so as to be able to prove that it has re-invested any surplus in educational activities.

Alternatively, a charity may wish to break the terms of VAT exemption by using at least some of its profits for non-educational purposes. This means it must charge VAT on its educational fees, but can recover VAT on its costs. This is particularly useful for charities that provide training to commercial organisations, which can recover VAT.

3.55   The provision of vocational training is also exempt when provided by an eligible body. Vocational training means training, retraining or the provision of work experience for any trade, profession or employment or for any voluntary work connected with education, health, safety or welfare, or the carrying out of activities of a charitable nature. This includes courses, conferences, lectures, workshops and seminars which train participants for future work or which add to their knowledge in order to improve their performance in their current work. Accordingly, training courses run by eligible bodies for charity trustees, for instance, are exempt from VAT.

3.56   The provision of education is also exempt to the extent that is ultimately provided under Learning and Skills Council budgets.

3.57   The provision of goods and services (eg materials, catering and accommodation) which are closely related to such education, training or retraining are exempt from VAT if:

•   the supply is made by or to the eligible body providing the education, training or retraining; and

•   the goods or services are for the direct use of the pupil, student or trainee receiving the principal supply; and

- where the supply is to the eligible body making the principal supply, it is made by another eligible body.

Hence, if the University of London runs an educational conference and provides a luncheon for the participants as part of the payment for the conference, the supply of the lunch will be exempt from VAT, as it is incidental to the training. However, if food was separately purchased from the University of London shop, or drinks purchased from the bar, these would be subject to VAT under normal rules. These points show that detail is all-important with VAT and professional advice should be sought.

Research

3.58 VAT is potentially relevant where a charity receives third party funding to carry out research. A cancer charity, for instance, may undertake research into cancer research or treatments. If the funding is a grant, rather than a contract, so that the funder retains no interest in the research, the grant will be non-business income outside the scope of VAT. Note that if the funder retains rights to own or exploit the intellectual property produced as a result of the research, the arrangement will not be a grant, but a contract, as the funds are not freely given (see **3.85**). If the arrangement is a contract, the arrangement falls within the scope of VAT.

3.59 Research is exempt from VAT if it is carried on by an eligible body and supplied to an eligible body (see **3.54** above). So, if the third party funding the research is an eligible body (eg another charity, or a university), the VAT exemption will apply. Research means original investigation undertaken in order to gain knowledge and understanding. If the intention at the start of a project is to advance knowledge and understanding, the supply is research. However, confirming existing knowledge and understanding is not research: HMRC does not regard the routine listing and analysis of materials, components and processes, for example, as VAT exempt. These supplies will therefore bear VAT at the standard rate.

3.60 Note that where a charity funds research, there are issues regarding the publication of the research, and the ownership of intellectual property rights, which need to be considered: these are explored more fully at **3.80–3.87**.

Sport

3.61 There are various VAT exemptions which may affect a charity providing sporting facilities. For instance, the letting of facilities designed or adapted for playing sport or taking part in physical recreation may be exempt from VAT if the letting is for over 24 hours or there is a series of lettings to the same person over a period of time.

3.62 Certain supplies by charities of services closely linked with and essential to sport or physical recreation to individuals taking part in the activity may also be VAT exempt. These include the use of changing rooms, showers, playing equipment, a playing area and multi-sport playing facilities, although the exemption is complicated and will depend on a number of factors, including the charity's membership arrangements. It should be noted that while there is a VAT exemption available for payments made by playing members of a sports charity, there is no such exemption for non-playing members. However, VAT exemption for their subscriptions may be achieved if the sports organisation behaves 'philanthropically' by looking beyond the interests of the members by doing good works in the community – e g by providing free coaching clinics at schools.

Nursery and crèche facilities

3.63 The provision of nursery and crèche facilities will generally fall within the VAT exemptions for education and/or welfare explained above and below. In addition, HMRC now accept that the supply of nursery and crèche facilities may, in certain circumstances, fall outside the scope of VAT, as it is not a business activity for VAT purposes. In *C&E Commissioners v Yarburgh Children's Trust* [2002] STC 207 a charity provided nursery and crèche facilities for pre-school age children as part of its charitable objectives. Its fees were set at a level designed to ensure it would simply cover its costs. The court decided that this was not a business supply. In *C&E Commissioners v St Paul's Community Project Ltd* [2005] STC 95 the court made a similar decision: it said that the intrinsic nature of the enterprise was not the carrying on of a business, and identified distinguishing features as social concern for the welfare of disadvantaged children, lack of commerciality in setting fees, and the overall intention simply to cover costs. These are important cases because they shattered the previously held HMRC view that the charging of fees automatically results in an activity being business activity for VAT purposes.

Health and welfare services

3.64 The supply of welfare services by a charity is exempt from VAT. Welfare services include:

(a) providing care, treatment or instruction designed to promote the physical or mental welfare of elderly, sick, distressed or disabled persons;

(b) protecting children and young persons;

(c) spiritual welfare provided by a religious institution as part of a course of instruction or retreat which, in either case, is not designed primarily as a recreation or holiday.

Supplies which have been exempted under this include residential accommodation at a centre for the study and practice of yoga, and the supply of food at a convention run by Jehovah's Witnesses.

3.65 The supply of accommodation or catering is excluded from the exemption unless it is ancillary to the provision of care, treatment or instruction. The supply of catering to elderly people in sheltered housing accommodation has been held to be ancillary (*Viewpoint Housing Association Ltd* (VTD 13148)) and thus within the scope of the exemption, as has the supply of hotel accommodation and catering to cancer patients and their families (*Trustees for the Macmillan Cancer Trust* (VTD 15603)).

3.66 By special concession, charities that provide welfare services at significantly below cost to distressed persons for the relief of their distress have the option of treating these supplies as non-business supplies, which fall outside the scope of VAT altogether. 'Distressed' in these circumstances means suffering pain, grief, anguish, severe poverty and so on. In order to qualify:

- the subsidy must be at least 15%;

- the subsidy must be available to all distressed persons, ie to both those who can and cannot afford to pay the full rate; and

- the services must be provided to the distressed individual (not, for example, to a local authority).

3.67 The supply of welfare advice and information by a charity may qualify for a reduced rate of VAT of 5%: for example, contracts to provide drug awareness advice, or the sale of educational DVDs for the parents of disabled children on how to manage their child's disability.

Rental and property

3.68 The supply of property is exempt from VAT. However, owners or landlords can opt to tax the supply of property unless it is used for a relevant residential or charitable purpose. A relevant residential purpose means domestic accommodation. A relevant charitable purpose means use otherwise than in the course of a business. HMRC regard non-business activity to be that which is not subject to fees. However, various court cases are suggesting that this is too restrictive a view, eg the *Yarburgh* and *St Paul's* cases mentioned at **3.63** above, as well as other cases involving Quarriers and Jeansfields Swifts Football Club. The courts are now suggesting that the motive behind the activity and the amount charged is a greater indication of whether an activity is a 'business'. HMRC have, however, still to accept this.

Zero rating

3.69 As explained in more detail at **2.65–2.66**, zero-rated supplies are taxable supplies which are charged to VAT at the rate of 0%. This enables a charity to claim back input tax on purchases made in connection with the supplies, even though it does not need to charge output tax.

3.70 Some supplies made in the course of primary purpose trading may be zero rated. These include certain types of food, books, leaflets and other publications, the supply of talking books for the blind and handicapped and wireless sets for the blind where supplied to other charities, and the supply of certain goods to the disabled and other charities. The latter includes adapted bathrooms, hoists, lifts, etc, and appliances designed for use by the disabled. The key here is the design purpose – appliances that the disabled find useful but which have a general commercial design purpose will not qualify for the VAT zero rate.

3.71 The sale of recovered pets to new homes by an animal rescue charity was recently confirmed as a VAT zero-rate supply where the animals have been donated for sale by members of the public, local authorities, etc (*Gables Farm Trust*).

RATE RELIEF

3.72 As explained in detail at **2.69–2.73**, where a charity occupies premises wholly or mainly for charitable purposes, it will be entitled to 80% mandatory relief from non-domestic rates. It will also qualify to be considered for additional discretionary relief of 20%.

3.73 Where a charity occupies premises for the purposes of carrying out primary purpose trading, it will be using the property wholly for charitable purposes, and the entitlement to rate relief will apply. Note that this will not be the case if the trading is carried out by a trading company (see **7.41–7.42**).

SORP

3.74 SORP (the Statement of Recommended Practice) requires that the gross income from primary purpose trading and the associated expenditure should be reported in the Statement of Financial Activity in the charity's accounts. Income from trading activities which are undertaken in furtherance of the charity's objects, ie primary purpose trading, will be categorised as 'incoming resources from charitable activities'. Similarly, the costs associated with primary purpose trading will fall under the heading of 'resources expended on charitable activities', as it represents resources applied by the charity in undertaking its work to meet its charitable objectives. See **2.74** for more information on SORP.

CHARITIES ACT 1993

3.75 Charities carrying out primary purpose trading will need to comply with s 5 of the Charities Act 1993 which requires that a registered charity with income of over £10,000 must state that it is a registered charity on various documents including advertisements, bills, invoices and receipts. The rules are explained in more detail at **2.75–2.77**.

PARTICULAR ISSUES – RIGHTS OF ADMISSION TO CHARITY PREMISES

3.76 Where a charity allows a member of the public to come onto its premises, or to view its property, in return for a fee, it will be trading. In most cases this will be primary purpose trading. Thus, although the National Trust may charge for admission to its properties, and Tate may charge for admission to some of its exhibitions, the profits from this should not be subject to direct tax.

3.77 Where a UK taxpayer makes a donation to a UK charity, the charity can generally recover tax on that donation under the gift aid regime. Do the gift aid rules apply to admission charges of this nature? On the face of it, clearly not, as the charity is receiving a fee, rather than a donation. However, when the gift aid regime was expanded in 2000, special rules were included in relation to rights to view the property of heritage and wildlife charities. These rules were changed again in 2006 (because some members of the government deemed them over-generous) and now appear in ITA 2007, s 420.

3.78 The position at the time of writing is that where a person makes a payment to a charity and in return receives a 'relevant right of admission' to the charity's premises or property, that right is disregarded for the purposes of the gift aid rules. Thus, if a supporter pays £10 in order to see an exhibition at a charitable art gallery (and the various conditions outlined below are complied with), and makes an appropriate gift aid declaration, not only is the £10 free of tax, but the charity can reclaim the basic rate tax paid. This is potentially a very useful concession.

3.79 The regime will only apply if certain conditions are complied with and HMRC is known to monitor this carefully. The conditions are:

(1)   A 'right of admission' is a right which:
   –   benefits the individual who makes the gift or that individual and one or more members of his or her family;
   –   authorises admission to premises or property to which the public are admitted on payment of an admission fee; and
   –   authorises admission to those premises or that property without payment of the fee, or on payment of a reduced fee.

(2)   The opportunity to make a gift and receive the right of admission in consequence must be available to the public. This means that the right of admission cannot be conditional on the individual making a gift aid declaration. So, if a charity running a nature reserve allows its supporters

to visit in return for a £5 donation, they must allow in those who make the donation even if they do not also make a gift aid declaration. Without the gift aid declaration the charity cannot reclaim the basic rate tax paid. This is a risk for the charity.

(3)   The right of admission must be a right granted by the charity for the purpose of viewing property preserved, maintained, kept or created by a charity for its charitable purposes. Examples include:
   –   the National Trust granting rights to see its historic properties;
   –   the Royal Society for the Protection of Birds charging for entry to its reserves;
   –   the Victoria and Albert Museum charging for entry to some of its collections.

(4)   A further condition is that either:
   –   the right of admission applies, during a period of 12 months, at all times at which the public can obtain admission: this would apply, therefore, where a charity makes a supporter a 'member' for a year, in return for his or her donation, with rights to see the charity's property for free during that year (the charity can exclude up to five special 'event' days per year from the right to free admission); or
   –   a member of the public could purchase the same right of admission, and the amount of the gift is greater than the amount which he would have to pay by at least 10%; this means that the charity must offer members of the public a chance to see the property or premises in return for a lower fee (not a donation) – eg supporters would have the option of paying the charity a £33 donation (on which gift aid relief could be claimed if the appropriate gift aid declaration were made), or a £30 fee.

Issues such as the scope of the right of admission, joint arrangements between charities and conferring other benefits on the donor are covered in the detailed rules and in HMRC's 'Detailed guidance notes for charities', ch 3, para 3.48.

RESEARCH

3.80   Charities which carry out research in return for funding from a third party must watch out for some particular issues.

3.81   The first question to ask is whether the activity is trading or not. Where a charity is grant funded to carry out research, and the arrangement really is a grant, then the charity will not be trading. But if the arrangement is a contract – under which the charity is expected to do something in return for a fee – then the arrangement is trading. The distinction between a grant and a contract can be very hard to draw, and we explore this in more detail at **3.105–3.116** below. In the context of research, note that if a charity is expected to assign intellectual property rights in the fruits of the research to the funder, or to allow the funder a share of the proceeds if the intellectual property rights are exploited, this may turn what might otherwise look like a grant arrangement into a contract (see **3.85**).

3.82 If the arrangement is trading, is it primary purpose trading? Research is not of itself a charitable purpose. It is instead a recognised means of achieving a charitable purpose. Thus, an educational charity might use research methods to investigate certain issues, and disseminate the results of the research in order to achieve its charitable object of advancing education. A charity set up to advance healthcare by preventing and treating a particular disease may carry out scientific research into possible cures and appropriate treatments. Charities which carry out research, as a trading activity, in a way which furthers their objects, are likely to be carrying out primary purpose trading. Charities that carry out research which does not further their primary purposes will be carrying out non-primary purpose trading. For example:

- A cancer research charity carries out research in return for funding from the NHS. The NHS has the rights to any resulting intellectual property. This will be primary purpose trading, as the research results are to be in the public domain.

- A cancer research charity receives funding from a commercial organisation to carry out research in which the commercial partner acquires all intellectual property rights. This is non-primary purpose trading, as the intellectual property is to be vested in a private organisation.

3.83 There are particular issues over the publication of research. Educational charities, by and large, should disseminate the results of any research they undertake. An educational charity which undertakes research which remains largely secret is not educating its beneficiaries, nor is it likely to be providing public benefit. This can give rise to tensions. First, a funder of charitable research may require that the results of the research be kept secret. This may be because it wishes to exploit the research commercially, or may be for other reasons: a government agency involved with defence work may require that research be kept secret in order to preserve state security. Second, secrecy can help with commercial exploitation of the research: if an invention is formally patented, it is best if it is kept confidential while the patent application is pending (see **9.91–9.99**). In such cases, trustees will need to take a finely balanced decision about what is best for the charity and its beneficiaries.

3.84 The tensions are similar, but less acute, where the charity does not have educational objects. The obligation on the trustees to disseminate the results of the research is less clear cut: they must act in a way which they reasonably feel best furthers their charity's purposes.

3.85 If the results of the research do have commercial value, to what extent should the financial rewards be shared between the charity and the funder of the research? The Association of Medical Research Charities has issued guidance on revenue sharing of commercially exploited charity funded research which may be helpful ('An Essential Partnership, Principles and Guidelines for Working with Industry', December 2007). Standard advice from AMRC is that research should be funded on the basis that an agreement should be reached once the project has come to fruition about how the financial benefit from any intellectual property rights will be shared. Lawyers call this 'an agreement to agree', because the precise formula for revenue sharing is not agreed at the outset. AMRC provides a suggested framework on which to base negotiations once the parties are ready to agree the detail of revenue sharing. HMRC is understood to accept that such an arrangement does not turn the relationship between the parties from a grant into a contract for VAT purposes (see **3.81**). Note, however, that if there is a precise agreement from the outset about how any revenue will be split, that might well mean the arrangement is a contract for VAT purposes (see **3.81**). Note too that exploitation of intellectual property rights once the research has been carried out may of itself be trading activity! – although this might be primary purpose trading. Again, charities must balance the costs and other implications of exploiting intellectual property rights commercially against the likely benefit to the charity.

3.86 Finally, any charity which becomes involved in a relationship with a commercial organisation must be aware of the impact which that relationship might have on its reputation. Chapter 5 gives some examples of the issues which charities should have regard to. This may be particularly important for medical research charities: AMRC guidance stresses the importance of independence, integrity and openness in any dealings with the commercial sector.

3.87 There may be situations where it would be inappropriate for research activity which amounts to trading to be carried out by the charity directly. The trustees may want to consider running the activity via a trading subsidiary. For example, Cancer Research UK employs a fully owned subsidiary company, Cancer Research Technology, to manage and commercially exploit intellectual property and materials resulting from research it has funded. Where a trading subsidiary is used, the parent charity should ensure that intellectual property rights are not transferred free of charge to the trading company, and should be cautious about allocating contracts to the trading company lest the whole balance of the charity is undermined by excessive use of the charity's assets for non-charitable purposes. Chapter 7 contains more detail about the use of trading subsidiaries.

PUBLIC BENEFIT

3.88 Charities which carry out primary purpose trading must also be alert to the rules on public benefit. This is an area which is in the process of change, following the implementation of the Charities Act 2006.

3.89 Under the Charities Act 2006, in order to be charitable a charity must:

–   have purposes which fall within the list of charitable purposes in s 2(2) of the 2006 Act (see **3.8–3.30** above); and

–   have purposes which are for the public benefit.

What this means is that all charities must show that they operate for the public benefit. This represents a change in the law: prior to implementation of this part of the 2006 Act in April 2008 it was presumed that educational, poverty and religious charities were for the public benefit. This meant that charities in these categories did not need to actively demonstrate that they benefited the public – it was presumed that they did.

3.90 The Charity Commission is charged with producing guidance on public benefit, and all charity trustees are obliged to have regard to the guidance when exercising any powers or duties to which the guidance is relevant (Charities Act 2006, s 4(6)). For financial years beginning on or after 1 April 2008, the trustees' report which accompanies the annual accounts must give details of the activities undertaken by the charity to further its charitable purposes for the public benefit (reg 40 of the Charities (Accounts and Reports) Regulations 2008 (SI 2008/629)). The level of detail required will depend on whether the charity is above or below the audit threshold.

3.91 The Charity Commission's general guidance on public benefit, published in January 2008, sets out two key public benefit principles:

•   There must be an identifiable benefit or benefits.

•   Benefit must be to the public, or a section of the public.

The Charity Commission lists some important factors to consider when deciding whether an organisation's aims meet the second of these two principles, including:

–   Where benefit is to a section of the public, the opportunity to benefit must not be unreasonably restricted by ability to pay any fees charged.

–   People in poverty must not be excluded from the opportunity to benefit.

–   Any private benefits must be incidental.

Charities which carry out primary purpose trading will need to bear these principles in mind.

Fee-charging

3.92   The Commission's general guidance states that while charities are able to charge fees for services and facilities which more than cover the cost of providing them, 'where, in practice, the charging restricts the benefits to only those who can afford to pay the fees charged, this may result in the benefits not being available to a sufficient section of the public'. Where fees are charged for services or facilities, the Commission will consider the following issues:

(1)   Whether the levels at which fees are set have the effect of preventing people who are unable to pay the fees from benefiting from the services or facilities.

(2)   If this is the case, whether it is possible to show that people who are unable to pay the fees are not excluded from the opportunity to benefit. According to the guidance:

> 'Where people are unable to benefit from a charity because they cannot afford to pay the fees charged for its services, there must be other material ways or opportunities, related to the aims, available to them to benefit.
>
> Fee-charging charities are encouraged to be positive, innovative and imaginative in considering how to maximise the benefits they can offer to the public and, in particular, to people who cannot afford to pay the fees charged.'

Examples given of where this might be the case include:
- where a charity provides concessions, subsidised or free places, such as fee-paying schools offering bursaries or assisted places, or theatres offering concessionary tickets;
- where other reliable sources of funding exist which are specifically made available to beneficiaries, such as a funding arrangement between an independent school and a separate, but linked, grant-making body, or where funding is offered by a local authority to pay for a place in a care home;
- where charities provide facilities or services for people other than those who pay fees for them, such as a charity lending equipment or staff to other charities or groups;
- where independent schools operate collaboration and partnership with state schools;
- where a private hospital gives free access to specialised medical equipment which would not otherwise be available locally to NHS patients;
- where a private hospital offers medical training to nurses or doctors at an NHS hospital which benefits the non-fee paying patients at that hospital.

(3)   Whether and how people who are unable to pay the fees may otherwise benefit from those services or facilities.

(4)   The nature and extent of the other benefits provided.

3.93 In December 2008 the Charity Commission published additional sub-sector guidance, after a process of consultation, explaining how the principles in its general guidance relate specifically to charities that charge fees for their services or facilities. The guidance makes a number of points, including the following:

> 'Fee-charging is likely to be a public benefit issue where:
>
> –   the service or facility that is charged for forms a significant part of the charity's aims, or the way it carries out those aims; and/or
> –   the fees that are charged for that service or facility are high.'

> 'where a charity charges low fees that most people can afford, then the fee-charging is unlikely to give rise to public benefit difficulties.'

> 'where a charity charges high fees that many people could not afford, the trustees … must … demonstrate that there is sufficient opportunity for people who cannot afford those fees to benefit in a material way that is related to the charity's aims.'

The guidance explains that offering free or subsidised access to the service or facilities is an obvious and, in many cases, the simplest, way to meet the requirement: however, the charity may also provide other significant opportunities to benefit. The guidance elaborates further on the issues the Commission will consider when assessing the public benefit of fee-charging charities, and explains how trustees of fee-charging charities should report on public benefit.

Private benefit

3.94 Where people or organisations, other than the charity's beneficiaries, receive private benefits from the charity, those private benefits must be 'incidental'. According to the Commission's guidance, private benefits will be incidental if it can be shown that they directly contribute towards achieving the charity's aims and/or are a necessary result or by-product of achieving those aims.

3.95 In practice, it will be very difficult in any particular case to determine whether a charity's activities actually provide only 'incidental' or a preponderance of private benefit. Take a hypothetical example. A charity, which has as its main object the improvement of the natural environment, is employed for a fee to re-landscape a back garden. The replanting is done in an ecologically sensitive manner. Native trees and shrubs are planted to attract birds and insects so as to encourage as rich a diversity of nature as possible. The environment has been improved as a result of the charity's work. Therefore, it can be claimed, there has been public benefit and the charity has traded in fulfilment of its primary purpose. But the owner of the back garden has also enjoyed a considerable benefit. He or she has a much better back garden. Has the work been done for the benefit of the public or the benefit of the landowner? Would the position be different if the works had been to his or her front garden, which abutted a busy road, with many passers-by?

3.96 The question of 'private benefit' can arise in a number of other areas such as the provision by a charity (in fulfilment of its main objects) of advice to an employer, for example, on how to meet its statutory obligations under health and safety legislation, or in providing training in first aid at work. Another example would be the provision by a charity of first aid cover at events, such as at races and football matches, so as to allow the owner of the ground to meet the legal obligation to have such cover available. In all these cases it can be argued that, in providing these services, a charity is fulfilling its objects, whilst at the same time enabling the purchaser of the service to meet its legal obligations – in the examples for the benefit of the public! Accordingly, the benefit derived by the employer or promoter of the event is incidental and not sufficient to disqualify the activity from being charitable. But this is a contentious area, where each case needs to be considered separately.

Complying with the public benefit rules

3.97 One undoubted implication of the change in the public benefit rules brought about by the Charities Act 2006 is that there will now be renewed focus on the extent to which charities charging fees for goods and services provide public benefit.

3.98 When the Charity Commission is registering new charities, it will require each organisation to show that it has charitable aims that are, and are carried out for, the public benefit. And the Commission will assess, on an ongoing basis, the public benefit of existing charities via a range of methods, including:

- Assessing the information provided in the trustees' annual reports.

- Carrying out public benefit research studies. The Commission's guidance implies that it will be looking, in particular, at poverty, educational and religious charities, including educational institutions and hospitals and other charities that charge high fees.

- Detailed assessments of individual charities. The Commission's public benefit assessment programme commenced in October 2008, with particular focus on independent schools and fee-charging residential care homes.

3.99 Failure to meet the public benefit requirement can have a number of consequences:

- the Commission may decide that the trustees are acting in breach of trust, and may take appropriate action which might include changing the trustees;

–   the charity's aims may need to be changed to cover charitable aims that will be for the public benefit; or

–   the Commission may decide that the charity was mistakenly registered as a charity and either ask the trustees to restructure the organisation or restate its objects, or remove it from the register – the latter course of action could well have significant tax implications, but it is highly unlikely.

3.100   In assessing whether a charity provides public benefit, each case will be considered separately, and the Commission will weigh up a range of factors. Assessment of public benefit will not necessarily be easy, and the law may change over time, particularly since the newly established Charity Tribunal – which deals with appeals from Charity Commission decisions – is expected to be asked to consider tricky public benefit questions.

3.101   Charities carrying out primary purpose trading, including charities involved in public service delivery (see **3.103–3.134**), will need to keep the public benefit rules in mind. Charities delivering public services are not necessarily, strictly speaking, fee-charging charities, since they are typically charging the body commissioning their services, rather than the end user of those services, but they should nonetheless ensure that the public benefit rules are observed.

3.102   Charity trustees are inevitably concerned about the impact of the public benefit rules. The vast majority of trustees should have nothing to fear from the Commission's guidance, but the following practical steps are recommended:

*   All charity trustees should ensure that they are properly briefed on the Commission's main guidance, and on any relevant sub-sector guidance, such as the guidance on public benefit and fee-charging.

*   Charities should use the guidance as an opportunity to review whether their aims and activities are for the public benefit, and should consider how to promote public benefit on an ongoing basis.

*   Charities should note that the Charity Commission's guidance is not a definitive statement of the law, but is the Commission's interpretation of the law. There will certainly be scope for argument in some situations as to whether the guidance represents an accurate statement of the law, particularly on difficult questions such as fee-charging.

*   The Commission's guidance itself states that if charities depart from the guidance they should be able to show good reasons for doing so. This implies that there may be cases where the trustees judge, quite properly, that compliance with charity law is not necessarily the same thing as compliance with the Commission's guidance. However, trustees should act with caution, and take appropriate professional advice.

- Charity trustees should be prepared to report on public benefit in their trustees' reports.

PUBLIC SERVICE DELIVERY

3.103   There is nothing new about charities delivering public services. Before the introduction of the welfare state, charities took on the task of providing many of the services, such as schools and healthcare, which we now see as the prerogative of the state. But in recent years, central and local government have increasingly contracted out the delivery of their services to voluntary sector organisations. NCVO's *The UK Civil Society Almanac 2008* reports that the voluntary and community sector's income from the public sector has increased steadily over the years, combined with a strong shift from grant funding to contract funding. In 2005/06 over 35% of the voluntary and community sector's funding originated from the public sector: a total of £11 billion. Of that, contract funding comprised 62% of the income from government: a percentage which has been on the rise.

3.104   Public service delivery is, in many cases, trading. Where charities are contracted to deliver a service, such as care, social housing or leisure services, they are trading. Provided the activity is carried out in the course of furthering the charity's main objects, it will be primary purpose trading. But there are some key considerations which charities involved in public service delivery should be alert to.

Are we operating under a contract or a grant arrangement?

3.105   Whenever a charity delivers public services under an arrangement with a public body, it is very important to be clear about the nature of that relationship. There are significant differences, in legal terms, between a contract, where the charity is promising to perform certain services in return for a fee, and a grant, where the charity is not obliged to do anything in return for the funding, simply to use it in a certain way. The distinction is not always easy to draw, and inappropriate use of the terms 'grant' and 'contract' only serves to exacerbate the confusion. The differing implications of operating under a grant or a contract are explored in more detail below. A charity operating under a grant arrangement is not, strictly speaking, trading and, crucially, while contracts are within the scope of the VAT regime, grants are not, as the charity is not treated as making a taxable supply.

3.106   There may be pros and cons to the arrangement being within the scope of VAT. If the supply of services is treated as a taxable supply, the charity should be able to recover input tax on its expenditure in relation to the supply. But the charity will need to account for output tax on the fee paid by the public body; if it has failed to negotiate that the public authority will pay both the fee and the VAT due on it, it may be faced with a VAT bill it cannot afford to pay.

How to distinguish a contract from a grant

3.107 It is not always possible to be 100% clear about whether an arrangement is a contract or a grant. There are many arrangements in the field of public service delivery which fall somewhere between the two, and it may be necessary to seek specialist advice, or even clearance from HMRC. The following are broad principles.

3.108 A contract typically involves a mutual bargain, where one party promises to do something for the other, in return for a fee. A contract is likely to include provisions allowing the parties to terminate the arrangement if the other party is in breach, or on giving a defined period of notice. A contract may include details of what the consequences of the breach are likely to be, such as suing for damages.

3.109 Under a grant arrangement, the funds are freely given and the charity is expected to do nothing except use the funds for the purposes for which they are given. If the terms of the grant arrangement are breached, the public authority may be able to claw back the funds, but should not be able to sue for any other type of damage.

3.110 Service level agreements set out what is required in a service and the basis for delivery and payment. They are usually more likely to be contracts than grants, even where they contain a statement that the arrangement is not a contract, although this is a grey area.

3.111 A particular case is where an agreement to fund medical research contains a provision requiring that any intellectual property developed as a result of the research should be the property of the funder. On the face of it, this looks like a contract as the funder is receiving a benefit in return for the award of funding (see **3.85**).

3.112 HMRC will regard an arrangement as falling outside the scope of VAT if the person supplying the funding is not benefiting from the arrangement. The following example is taken from HMRC publication 701/1. HMRC suggests that the example 'may help to illustrate the difference between "grant funding" which falls outside the scope of VAT and "third party funding" which is payment by one party on behalf of someone else and is subject to VAT'.

'A Citizens Advice Bureau (CAB) provided free legal, and other, advice. It received grant funding from, amongst others, the local authority. The local authority, as a condition of grant funding, required a service level agreement to be entered into by the CAB, detailing opening times, levels of service, etc. On this basis the CAB viewed the funding, and linked agreement, to be consideration for a taxable supply of services to the local authority.

On appeal to the VAT tribunal it was found that there was nothing in the service level agreement to support the CAB's view. In the Tribunal's view, although strings were attached to the grant given by the local authority, that in itself did not create a supply. This was because the local authority did not derive any direct benefit from the advice given. Its only benefit was the indirect knowledge that it had helped fund a service that might be of benefit to its citizens. The strings attached to the grant funding were simply good housekeeping measures by the local authority. The only supplies made were to the local citizens and, as these were mainly free of charge, there was no supply for VAT purposes.

The only exception is where legal advice is given by a CAB to a citizen who qualifies for legal aid. In such cases the legal advice given is subject to VAT. This is because the CAB has received specific payment, from a third party, for specific advice given to a citizen.'

3.113 The example illustrates, in fact, how difficult the distinction can be to draw. Other key cases include the VAT Tribunal case of *Bowthorpe Community Trust* (1994) and the ECJ case of *Mohr v Finanzamt Bad Segeberg* [1996] STC 328.

3.114 In the former case the Bowthorpe Community Trust, a registered charity, received funding from Norfolk County Council towards its work with disabled people. Initially, the charity was simply required to provide the council with its accounts, showing how the funds had been used, but in 1992 the charity was asked to enter into a more formal agreement covering the work experience places it would provide for disabled people, and requiring the charity to provide guaranteed places on its programme for people referred by the council. The VAT Tribunal decided that notwithstanding the more detailed agreement from 1992 onwards, the arrangement remained a grant:

'The trust is supplying services to [the individuals attending its workshops]. Those individuals referred to the trust by the Council's Social Services have priority in the selection of persons to receive training, and the Council is given certain monitoring rights to see that they do and that the trust fulfils its other obligations in providing those benefits, but that does not mean that the trust is supplying the training services which the grant supports to the Council.'

3.115 The *Mohr* case concerned payment by the German state of agreed compensation to a farmer who had agreed to discontinue milk production. The European Court of Justice held that this payment was outside the scope of VAT. The German authorities were not, in making the payment, acquiring anything for their own use but instead acting in the common interest of promoting the proper functioning of the European milk market. They were not receiving any benefit which would enable them to be consumers of a service.

3.116 However, a VAT Tribunal case decided shortly before this book went to print may pave the way for a different approach. In *Bath Festivals Trust Ltd v Revenue and Customs* [2008] UKVA V20840 (22 October 2008) the Tribunal decided that agreeing to take over a job previously undertaken by a local authority could amount to a supply of services, where that activity fell within the scope of the council's strategy relating to the promotion or improvement of the social wellbeing of its area. This case will need to be watched closely to see whether it represents a change in what was previously understood to be the law.

Mission drift

3.117 In the summer of 2006 the Charity Commission conducted a survey of charities concerning their participation in public service delivery. The results appear in the Commission's research report, RS15 Stand and Deliver – The future for charities delivering public services. The research findings showed that of the charities responding to the survey, those involved in public service delivery were significantly less likely than other charities to agree:

(a)   that their charitable activities were determined by their mission rather than their funding opportunities;

(b)   that they were free to make decisions without pressure to conform to the wishes of funders; and

(c)   that the trustees were always involved in decisions about what activities or projects to undertake.

3.118 The Commission was concerned about the pressure on charities undertaking public services to focus on the wishes of the public authority funding them, rather than their own objects and, in turn, the needs of their beneficiaries. The Commission's guidance on charities and public service delivery, published simultaneously with the research findings (CC37 – Charities and Public Service Delivery – An Introduction and Overview) reminds charities that:

> 'Decisions about activities or services must be directed by the charity's objects, and should follow its mission and planned priorities rather than funding opportunities. Funding considerations may well be a factor, but they should not drive or determine the mission.'

Negotiation of terms

3.119 A further issue for charities undertaking public service delivery is the negotiation of contracts with the public authority.

3.120 In its guidance on public service delivery, the Charity Commission urges charities to be fully informed about the financial aspects of public service delivery. In particular, they should understand the full cost to the charity of providing the services, recognise the charity's scope to deliver and any limitations, identify any unique or distinctive qualities of the charity's services, and use these and other relevant factors to set a price for the services.

3.121 It is perfectly acceptable for the charity to make a surplus on the arrangement. Equally, provided the trustees are happy that the arrangement is in the interests of the charity's beneficiaries, it is acceptable for it to provide services at less than full cost recovery, ie to effectively make a loss on the contract.

3.122 In 1998 the government launched the 'Compact' – a framework for partnership working between government and the voluntary and community sector. The Compact sprang from recommendations in the 1996 Deakin Commission report on the Future of the Voluntary Sector to the effect that the government should recognise the legitimacy of the voluntary and community sector's diverse roles and its own responsibility to promote a healthy sector. The Deakin Commission proposed a 'concordat' drawn up between representatives of government and the sector, laying down basic principles for future relations.

3.123 The Compact, which resulted from consultation across the sectors, sets out key principles underpinning the relationship between government and the voluntary and community sectors. Government undertakes to respect the independence of the voluntary and community sector, to consult early enough to make a difference and to recognise the cost of doing business when funding public service delivery. In turn, the voluntary and community sector undertakes to involve all stakeholders and embrace diversity and to contribute constructively to public policy. All sectors undertake to work together to improve outcomes for the community.

3.124 The Compact is supported by five Codes of Good Practice, including a Code on Funding and Procurement. Local compacts, which now cover most of the United Kingdom, deal with the relationship between local government, local public bodies and voluntary and community sectors.

3.125 The Compact is aimed at ensuring a positive working relationship between government and the voluntary sector. In 2007 the Commission for the Compact was established in response to a widespread recognition that the Compact was not being properly implemented. The Commission is an independent body which aims to raise awareness of the Compact locally and nationally, and to promote compliance. The Compact Advocacy Programme run by the NCVO provides practical support and wider campaigning to the sector where the government has breached the Compact.

3.126 The Compact is the subject of constant debate and controversy across the voluntary and community sector. There is a widespread concern that the principles of the Compact are not generally adhered to by public authorities, and that in practice, in its day to day dealings with charities, government continues to believe that charities should subsidise public services, rather than perform them to specification for a fair contract price, and that 'full cost recovery' precludes, rather than demands, a reasonable surplus to support future service viability and development.

3.127 As well as ensuring that they are properly informed about the overall implications of the contract with the public authority for their organisation, charities should be happy with the specific contractual terms. Particular issues to be alert to are:

– ensuring that the payment terms are appropriate;

– having particular regard to any terms which might allow for recovery of the fee or delayed payment;

– making sure that the contract specification is very clear about what is expected from the charity;

– checking the powers which the public authority has in the event of a breach of contract;

– the termination provisions;

– the cost implications of monitoring requirements.

Chapter 8 gives more detail about issues to be aware of when negotiating charity contracts generally.

3.128 The Charity Commission's guidance on public service delivery lists further risks which charities involved in public service delivery should be aware of, including the frequently short-term nature of public funding, payment in arrears which can give rise to cash-flow problems, and the possibility of becoming responsible for additional staff under the Transfer of Undertakings (Protection of Employment) Regulations ('TUPE'). A further risk (as mentioned at **3.117–3.118**) is the temptation for charities to bow to pressure from public authorities to influence or direct their decision-making, as well as the possibility that a charity which is receiving funding from a public authority may be compromising its independence.

Public procurement

3.129 A further major issue for charities contracting with public authorities to bear in mind is the prescriptive procedural regime to which public sector organisations are subject and to which charities must appropriately respond. All public bodies have an inherent public duty to secure contracts which provide 'best value' to the public, and internal procedures to ensure decisions are made with due objectivity to this end. In addition, there are prescriptive procedural requirements which apply through European Union legislation designed to ensure that all prospective suppliers of services have a fair and equal opportunity to secure available public sector contracts. Detailed procedural rules apply under the public procurement regulations, which implement the relevant EU directive, for specified types of goods, works or services contracts above specified contractual value thresholds. Such contracts are 'Part A' contracts under the regulations. The rules applicable to Part A contracts set out the processes which must be followed when advertising, tendering for, negotiating and finalising the regulated type of contract. For all contracts by public authorities, general principles apply requiring fair, transparent and objective procedures giving assurance that all prospective suppliers receive equal treatment. These general principles apply, without the additional Part A prescriptions, to all other types of contract and all contracts below the Part A value thresholds. Often the application of the general principles will mean procedures similar to those required for a Part A contract are followed, without this being strictly required, for a Part B contract (see below). A detailed explanation of the procurement rules is beyond the scope of this book, but the broad principles are as follows:

- The essence of the regime is to ensure that prospective providers are treated equally, and that the process of awarding the contract is objective, open, transparent and proportionate.

- The rules apply to the award of contracts by central and local government and other public bodies, as well as organisations controlled by them. This will include local authorities, central government departments and other public bodies, such as primary care trusts.

- Failure to comply with the rules allows the award of the contract to be challenged. While this represents a risk for the contracting parties, it can also be an opportunity for a charity which has failed to secure the contract to challenge it.

- The Part A thresholds vary depending on the nature of the contract: at the time of writing the threshold for service contracts was €206,000. However, lower value contracts are still subject to principles of fair contracting appropriate in the circumstances: the European Commission has published guidance on how to interpret this principle in a Commission Interpretative Communication (2006/C 179/02).

- Where the public authority is required to comply with the full procurement procedures, the process will include:
    - advertisement of the contract at various stages in the Official Journal of the European Union;
    - compliance with prescribed procedures for inviting tenders;
    - compliance with prescribed provisions about the technical specifications in the contract;
    - publication of contract awards in a prescribed form in the Official Journal;
    - debrief to unsuccessful tenderers.

- Part B services include various services typically provided by charities, including educational, health, recreational and cultural services.

- A typical procedure, whether for a Part A or Part B contract, might involve necessary/appropriate advertisement of the opportunity; a prequalification questionnaire; an invitation to tender issued to those fulfilling objective prequalification eligibility criteria; submission of tenders; objective assessment of the tenders by reference to assessment criteria (which should be apparent from the invitation to tender); the contract award and notification.

- Variations to this procedure might involve an invitation to tender without a prequalification questionnaire; a process during the consideration of tenders which involves dialogue leading to refinement of final bids; engagement in relation to the appropriate terms and conditions, which might otherwise be prescribed; direct engagement with the manifestly best potential provider or providers; the establishment of a framework contract, which establishes general terms and conditions under which particular further contracts are awarded by the public authority without the need for a further procurement exercise.

- A key principle in relation to fairness and equality of treatment is that all information provided to one tenderer should be provided to all.

- A further key principle is that scope for further negotiation of the contract after the tender process is limited by the obligation to ensure that all tenderers had the same opportunity.

3.130 Importantly, the public procurement regulations also apply to organisations which are wholly or mainly funded by public authorities (by contract and/or grant), which means charities can themselves be subject to the rules in contracts they enter into, being considered to be in effect 'public authorities' for these purposes. In addition, obligations upon charities to comply with the regulations in their own contracts and subcontracts may well be imposed under the terms and conditions of a primary public sector contract.

3.131 Charities interested in delivering public services should ensure that they familiarise themselves with the procurement regime and/or policy which applies to the services they wish to deliver. The simplest way to achieve this may be to arrange a meeting with the relevant procurement officer at an early stage.

3.132 The procurement rules are only relevant where a public authority is contracting for the delivery of services. Where funding is awarded by way of grant, rather than by way of contract, the procurement rules do not apply. (Such an arrangement is not regarded as trading and is outside the scope of VAT (see **3.105–3.116**).) However, a charity in this situation will need to be alert to the rules prohibiting state aid, which are explored below. Public authorities can describe what are in reality contracts as grants. Terminology is not determining, so a contract wrongly labelled as a grant could give rise to VAT problems (see **3.106**). But if a contract is properly restructured as a grant, this can mean that the supplying charity as a consequence has irrecoverable VAT problems!

State aid

3.133 The European Union Treaty prohibits the supply of 'aid', ie subsidy by a member state to an economic undertaking which might have the cause or effect of distorting free competition and, consequently, trade between member states. This may affect charities which receive funding from public authorities. The prohibition is potentially relevant where a charity receives grant funding, which is not trading (see **3.105–3.116** above). But it may also be relevant where a public authority has awarded a contract to a charity on preferential terms, although such circumstances may alternatively amount to a breach of the procurement requirement of equal treatment between potential suppliers.

3.134 If a charity is legally determined to have received unlawful state aid, the funding must be clawed back by government. This is not a realistic prospect for most charities, and indeed for most charities there should be a clear reason why the state aid rules are not applicable in relation to the receipt of public sector grants. However, there can be practical difficulties in obtaining satisfactory assurance that state aid rules do not have a material application to a particular grant. For example, grant (and, misleadingly, contract) conditions can include reference to the charity providing an indemnity to the local authority in relation to state aid which looks alarming and needs explaining. State aid compliance is the responsibility of the public authority, but can, nevertheless, become something to which the potential grant recipient needs to apply itself. Until the general interpretation of state aid rules to charity grants is more developed and public authorities are more confident in applying the rules, practical issues may continue to arise. The solution in a number of cases has been to obtain an expert analysis and interpretation from legal counsel specialising in European competition law. (See also **8.145–8.147** in relation to state aid.)

ANCILLARY TRADING

3.135 Some charities undertake trading activities which are *not* in fulfilment of one of their primary purposes, but which are in some way complementary to or derived from those purposes. Examples include:

- running a café open to visitors at a museum or gallery;

- a school or college providing a crèche for children of students;

- a hospital selling confectionery and flowers to patients and their visitors.

Both the Charity Commission and HMRC accept that ancillary trading is part and parcel of primary purpose trading. The key is that the trading contributes – albeit indirectly – towards the primary purposes of the charity. Thus, from a charity law perspective, provided its constitution gives it the necessary powers to carry out the activity in question, it is perfectly proper for a charity to carry out ancillary trading. From a tax point of view, HMRC regards ancillary trading as falling within ICTA 1988, s 505 and ITA 2007, ss 524 and 525 (see **3.35–3.47** above).

3.136 Note that the trading must be ancillary to a primary purpose *trade*, ie for the ancillary trading exemption to apply it is not enough for the charity simply to be carrying out its primary purposes: it must actually be trading in the course of doing so. For example, if a museum charges for entrance, it is trading in furtherance of its primary purposes; if it runs a café for its visitors, the café will be treated as an ancillary trade. But if entrance to the museum is always free, there is no primary purpose trade, so the café will not fall within the ancillary trading exemption.

3.137 The VAT implications of ancillary trading are the same as those of primary purpose trading (see **3.48–3.71** above).

3.138 Note also that, as with many elements of charity trading, with ancillary trading the devil is in the detail. It is inevitably difficult to discern whether a particular trading activity is 'ancillary' or is of a nature or extent which has turned it into non-primary purpose trading. If the ancillary trade is a café at a museum, is it truly only open to visitors to the charity's premises, or can other people come in off the street to have a cup of coffee without visiting the museum? Each case will need to be looked at individually. The Charity Commission's guidance on trading (CC35 'Trustees, trading and tax') states at para C7 that the level of annual turnover from this type of trading 'may have a bearing on the question whether the trading really is ancillary, but there is no specific level of annual turnover beyond which trading will definitely not be regarded as ancillary'.

3.139 Charities should bear in mind that 'ancillary' here means 'as an appendix to', 'as an extension to' the primary purpose trade. Ancillary income should therefore be relatively small compared with primary purpose income. If the ancillary element is greater than the primary purpose element, HMRC could question this.

MIXED TRADING

What is mixed trading?

3.140 There will be situations where charities are carrying out trading which is both primary purpose (or ancillary to a primary purpose) and non-primary purpose. For instance, a shop in a charitable art gallery may sell a range of goods. The sale of items which have a bearing on the charity's primary purposes, such as exhibition catalogues, postcards with pictures of work at the gallery, other items such as mugs displaying the gallery's work, and general publications about art, is likely to be primary purpose or ancillary trading. The sale of other items, such as toys, pens and mugs with the gallery's name and logo on them, and stamps, is very likely to be regarded as non-primary purpose trading.

Charity law

3.141   As far as charity law is concerned, a mixed trade of this nature will be treated as two separate trades. The rules on primary purpose trading will apply to the primary purpose and ancillary trading: namely, that it is permitted provided it is allowed by the charity's constitution (see **3.31–3.33**). Under the terms of the Charity Commission's current guidance, the non-primary purpose element of the trade will be allowed if it does not involve significant risk to the resources of the charity (see **2.21–2.33**).

Tax

3.142   The rules on mixed trades have recently changed. Prior to 2006 HMRC took a relatively relaxed attitude towards mixed trade, and would allow the charity to treat all the profits as falling within the primary purpose exemption, provided the turnover of the non-primary purpose part of the trade was below £50,000 per year, and represented less than 10% of the turnover of the combined trade. For accounting periods beginning on or after 22 March 2006, the two distinct parts of the trade must be treated as two separate trades: ICTA 1988, s 505(1B) and ITA 2007, s 525(2). The receipts or expenses should be apportioned on a reasonable basis: ICTA 1988, s 505(1B); ITA 2007, s 525(4). This means that separate accounting records must be kept for the two trades, and the profits of the non-primary purpose trading will be taxable unless they fall within another tax exemption, eg the small-scale trading exemption (see **2.41–2.50**). Clearly, this may have significant cost implications for the charity, which may find it simpler to run the whole enterprise through a subsidiary trading company (see Chapter 7). Similar rules apply where the trading is a mixture of work carried out by the beneficiaries of the charity (which is exempt from tax) and non-primary purpose trading. The two different elements of the trade must now be treated separately, and separate accounting records must be kept.

3.143   In both cases, there will inevitably be situations where it is difficult to tell what is primary purpose or ancillary trading and what is not. For example, if a charitable museum runs a shop, how closely connected is each particular item in the shop to the work of the museum?

VAT

3.144 The VAT treatment of supplies made in the course of mixed trading will depend on the nature of the supply rather than whether it is primary purpose or non-primary purpose trading (see **3.48–3.71** above).

CONCLUSION

3.145 In many ways primary purpose trading is the Holy Grail of charity trading. It can be carried out without risk of breaching charity law, and with no direct tax consequences. Primary purpose trading does not affect a charity's relief from business rates. However, charities should be alert to the VAT implications of their primary purpose trading. They should also be alert to the risks. Whilst it is perfectly acceptable for charities to make a loss on primary purpose trading activity, as the activity by definition furthers the charity's objects, there may be situations where trustees choose to run even primary purpose activities through a trading company.

Chapter 4

CHARITY SALES ACTIVITY

4.1   *In this chapter we explore sales activity by charities. We look at the situations where sales might amount to primary purpose trading, or fall within the tax and VAT exemption for fundraising events. We examine the special issues which apply to the sale of donated goods, and examine the pros and cons of recent schemes involving charities selling donated goods on behalf of their supporters. We look at the circumstances in which mandatory rate relief can be compromised. We also mention specific types of charity sales, including concessions, Christmas cards, charity auctions and so-called 'Good' gifts.*

INTRODUCTION

4.2   A major source of income for charities is the business of selling things. Charities sell a vast range of items, including second-hand clothes and books, aids especially adapted for the charity's beneficiaries, items made by the charity's beneficiaries, postcards of works of art owned by the charity, Christmas cards and mugs. This is, for the most part, trading activity fair and square.

4.3   As with any trading activity, the charity must ask itself some key questions:

(1)   Is this primary purpose or non-primary purpose trading?

(2)   Do we have constitutional power to carry out this activity?

(3)   What are the charity law implications of what we are doing?

(4)   What are the tax and VAT consequences?

See the commentary and flow-charts in Chapter 2 for more detail on these preliminary questions.

4.4   Charity sales will span primary purpose and non-primary purpose activity. Sales at charity fundraising events may qualify for the fundraising event tax and VAT exemption. And there are very particular rules which apply to the sale of donated goods – which is, in fact, not considered by the Charity Commission or HMRC to be trading at all! Charity sales also give rise to important issues regarding the availability of relief from business rates: while charities generally attract mandatory 80% rate relief, the availability of the relief may be prejudiced if the sales activity carried out on the premises is either non-primary purpose trading or carried out by a trading subsidiary.

4.5   The same charity law and tax principles apply whether the sale takes place in a shop, via a catalogue, or over the internet.

4.6   In this chapter we deal separately with the sale of goods charities have manufactured, or bought, themselves, and the sale of donated goods.

THE SALE OF BOUGHT-IN OR MANUFACTURED GOODS

4.7   This section covers goods which charities buy in with the purpose of selling, or make, or commission, themselves.

Primary purpose trading

4.8   As we explain in Chapter 3, the tax and charity law treatment of trading varies significantly depending on whether the trading activity is primary purpose or non-primary purpose. The charity's purposes, the nature of the item sold and, in some cases, the way in which the item was made, will affect whether or not the sale is primary purpose trading.

4.9   Primary purpose trading is trading which is carried out in fulfilment of a charity's main or primary purpose. Trading in which the work is mainly carried out by the charity's beneficiaries is also primary purpose trading. Trading which is ancillary to primary purpose trading (ie in some way complementary to it) is treated in the same way as primary purpose trading.

4.10   The following are examples of sales which amount to primary purpose trading:

(1)   The Royal National Institute of Blind People sells a range of products designed to help the blind and partially sighted, such as easy-to-see and tactile watches, and resources for learning Braille.

(2)   The Red Cross sells first aid products, and items such as walking sticks which help with independent living.

(3)   The sale of fair trade goods can be primary purpose trading. In 1995, the Charity Commission agreed to register the Fairtrade Foundation as a charity. The Foundation licenses the use of the FAIRTRADE Mark on products in the UK in accordance with internationally agreed fair trade standards. In registering the Foundation as a charity, the Charity Commission accepted that there is a link between the charitable purpose

of relieving poverty and the activity of encouraging fair trade. Commenting on its decision (in RR1a Recognising New Charitable Purposes), the Commission said:

> 'We ... were convinced by ... detailed evidence that there was ... a principal aim to relieve poverty by a fresh and imaginative mechanism which was responding to a widely felt desire to help on the part of many consumers in this country. In particular, we were convinced by evidence that the organisation, when established, would be able to show that there was a direct connection between the award of the fair trade mark and an actual and observable improvement of conditions in the third world ... We therefore decided that this means of putting into practical effect the desire, of a substantial number of consumers, for improved conditions of life for deprived producers and workers should be formally recognised as charitable.'

It is therefore likely that where the charity's aim includes the relief of poverty, sale of fair trade products will be regarded as primary purpose trading.

(4) Oxfam sells goods made by its beneficiaries in its workshops in the developing world.

(5) A children's charity sells Christmas cards designed by children falling within the charity's class of beneficiaries.

(6) A Christian charity sells Bibles and other religious books.

(7) An art gallery sells postcards, mugs and T-shirts bearing pictures of the work which it displays.

(8) The Royal Society for the Protection of Birds sells bird feeders. Note that if a charity which is not devoted to helping protect birds sells bird feeders – a human rights charity in its Christmas catalogue, for example – the activity would not amount to primary purpose trading!

(9) The sale of sweets to patients and their visitors at a charitable hospital may be ancillary trading.

4.11 Broadly speaking, primary purpose and ancillary trading may be carried out by charities without undue restriction under the charity law and tax rules: both are explored in detail in Chapter 3. The sale of bought-in and manufactured goods, which does not qualify as primary purpose trading, will be subject to more stringent charity and tax law requirements, unless another exemption applies.

Sales at fundraising events

4.12   Charities often sell items at fundraising events. A human rights charity organising a rally may sell T-shirts, souvenirs or commemorative brochures. An open-air concert run by a charity may involve sales of CDs and refreshments. A village hall organising an annual fete may have several stalls: bric-a-brac, home-made cakes, Christmas cards and so on. Not all of these sales will qualify as primary purpose trading, although the bric-a-brac stall and the cake stall may amount to the sale of donated goods.

4.13   However, as explained in some detail at **5.36–5.54**, tax will not be charged on the profits of fundraising events which fall within the specific tax and VAT exemption. Provided the sales are carried out at a qualifying event, tax will not be an issue and the proceeds of the sale will be exempt from VAT. Note that the event must be a fundraising event: it must be clearly organised and promoted to raise money for the charity. Note also that the sales must take place at the event: sales of souvenirs after the event will not be covered.

4.14   As far as charity law is concerned, if the sales activity takes place at a fundraising event, the trustees must consider whether the charity's constitution permits the activity (see **2.5–2.19** for more details) and whether any constraints are imposed by charity law. The Charity Commission's current approach is that where non-primary purpose trading of this nature involves significant risk to the resources of the charity, it should not be carried out directly by the charity (see **2.20–2.33** for more details).

Small scale exemption

4.15   Non-primary purpose sales activity which is not carried out at a qualifying fundraising event will, in principle, be subject to tax. Examples of such activity might include:

(1)   The sale of bought-in items such as jewellery or stationery at a charity shop.

(2)   The sale of Christmas cards.

(3)   The sale of soap and bubble bath in a charity Christmas catalogue.

(4)   The sale of cuddly toys at the shop in a charitable art gallery.

4.16   If the trading activity is relatively small, it may fall within the small scale trading exemption described in detail at **2.41–2.50**. If not, the profits from the sales activity will be subject to tax. The trustees will need to consider running the sales through a trading company (see Chapter 7).

4.17   In all cases, the trustees should ensure that the charity has the constitutional capacity to carry out the activity (see **2.5–2.19**). They should also have regard to the level of risk involved: if the activity involves significant risk to the resources of the charity, the Charity Commission may recommend the use of a trading company (see **2.20–2.33**).

VAT

4.18   The sale of bought-in or manufactured goods is within the scope of VAT, whether or not the sales qualify as primary purpose trading. So, where a charity's trading supplies exceed the registration threshold, it will generally need to account for output VAT on these sales. There are some exceptions. Where the goods are sold at a fundraising event, the special VAT exemption may apply (see **5.36–5.53**), and some sales, such as sales of books, may be zero rated (see **2.65–2.66** and **3.69–3.71** for more details).

4.19   Charities will need to be conscious of the VAT implications of the sales they are making, and take detailed advice as appropriate. For the most part the VAT implications will be the same whether the selling is carried on by the charity or by a trading subsidiary.

Rate relief

4.20   As explained at **2.69–2.73**, 80% mandatory rate relief from non-domestic rates is available if a charity 'wholly or mainly' occupies a property for charitable purposes. The sale of bought-in goods will fall within the scope of the relief where it counts as primary purpose trading, but not otherwise. So the sale of bought-in goods may affect a charity's entitlement to rate relief on shop premises. At **4.58–4.68** we explore the implications of a sales operation combining different types of sales activity.

Trading companies

4.21   In many cases, it will be appropriate for a sales operation to be conducted via a trading subsidiary. Trading subsidiaries are discussed in detail in Chapter 7.

4.22   Some charities apparently believe that it is perfectly legitimate for the charity to conduct a business of selling bought-in goods as agent on behalf of the trading company. This has the merit of allowing the charity to occupy the premises (hence stopping any arguments about the loss of rate relief as a result of occupation by a trading company: see **2.71**). Unfortunately, this belief is misguided. It makes no difference whether the charity receives income through selling goods it owns as principal or from commission received from selling goods as agent. In either case, the profits (not being derived from primary purpose trading) will be taxable. And if such activity represents more than half of the activity on the premises, the rate relief may be prejudiced (see **2.69–2.73** and **4.61–4.64**).

THE SALE OF DONATED GOODS

4.23   Many charities seek to raise money by encouraging their supporters and the general public to donate surplus clothes or other items for resale. This has proved to be a method which both generates income for charities and attracts public interest in their work.

4.24   The vast majority of donated goods are sold via charity shops: the first charity shop was opened by Oxfam in the late 1940s, as a way of selling the surplus second-hand goods it had been given following its appeal for aid to alleviate the situation in Greece after the 1939–45 war. There are now an estimated 7,500 charity shops nationwide, many occupying prime trading locations in high streets. Charity shops bring in an estimated £110 million per year to the sector. Many charity shops offer serious competition to purely commercial operations: Oxfam is one of the largest book-selling chains in the UK.

4.25   Charity shops are popular because they raise money for charity, their goods are generally very reasonably priced and, increasingly, because they offer an environmentally friendly alternative to buying brand-new goods. For many charities, their shops are more than a means of attracting and selling donated goods. The presence of a shop bearing the charity's name and logo in a high street can be a valuable source of publicity, reminding the public of the charity's existence. This can (and does) lead many individuals not only to purchase goods at charity shops but also to make a donation at the same time – or even to leave a legacy in their will.

4.26   Charities also sell donated goods online, either on their own websites, such as Oxfam's online second-hand store, or via an intermediary such as eBay for Charity.

4.27   The Association of Charity Shops, which has 300 members representing over 90% of the charity shops sector, provides information and support to charity shops (see www.charityshops.org.uk).

Does the sale of donated goods constitute trading?

4.28   If the badges of trade (explored at **5.9–5.23**) are applied to the sale of donated goods by a charity, it is clear that the charity is carrying on a trade:

- There is a profit motive.

- There is repetition.

- There is a selling organisation.

- The goods will generally be acquired (albeit not for a fee) with a view to their sale.

- The items are unlikely to have a value to the charity unless they are sold.

- The items may not necessarily be adapted before sale (although see **4.31–4.33** below).

- The items are likely to be sold relatively quickly.

- A charity may have a number of charity shops.

4.29 Notwithstanding this, HMRC has accepted that the sale of donated goods does *not* constitute a trade. Instead, HMRC regards it simply as a case of the charity converting a donation it has received in kind into cash. HMRC will not seek to tax the profits derived from the sale of donated goods. HMRC's 'Detailed guidance notes for charities' (Annex IV, para 23) read as follows:

> 'Traders usually sell goods that they have manufactured, or have purchased for resale; they do not usually receive goods by way of donation as charities do. For the charity it is simply a realisation of the value of a gift. For this reason the sale of donated goods is generally not regarded as a trade for tax purposes.'

4.30 The Charity Commission adopts the same view. Its guidance (CC35 'Trustees, trading and tax', para C3) states that 'the sale, or letting on hire, by a charity of goods donated to it with the intention that they should be sold (or let) is not normally "trading"'. Thus, as far as charity law is concerned, charities can sell, and hire out, goods that have been donated to them without involving a subsidiary trading company.

Alterations and improvements

4.31 Note, however, that the tax and charity law treatment will be different where the donated goods are substantially altered or improved prior to sale. HMRC accepts that there will be no trade where the donated items are simply 'sorted, cleaned and given minor repairs'. But its 'Detailed guidance notes for charities', Annex IV, para 23 states:

> 'If the goods are subjected to significant refurbishment or to any process which brings them into a different condition for sale purposes than that in which they were donated, the sale proceeds may be regarded as trading income. For example, where donated cloth is made into garments for sale this will amount to a trade.'

This is also echoed in the Charity Commission's guidance (CC35, para C3).

4.32 Thus, if clothes are donated to a charity, and they are simply tidied up in order to be sold on, there will be no trade from a tax or charity law perspective. But if the clothes are revamped and made into something very different, then selling them to the public may well constitute trading.

4.33 In some cases, though, this may be primary purpose trading (see Chapter 3). For example, a charity working with people recovering from drug or alcohol dependency runs a project giving employment opportunities and training to its beneficiaries through workshops turning donated clothes into fashion items, which are then sold by the charity. Although this will probably be trading – depending on the degree to which the items are altered – it will probably qualify as primary purpose trading.

VAT

4.34   The sale of donated goods is zero rated for VAT purposes. This means that the charity does not need to charge VAT on the sale of the goods, but any input VAT incurred by the charity on the cost of the sale is wholly recoverable. This is generally a good position for the charity to be in. Note that zero-rated supplies will count towards the charity's total supplies in establishing whether it needs to register for VAT. (See **2.65–2.66** for an introduction to zero rating.)

4.35   Various conditions must be met if the zero rating is to apply:

(1)   The goods must have been donated for sale or letting, or any combination of these two, or for export.

(2)   The goods must generally be made available to the general public, eg at a charity shop, online, or via an auction. However, zero rating will also apply where sales are restricted to certain categories of the public, namely the disabled or individuals on certain benefits (see HMRC's V1-9 'Charities', para 7.3.4).

(3)   Zero rating will still apply where the goods are sold at a fundraising event which qualifies for the VAT exemption (see **5.36–5.53**), provided all the goods at the relevant stall have been donated.

(4)   Where the goods cannot be sold (eg because they are of such poor quality or the charity is unlikely to be able to sell them because of trading standards regulations), they can be sold to scrap merchants or the like at the zero rate.

(5)   The goods can be cleaned or repaired, as long as this does not alter their structure or original use.

(6)   The goods need not be sold immediately if they are cleaned or repaired, or hired out, before being sold. But the charity cannot use them in the meantime. HMRC's V1-9 'Charities', para 7.2.2 gives the example of the sale of donated paintings which have hung in the charity's offices for many years. The sale would be standard rated (unless any other VAT reliefs applied).

(7)   The relief applies only to goods, so it will not apply to services. It does not include items deemed to be goods under other parts of the VAT rules (eg land and buildings).

(8)   The goods may be new or second-hand, but they must have been donated to the charity.

4.36   The sale of donated goods by a trading subsidiary owned 100% by a charity will also be zero rated, provided the company has agreed in writing (whether by deed or simple letter) to transfer to a charity its profits from the supply of the goods, or the profits from the supply of the goods are otherwise payable to charity.

4.37   Hence, so far as VAT is concerned, provided the trading company has entered into a deed of covenant or other written agreement to give 100% of its profits from selling donated goods to the charity, it makes no difference if the charity or trading company sells the donated goods. However, if there is no covenant/letter of agreement, or the trading company merely intends to pay over its profits by gift aid or dividend (see Chapter 7) or intends to retain all or part of its profits, this VAT zero rate will not apply. VAT will then have to be charged at the standard rate on the sale of donated goods.

Rate relief

4.38   80% mandatory rate relief is obtainable if a charity 'wholly or mainly' occupies a property for charitable purposes (see **2.69–2.73**). The sale of donated goods at a premises will qualify as occupation for charitable purposes. Section 64(10) of the Local Government Finance Act 1988 (which deals with rate relief for charities) provides specifically that a property:

> 'shall be treated as wholly or mainly used for charitable purposes at any time if at the time it is wholly or mainly used for the sale of goods donated to a charity and the proceeds of sale of the goods (after any deduction of expenses) are applied for the purposes of a charity.'

4.39   The availability of rate relief is a key advantage for charity shop operations. Where the sale of donated goods by a charity is combined with the sale of new goods, sales on behalf of supporters (see **4.43–4.57** below) and sales by a charity's trading subsidiary, rate relief may be compromised: this is explored in more detail at **4.61–4.64** below.

Use of a trading company for the sale of donated goods

4.40   As we have seen, both the Charity Commission and HMRC accept that the sale of donated goods may be carried out by the charity directly, without any adverse tax consequences. But some charities do, nonetheless, operate the sale of donated goods through a separate, non-charitable trading company. It is thought that these charities are in the minority: most of the larger charities, including Oxfam, Scope, Cancer Research UK and British Heart Foundation, run their sales of donated goods through the main charity.

4.41 At **7.13–7.37** we explain that tax and charity law are not the only reasons for using a trading subsidiary. A key factor is that using a trading company can insulate the charity from the potential risks attached to selling goods. At first glance, such risks may seem negligible, but on closer analysis it is clear that establishing a network of charity shops selling donated goods can constitute a risk for the charity. The risks include:

(1) The operation may make a loss. If the activity is conducted directly by the charity, the charity will have to finance it. If it is run through a separate trading company, any losses will be incurred by the trading company and not by the charity. However, to the extent that the trading company has been financed by the parent charity, which is highly likely, the charity will be bearing the loss. And where a trading company makes significant losses, this may give rise to questions as to whether the trustees acted prudently in investing in the trading company in the first place.

(2) The shops are likely to be run from commercially leased premises. Leases carry short- and long-term risks for the tenant.

(3) The sale of goods invokes a raft of consumer protection and other legislation which can impose liabilities on the seller or producer of the goods (see Chapter 8). The charity may well wish to be insulated from the attendant risks.

(See Chapter 7 for more detail on the reasons for establishing a trading subsidiary.)

4.42 In Chapter 7 we explore the relationship between the charity and a trading subsidiary in detail. But there are particular issues where a charity is considering running a donated goods operation via a trading subsidiary.

(a) The goods donated to a charity are part of the charity's assets. They are given to the charity for *it* to sell and apply the proceeds to the charity's purposes. The charity cannot give away its property to a trading company, even though it owns the company, as to do so would be a breach of the duties of the trustees of the charity to exploit the charity's assets so as to obtain a proper return. Thus, the charity should charge a reasonable price to its trading company if the charity transfers donated goods to the trading company for it to sell on.

(b) This raises the question of VAT. The sale of donated goods by a charity is zero rated for VAT purposes, provided the sale is to the general public, or two or more disabled people, or people claiming various benefits (see **4.35** above). A bulk sale to a trading company of donated goods by the charity will be subject to VAT at the standard rate. This should not be a problem for the trading company, as (provided it is VAT registered) it will be able to recover this VAT.

However, although the sale of donated goods by a trading company can be zero rated (see **4.36–4.37**), if the trading company has purchased the goods from the charity, so as to comply with the obligations of charity law that trustees should only dispose of assets at a proper price, the trading company will not be selling donated goods. It will be selling bought-in (albeit second-hand) goods, and the sale of such goods is not zero rated!

The trading company will be required to register for VAT and charge VAT on the sale proceeds if its annual turnover exceeds the VAT registration threshold. So, whilst it might appear to be sensible for a charity to pass its donated goods over to its trading company so as to minimise risk, this in turn can cause tax complications – the need to register for and charge VAT – which will force the trading company either to increase its prices or squeeze its profit margins (or both) so as to meet the VAT charge.

(c)   The position will be different if the goods are donated to the trading company, but care must be taken to ensure that this is what happens – for example, collecting bags should bear the trading company's name and not the charity's. It is very likely that in practice this distinction will be blurred. The shop should have a prominent notice stating that it is run by the trading company and that all profits are donated to the charity.

(d)   Sales of goods by a trading subsidiary will not qualify for automatic rate relief, although the local authority may be persuaded to grant discretionary relief to a trading subsidiary (see **2.69–2.73**).

Charities thinking of running sales of donated goods via a trading company must be aware of these complications.

The gift aid scheme for sales of donated goods

4.43   In this section we explore the pros and cons of a relatively new scheme designed to deal with the sale of donated goods.

How does the scheme work?

4.44   Where goods are donated to a charity so that the charity may sell them on, there may be scope to use the gift aid scheme to maximise the income from the donation. The process works in the following way:

(a)   Instead of simply donating goods to a charity, a supporter asks the charity to sell the goods on his or her behalf.

(b)   This means that when selling the goods the charity is acting as the supporter's agent.

(c)   Once the goods are sold, the supporter is told how much has been raised. Provided the supporter does not object, the charity can keep the proceeds.

(d)   The proceeds are treated as a gift from the supporter to the charity. Provided the supporter has made a valid gift aid declaration, and the usual conditions applying to gift aid are fulfilled, the charity can claim tax relief on the donation under the gift aid scheme, and if the supporter is a higher rate tax payer he or she can also claim tax relief. This means more income for the charity.

4.45   While HMRC has accepted that this scheme can work (see its 'Detailed guidance notes for charities', ch 3, para 3.51), it does have some disadvantages.

4.46   Once the goods have been sold, the charity must give the supporter the opportunity to claim all or part of the proceeds themselves, rather than giving them to the charity. There is a risk that the supporter will decide to keep the proceeds. The charity can agree in advance to charge commission on the sale, so that it makes some money on the arrangement even if the supporter keeps the sale proceeds, but the commission will be trading income, subject to VAT, which would have tax and charity law implications.

4.47   If the goods are especially valuable, there may be a charge to capital gains tax when they are sold. Because the sale is being made by the supporter, he or she will be liable for any capital gains tax. This would not be the case if the goods were simply given to the charity: gifts to charity do not attract capital gains tax, and the charity would not pay any capital gains tax on the sale either.

4.48   The charity will need to keep appropriate records, including evidence of the agreement with the supporter. (More detail is available in HMRC's 'Detailed guidance notes for charities', ch 3, para 3.51.)

4.49   A further concern is the level of resources required to train charity staff and volunteers to operate the scheme properly, particularly given the scope for the scheme to fail if HMRC's detailed conditions are not complied with.

4.50   Perhaps most importantly, HMRC recently updated its guidance in this area to include the warning that arranging for goods to be sold in this way is not charitable activity. This means that anything the charity spends in carrying out the activity may be 'non-charitable expenditure'. As explained at **7.96–7.97**, where a charity incurs non-charitable expenditure, it may well incur a tax liability on its income. The guidance reads:

> 'regardless of whether a commission is charged, all direct and indirect costs incurred in selling these goods will be non-charitable expenditure, and may affect the charity's entitlement to tax exemption.'

This is not a concern where the charity is simply selling, on its own behalf, goods which have been donated to it: in that case, because the selling activity is not trading, expenditure in connection with it will be regarded as charitable expenditure, ie expenditure incurred in realising the value of a gift.

4.51 HMRC explains that costs incurred in selling the goods will not only include any advertising expenses and insurance cover, but also a proportionate share of any overheads. Thus, if a charity shop sells some donated goods on its own behalf, and some goods on behalf of supporters in order to take advantage of the gift aid rules, the shop's overheads must be divided between the two activities (HMRC says that they must be apportioned 'by the most appropriate method'). The overheads attributable to selling goods on behalf of supporters will be non-charitable expenditure.

4.52 Where a supporter asks the charity to sell the goods as his or her agent, the VAT treatment will be different from that which applies to a straightforward sale of goods donated to the charity (see **4.34–4.37**). Where the charity charges a commission on the sale, it is making a taxable supply. If the charity is VAT registered, it will need to charge VAT on the supply at the standard rate. If the charity does not make a charge (ie where the supporter voluntarily agrees to make a donation to the charity from the sale proceeds after the goods have been sold), the work that the charity has done is outside the scope of VAT because it will be regarded as a non-business transaction. The charity will not be able to reclaim VAT on costs directly incurred in selling the goods, or on associated overheads. This, again, is a real disadvantage of the scheme.

Rate relief

4.53 As explained at **2.69–2.73**, 80% mandatory relief from non-domestic rates is available where a charity 'wholly or mainly' occupies a property for charitable purposes. While the sale of donated goods qualifies as occupation for charitable purposes, the operation of the gift aid scheme does not, so this scheme may affect the availability of the relief (see **4.61–4.64**).

Charity law

4.54 The charity trustees must be able to show that the likely proceeds of running the scheme are reasonably likely to exceed costs. Charities should also consider in advance what their position would be should they be duped into selling stolen goods, or goods on behalf of another trader.

Use of a trading subsidiary

4.55 Some of the disadvantages of the scheme could be avoided by involving a trading subsidiary. The trading subsidiary sells the item on behalf of the donor. The donor donates the proceeds to the charity under gift aid. This avoids the charity incurring non-charitable expenditure, or putting charitable funds at risk, but the VAT and rating concerns remain, and this involves added administration and costs, thus reducing the real gain of operating the scheme.

Conclusion

4.56   The scheme is a complex tax minefield. Gains for gift aid on the one hand can be substantially eroded by the loss of other tax reliefs and the substantial administration required. For this reason, at the time of writing, only some charities have taken on the scheme: the Charity Finance Charity Shops Survey 2008 reported that 16% of the respondents to the survey claimed gift aid on items sold.

4.57   HMRC, while accepting the scheme can work for gift aid, has put up other taxation barriers in what some see as a deliberate attempt to put charities off the scheme. Cynically, one wonders whether they want the scheme to fail. The position may change once the Government has concluded its review of gift aid generally, which is under way at the time of writing. But all charities interested in implementing this scheme should take advice and think carefully about the pros and cons, and the various complexities, before going ahead.

MIXED SALES ACTIVITY

The complications

4.58   We have seen that charity sales activity may involve a mixture of taxable and non-taxable trades. For example, a charity shop may sell a combination of donated goods, goods made by the charity's beneficiaries and bought-in items. The shop may also operate the gift aid scheme described at **4.43–4.57** above.

4.59   The sale of donated goods, and items made by the charity's beneficiaries can all generally be carried out by the charity without any adverse tax implications. The sale of bought–in items will attract tax if carried out by the charity, and operation of the gift aid scheme will also have tax complications.

4.60   Equally, the various sales will be treated differently for VAT purposes. The sale of donated goods is zero rated, while the sale of bought-in goods, even if their sale constitutes primary purpose trading, will be standard-rated unless the particular goods sold are zero rated for other reasons (e g books).

Rate relief

4.61   This is complicated enough, and means that the charity will need to set up different systems in order to deal with the different types of sale. However, a further major implication of carrying out different types of sales activity side by side is the impact on rate relief. As explained previously, 80% mandatory rate relief is available if a charity 'wholly or mainly' occupies a property for charitable purposes. The sale of donated goods and sales amounting to primary purpose trading will qualify as occupying property for charitable purposes. But the sale of bought-in goods, and activity involving the sale of donated goods on behalf of supporters under the gift aid scheme will not. Nor will the sale of goods by a trading subsidiary rather than the parent charity.

4.62 This means that the 'wholly or mainly' part of the concession becomes crucial. How is this test operated in practice? Is this based on a percentage of turnover, floor area, or something else?

4.63 Since there has been no court ruling on this question, one has to rely on the practices of different rating authorities. These vary from place to place, so it is impossible to advise definitively on what a court might consider an appropriate level of sales of donated goods to constitute 'mainly' donated goods. However, in *Fawcett Properties v Buckingham* [1960] 3 All ER 503, Lord Morton said that 'mainly' means 'probably … more than half'. On this line of argument, if 49% or less of the turnover of a charity shop is attributable to non-primary purpose sales of non-donated goods, with the balance made up of the sale of donated goods, this should mean that the shop is 'mainly' occupied for charitable purposes and should continue to enjoy the 80% mandatory rate exemption.

4.64 It is the authors' experience that the use of the shop floorspace is also a good guide accepted by many local authorities; ie provided less than 50% of the floorspace is used for non-primary purpose sales of non-donated goods, then mandatory rate relief will apply. Equally, if over 50% of turnover or floorspace relates to the sale of donated goods by the charity, while the balance is attributable to sales by a trading subsidiary, the exemption should be available. Percentages of profit and individual items sold may also be relevant.

Trading subsidiary

4.65 In many ways, the complications involved in carrying out mixed sales activity would be simplified if the whole sales operation was run through a trading subsidiary. But this would have the VAT complications mentioned at **4.40–4.42** in relation to the sale of donated goods and the 80% mandatory rate relief would be lost.

What happens in practice?

4.66 Charities vary in how they deal with these complications in practice. Most charity shops deal mainly in donated goods: the Association of Charity Shops reports that 95% of goods sold by charity shops are donated. The sales operations are therefore more likely to be run by the charity itself, in order to maximise the availability of rate relief.

4.67 Bigger charities may split the trading between the charity and the trading subsidiary. The donated goods would be sold by the charity. The bought-in goods would be sold by the trading subsidiary. A sophisticated till system is used to ensure that the sales are correctly logged in the accounting system. This also ensures accurate recording for VAT purposes. Some charities use an electronic point of sale IT system which logs sales onto a central accounting database via the tills. Staff and volunteers must be trained to ensure that they can distinguish between the various types of sale. The charity occupies the shop premises, and charges the trading subsidiary for its share of the shop's resources, such as rent, staff costs and general overheads. This must be correctly calculated to ensure no element of subsidy of the trading company by the charity, and no element of profit by the charity. The sharing of resources by a charity and its trading subsidiary are discussed in detail at **7.190–7.224**: the same principles apply here. Note that rate relief will remain an issue: to the extent that sales conducted for the trading subsidiary mean that the premises are no longer occupied wholly or mainly for charitable purposes, the mandatory rate relief may be lost, so charities must keep a wary eye on the proportion of sales.

4.68 If the sales operation is small, where the income from a sale of non-donated non-primary purpose goods does not take the charity's income over the small scale exemption (see **2.41–2.50**) the charity may simply continue to run all the sales activity through the charity. Equally, where the costs associated with establishing and running a trading subsidiary would be significant in comparison to the likely tax saving, the charity trustees may decide to live with a small tax bill. The Charity Commission guidance (CC35 'Trustees, trading and tax', para D2) accepts that this would be legitimate.

CHARITIES ACT 1993

4.69 As explained at **2.75–2.77**, under s 5 of the Charities Act 1993, a registered charity with a gross income in its last financial year of more than £10,000 must state in English or Welsh in legible characters the fact that it is a registered charity on various documents, including cheques, orders for goods, invoices and receipts. Breach of s 5 is a criminal offence. The offence will be committed (in the case of a cheque or an order) by the person who signs the offending item, and in the case of receipts or notices soliciting donations of goods, by the person who issues or *authorises the issue* of the relevant document. The maximum penalty is a fine of £1,000. This means that if a registered charity runs a shop, the till receipts must contain the magic phrase 'a registered charity'. Advertisements encouraging donors to give goods to or for the benefit of the charity must contain a similar statement.

SPECIAL CASES

Concessions

4.70 Manufacturers often use charity shops as concession outlets for the sale of new goods. A stand displaying the manufacturer's name will display the goods. These goods continue to belong to the manufacturer until they are sold: at that point the sale proceeds will be paid to the charity (or more usually its trading company, as this is non-primary purpose trading); the charity/trading company will keep a commission out of the proceeds and pay the balance to the manufacturer. If the charity/trading company is registered for VAT, then VAT must be charged on this commission.

4.71 Given that charities raising funds via this route are carrying out non-primary purpose trading, they need to consider the constitutional and charity law implications (see **2.5–2.33**), and the profit from the activity will be taxable. The activity does not qualify as charitable activity under the rating rules, so will count against the charity when assessing whether a property is occupied 'wholly or mainly' for charitable purposes.

4.72 Larger charities may consider running these concessions via a trading subsidiary. The issues discussed at **4.58–4.68** will apply equally here.

Christmas cards

4.73 Christmas cards are worth a special mention because the sale of Christmas cards is a popular form of trading. The scale of this activity varies from the sale of a few cards made by pupils of a school to the very high volume of cards sold on behalf of leading national charities.

4.74 For some charities the sale of Christmas cards can constitute primary purpose trading (see **4.8–4.11**). The following are some examples. Where a museum, set up to educate the public, sells cards illustrated by pictures from its collection, it can be argued that the card is a form of educational material and its sale is in fulfilment of the charity's primary purpose. This would apply to the National Gallery, Tate, the British Museum and so on. Or a charity may be established to educate the public in the work of local artists, and the sale of cards designed by such local artists would be in fulfilment of a primary purpose. Alternatively, a charity may sell cards which have been designed or made by beneficiaries of the charity – the cards might have been drawn by clients of an art therapy charity or pupils at a school.

4.75 The circumstances in which the sale of cards is a primary purpose activity are fairly limited. In most cases cards will be bought in and sold with the sole objective of raising money for the charity. This is not primary purpose trading. It will be subject to the charity law and tax complications explored at **2.20–2.58**. It is possible that the sale of the Christmas cards will fall within the scope of the small scale tax exemption (see **2.41–2.50**). In this case, since the sale of Christmas cards is unlikely to give rise to any great risk to the resources of the charity, the Charity Commission will probably accept that the activity can be carried out directly by the charity. For larger scale Christmas card sales, the activity should probably be conducted via a trading subsidiary.

4.76 The charity should also determine whether or not it makes any profit at all from the sale of the cards. It should attribute the proper costs of the sales, including a fair apportionment of overheads and staff time, against the profits. If there are no profits at all or if these are very small, the trustees should review the position carefully. Selling Christmas cards at a loss may well be a breach of their duty as trustees to act in the best interests of the charity. However, against this it might be argued (perfectly legitimately) that although the sale of cards is run at a loss, the intangible benefit of the publicity which the charity gains as a result more than outweighs the loss. In any event, the trustees of the charity should monitor and review regularly any such loss-making sales.

4.77 The requirement in s 5 of the Charities Act 1993 for a registered charity with income over £10,000 to state its registered name on notices, advertisements and documents issued by or on behalf of the charity and soliciting money or other property for the benefit of the charity is explained at **2.75–2.77**. Does this requirement apply to cards sold on behalf of a charity? It all depends on who issues the card and what is printed on it. Consider the following examples:

(a)   The sale of a card by the XYZ Gallery, a charity, using a picture in the gallery's collection, which states: '*Sold in aid of the XYZ Gallery*'. Is the card 'a notice, advertisement' or 'other document' issued 'by or on behalf of the charity'? A notice has a definite legal meaning which would not include a card. But although an 'advertisement' has not apparently been defined at common law, various statutes give it a very wide meaning. Equally, 'document' has been generously interpreted: 'I should say that any written thing capable of being evidence is properly described as a document' per Darling J in *R v Daye* [1908] 2 KB 333 at 340. In that case it was ruled that a sealed envelope was a document. The authors' view, therefore, is that a card is a document and potentially subject to CA 1993, s 5.

But for CA 1993, s 5 to apply, the document also has to 'solicit money or other property'. Does the phrase 'sold in aid of' solicit money or other property for the benefit of the charity? Bearing in mind that s 5(3) states that s 5 has effect whether the solicitation is 'express' or 'implied', it is the authors' view that it does. People are encouraged to purchase the card by the statement that the card is sold in aid of the charity. The statement may well affect a consumer's decision on which card to buy when faced with a choice between a 'charity' card and a 'commercial' card. The card solicits money for the charity. Thus, the card should comply with s 5 and state the fact that XYZ charity is a registered charity.

(b)   What if the card states 'the XYZ Gallery' and nothing else? Does the phrase 'the XYZ Gallery' amount to an implied solicitation that the price of the card will be applied 'for the benefit of the charity'? For the reasons set out above, the fact that the charity's name appears on the card is an inducement to the purchaser to buy the card. Hence the authors consider that this is an implied solicitation, and the card must comply with s 5 and state 'XYZ Gallery, a registered charity'.

(c)   Section 5 also applies to a trading company owned by a charity that sells cards which state 'sold in aid of XYZ Charity'. This is because, since the card bears the charity's name, it will be deemed to be issued 'on behalf of the charity' (see s 5(2)) and the analysis at **4.77**(b) above will apply.

4.78 An increasingly common practice is for commercial retail organisations to sell Christmas cards with a representation that part of the proceeds will be paid to charity. This is a form of cause-related marketing, and the retailer is likely to be a commercial participator under the Charities Act 1992. Such relationships are covered in detail at **5.84–5.152**.

'Suggested donation' sales

4.79 It is not unusual to see goods – typically badges or key rings – offered to the public on the basis that a 'minimum' or 'suggested' donation be made in return for the items. Does this constitute trading activity? Where people are invited to make a 'minimum' donation in return for something, this is trading. The items are essentially being sold for the 'minimum' amount requested. There is, in fact, no donation, but a price. The position is different where the charity simply suggests that a donation of a certain amount be made: members of the public are able to take the items away for free if they wish to. Here the 'donation' really is a donation and no trading is involved. HMRC will look carefully at the wording of the promotion in order to establish whether the activity is trading, and hence potentially subject to tax and VAT.

Charity catalogues and internet sales

4.80 Many charities, particularly at Christmas time, sell goods via catalogue, or over the internet, rather than in charity shops. In most cases, these goods will be bought-in rather than donated, although some charities do sell donated goods online: Oxfam, for instance, has a range of donated goods for sale on its website. In some instances the sale of the goods will represent primary purpose trading, eg where the goods are made by the charity's beneficiaries in the developing world, or where a horticultural charity sells gardening products. However, in many cases, the sale will not be primary purpose trading, but straightforward non-primary purpose trading designed to raise funds for the charity. For instance, the Parkinson's Disease Society produces a catalogue each year selling gifts, wrapping paper and Christmas cards.

4.81 Catalogue and internet sales are subject to the principles set out in this chapter. Primary purpose sales can be carried out by the charity. So can sales of donated goods. The sale of bought-in goods, where it does not represent primary purpose trading, may need to be carried out via a trading subsidiary. While additional considerations, such as the distance selling rules and rules on internet and electronic trading (described in more detail at **8.94–8.123**), may apply to catalogue and internet sales, the charity law and tax principles remain the same. We have seen how the availability of rating relief may play a major role in deciding how sales in charity shops should be structured: this should also be considered where distance selling is involved.

4.82 Often, where supporters buy goods from charity catalogues, or over the internet, they will be invited to make an additional donation to the charity. In order to ensure that the gift aid regime can apply to these donations, provided the appropriate gift aid declarations are made and other conditions are complied with, the donation must be made to the charity, even where the selling is conducted by a trading subsidiary. The trading company will need to hold the donations on trust for the charity and account to the charity for them.

Charity auctions

4.83 A popular method of fundraising is a charity auction: selling items either at a charity event or online. The principles described in this chapter apply equally to sales at these auctions. Where the auction is held at a fundraising event which qualifies for the fundraising exemption, there should be no tax and VAT implications (see **5.36–5.54** for more details). In many cases, the sales at an auction will be sales of donated goods, eg the sale of donated tickets, or a celebrity's time.

4.84 HMRC accepts that, in certain circumstances, all or part of the price of the item sold at a charity auction may qualify as a gift aid payment payment; see 'Detailed guidance notes for charities', ch 3, para 3.49.2:

> 'HMRC recognises that when a person purchases a lot at a charity auction they may intentionally pay more than it is worth in order to support the charity. So, on that basis, we are prepared to treat a payment for an auction item as a donation to the charity.'

This will only apply where the price paid is more than the market price. So a £500 winning bid for a tour of an office building would qualify, while a £100 winning bid for a trip to Estonia would not. The supporter needs to know the commercial value of the item they are bidding for up front, so that they know that they are paying more than the asking price. Note that this treatment will not apply where the item in question is not commercially available: eg a football signed by the local team, which is not available in the shops.

4.85 The usual requirements of the gift aid regime apply: a gift aid declaration will be needed, and gift aid will not be available where the value of the item exceeds the gift aid benefit limits (see **5.70–5.71**). However, there may be scope to split the payment and effectively 'buy' the benefit. More detail is available in HMRC's 'Detailed guidance notes for charities', ch 3, para 3.49.

'Good' gifts

4.86 A relatively recent innovation is the opportunity for charity supporters to buy 'gifts' which in reality support the charity's beneficiaries. The Good Gifts Catalogue, for instance, is an initiative of the Charities Advisory Trust, which allows supporters to pay for a range of projects as 'gifts' for others, including planting a bluebell wood or providing food for an abandoned donkey. The Oxfam Unwrapped promotion allows supporters to buy a selection of gifts, from bags of seeds for poor farming communities to the tools needed to build an emergency shelter in a disaster zone. The supporter generally receives a certificate confirming that the gift has been 'purchased', which can be sent on to family and friends as a present. This is not trading. It is a donation of funds for a specific purpose. Provided the benefits to the supporter are within the gift aid limits, the gift aid regime can apply to the 'price' paid.

CONCLUSION

4.87 The tax and charity law treatment of charity sales depends on an analysis of the item being sold: in many cases a sales operation may involve a combination of primary purpose trading, the sale of donated goods and the sale of other items. Charity sales operations should be structured to take account of the different rules.

Chapter 5

FUNDRAISING

5.1 *This chapter deals with trading activity aimed purely at raising funds, including fundraising events, relationships with businesses and lotteries. We examine when fundraising activity is likely to be trading. We look at the tax and VAT concession for fundraising events and general issues for events organisers. We explore the considerations which charities going into partnership with businesses for fundraising purposes need to have in mind, and include a dedicated section on affinity cards.*

INTRODUCTION

5.2 Charity fundraising covers a vast spectrum of activity: the sector is awash with ever more imaginative ways of raising funds. From soliciting donations to teaming up with credit card companies, from running coffee mornings to seeking sponsorship for publications or events, the range of fundraising activities undertaken by charities is huge.

5.3 In many cases fundraising activity will be just that: raising funds. But very often fundraising does involve trading. The trading rules can be a real trap for charity fundraisers: there is a risk that what seems to be a straightforward fundraising activity may actually be non-charitable trading, with all the tax and charity law complications that that involves. It is therefore important that charity fundraisers are able to identify what is pure fundraising activity, and what is trading.

5.4 In one sense, any trading carried out by a charity is a form of fundraising, as it is designed to do just that – namely, raise funds for the charity. Charity fundraisers might deal with a range of trading activities. For example, a charity relieving poverty in the developing world might raise funds by selling goods made by its beneficiaries (which would qualify as primary purpose trading: see Chapter 3) and bought-in trinkets (which is non-primary purpose sales activity: see Chapter 4), and by running sponsored challenge events (which are covered in this chapter). There is therefore a degree of overlap between this chapter and Chapters 3 and 4. In this chapter we deal with trading activity which might typically fall within the remit of the fundraising team in a larger charity, including event fundraising, partnerships with commercial businesses and lotteries, and we cross-refer to Chapters 3 and 4 where appropriate.

IS FUNDRAISING TRADING?

5.5   In some cases, it will not be necessary to go through a detailed analysis of whether an activity does actually qualify as trading. Primary purpose trading is treated, by and large, in the same way as other charitable activity: this is explored in detail in Chapter 3. While selling things will generally be trading, the sale of donated goods is not regarded as trading by HMRC, as we explain in Chapter 4. But in other situations – again those typically dealt with by a fundraising team – a precise analysis of whether a particular activity designed to raise funds is or is not trading may be crucial.

5.6   Fundraising which does not amount to trading typically covers such activities as public appeals for donations (whether of money or goods) – the annual Poppy Appeal, for example, television appeals, sponsored walks, and soliciting legacies and donations.

5.7   But people's altruism is limited. Getting people to give something for nothing is not the only way of getting support. Charities also raise funds by giving something in return to their supporters. Hence the proliferation of jumble sales, carnivals, balls and quiz nights, all of which may involve trading activity.

5.8   What, therefore, is trading? Section 832(1) of the Income and Corporation Taxes Act 1988 ('ICTA 1988') defines 'trade' as follows:

> '"Trade" includes every trade, manufacture, adventure or concern in the nature of trade.'

This is a wonderfully circular definition and a statement of the obvious. The term 'trade' is used twice in the definition. 'Trade' = 'trade' = 'trade'! Trade is said to include trade, but other activities may be caught as well. Hence, ICTA 1988 does not assist much in arriving at a definition.

5.9   The courts have considered this question on many occasions over the last century since the definition quoted first became law and have worked out certain hallmarks or 'badges' which indicate the type of transactions that constitute a trade. It is necessary to apply these tests to the income-generating activities undertaken by a charity to determine whether or not the activities are 'fundraising' or whether they amount to trading.

5.10   There are nine badges of trade, which are explored in more detail at **5.11–5.22** below. For a trade to be carried out, it is not necessary for a particular activity to display all of the 'badges' listed below. If one or more is present, then that may be sufficient to establish that there is a trade.

Profit motive

5.11 An intention to make a profit is supportive of the activity being trading, but is not necessarily conclusive. Charities will enter into many different arrangements to make a profit (eg the sale of Christmas cards). The fact that a charity will have other motives (eg applying the profits to charitable purposes) is irrelevant.

5.12 The case of *Oxfam v City of Birmingham District Council* (1979) AC 126 illustrates the fact that applying the profits to charitable purposes does not rule out a profit motive. The Court of Appeal held that the occupation by Oxfam of premises for the sale of donated goods was not occupation of the property for charitable purposes. This decision subsequently led to a change in the law: as we have seen in Chapter 4, the sale of donated goods does now qualify as occupation for charitable purposes. But the case illustrates the principle that the courts and HMRC distinguish between the *purposes* of the charity and the *means* by which monies are raised in order to carry out those purposes (eg sale of mugs, T-shirts, holding of pop concerts, etc).

5.13 But beware. As mentioned above, not all of the badges of trade need to be displayed in order for the activity to be trading: a trade may be carried on even though there is no intention of making a profit. If a trade is being carried out and a profit is made – even though this was not intended – HMRC can seek to tax any profit arising. In *Incorporated Council of Law Reporting for England and Wales, In re Duty on the Estate of* (1888) 22 QBD 279 (DC), a case involving whether the Council for Law Reporting was carrying on a trade or business, Lord Coleridge CJ said (at 293):

> 'I should have thought it capable of strong argument that they carried on a trade, because it is not essential to the carrying on of a trade that the persons engaged in it should make, or desire to make, a profit from it.'

Repetition

5.14 Systematic repetition of a transaction is a pointer towards trading. A one-off transaction (eg a ball to raise funds for a charity) is unlikely to amount to trading; in contrast, it was established in *British Legion, Peterhead Branch, Remembrance and Welcome Home Fund v IRC* (1953) 3 STC 84 that running dances regularly on Saturday nights *did* amount to trading (see **3.40**).

5.15 But the position is not always so simple. Again, lack of repetition by itself does not rule out the possibility of a trading activity. In one case, an individual who ran a cinema purchased and sold a quantity of toilet paper in a single job lot, thereby making a profit (*Rutledge v IRC* (1929) SC 379). He was taxed on the profits of the sale – because there was a profit motive and because of the nature of the goods involved. In another case, two linked transactions involving the purchase and resale of silver bullion by the comedian Norman Wisdom were held by the Court of Appeal to amount to trading for tax purposes (*Wisdom v Chamberlain (HM Inspector of Taxes)* (1968) 45 TC 92).

Selling organisation

5.16 The existence of a mechanism for selling (such as a physical or online shop, or a catalogue) will point to a trade being carried out. But, as explained in detail in Chapter 4, if a charity shop only sells donated goods, this is not regarded as trading, but as the conversion of a donation made by a supporter into cash.

Method of acquisition

5.17 Where goods are purchased with a view to resale, there is a strong presumption of trading. The sale of items (such as Christmas cards and T-shirts) which are acquired to be sold will point to a trading activity. The sale of milk from a cow on a city farm would *not* be trading, unless the cow was being kept for the purpose of producing milk. It would simply be the disposal of an item produced as a consequence of having the cow on the farm! In such cases clear records should be kept showing the purpose of the acquisition of the cow.

Nature of the asset

5.18 Some assets, which only generate a benefit by being sold, are more likely to be regarded as trading stock than others. For example, if a charitable art gallery sells souvenir mugs in its shop, it is likely to be trading, but it is less likely to be trading if it is selling a painting in its collection.

Whether work was done on an object before resale

5.19 The adaptation of an object prior to resale can be an indication of trading activity. This will be relevant to charities making significant alterations to donated goods (see **4.31–4.33**).

Interval between purchase and sale

5.20 If an item is held for some time prior to sale (for instance, if a painting is hung in a charity's premises or is used by the charity before it is sold), there is less likely to be trading.

Existing connections

5.21 A transaction related to the trade of the taxpayer is more likely to be a trade. A charity which engages in a series of similar fundraising activities is therefore more likely to be trading than a charity which carries out a one-off campaign.

The source of finance

5.22   If an activity is financed by means of a short-term loan, HMRC are more likely to regard it as trading. In the *Norman Wisdom* case (see **5.15**), it was relevant that the silver bullion had been purchased with the aid of high interest loans.

5.23   The badges of trade will be applied to the activity by HMRC, but it is the overall picture, rather than a precise 'tick box' approach to each of the badges, which is important. The cinema owner with his job lot of toilet paper did not repeat the exercise and did not have a selling organisation: the presence of the profit motive and the nature of the goods being bought and re-sold were sufficient in that case to allow HMRC to establish that there was a trading activity.

5.24   The following examples show how the badges of trade can be applied to particular activities:

(a)   Sale of tickets to an annual ball.
   - There is a profit motive.
   - Although the ball is run annually, that amount of repetition will not constitute trading.
   - There is no formal selling organisation.
   - There are no items purchased with a view to resale.
   - The charity is not in the business of running balls.
   This is unlikely to be trading. Note that in any event the tax and VAT fundraising exemption (see **5.36–5.54** below) may well apply to fundraising balls.

(b)   Sale of Christmas cards.
   - There is a profit motive.
   - Unlike an annual ball (which takes place on one night of the year), the sale of cards is repeated over a period of weeks or months.
   - There is a selling organisation – through shops, or in halls, or to retailers, or through a network of supporters.
   - The goods are purchased with the intention that they be resold.
   - The cards are unlikely to be adapted before sale.
   - The cards will probably have no use other than subsequent sale.
   - The charity may carry out the sale of Christmas cards every year.
   This is trading.

(c)   Sale of tickets by a charitable theatre.
   - There is probably a profit motive (even if the theatre is also supported by grants or sponsorship) but the absence is not fatal to the argument that there is trading (see **5.13**).
   - There is repetition.
   - There is a selling organisation.
   - The tickets do not have any value unless they are sold.

- The activity is related to the business of the charity.

This is trading, but it will almost certainly be primary purpose trading (see Chapter 3).

(d) Sale of educational books by a charitable university press.
  - There is probably a profit motive (see the point above concerning the charitable theatre).
  - There is repetition.
  - There is a selling organisation.
  - The books are acquired, or produced with a view to resale.
  - The assets are likely to generate a benefit only if they are sold.
  - The activity is related to the business of the charity.

This is trading but, again, it is likely to be primary purpose trading.

(e) The provision by a charity under contract to a Primary Care Trust of services to help alcohol and drug abusers.
  - The charity structures its prices to make a surplus, ie it has a profit motive.
  - The service is supplied continuously for the period of the contract, hence there is repetition.
  - There is no selling organisation such as a shop.
  - The services are arranged by the charity with a view to charging for them.
  - The activity is related to the business of the charity.

This is trading, but is likely to be primary purpose trading, depending on the charity's purposes.

(f) A charity receives funding for the development of its website from a commercial sponsor: in return it publicises the sponsor's business. The charity is effectively advertising the sponsor's business.
  - The charity has a profit motive.
  - There is, potentially, repetition: the trading is repeated each time the charity advertises the sponsor.
  - There is no formal selling organisation.
  - The services sold are clearly of a commercial nature.

This is likely to be trading, although this will depend on the nature and level of the advertising (see **5.153–5.183**).

(g) A 'charity of the year' arrangement under which a charity receives funding from a supermarket in return for allowing it to use the charity's name or logo on its bags and other promotional material.
  - The charity has a profit motive, as it is entering into the arrangement to raise funds.
  - There is repetition.
  - There is no selling organisation.
  - The arrangement is clearly a commercial one.

This is trading.

5.25 A further example of the subtle borderline that divides fundraising from trading is the creation of databases for charities. The use of a database comprising the names and addresses of potential or actual donors is a vital part of modern fundraising. Subject to the data protection rules (see Chapter 9), it allows a charity to send fundraising material by post or email, or to telephone potential donors in order to solicit donations. For many charities income derived from such fundraising activities constitutes a major part of their total revenue.

5.26 But in order to create such a database, a charity may have to expend very considerable amounts of money, on renting lists of names of potential donors, or by paying a fundraising agency to compile such a list by telephoning potential donors. This initial expenditure will be categorised by the fundraiser as an 'investment'. Indeed, the charity may well lose money on the initial fundraising if the expenditure is contrasted with the immediate income generated. The sums involved can be very considerable, but this is not an investment in the commercial sense. A charity could spend many thousands of pounds in building a database, but so long as the charity is not carrying on a trade of creating and selling databases, the creation of the database is not a trading activity, but rather an expense of fundraising. If, however, a charity hired out its own database on a commercial basis, as some charities have done in the past, it would be trading. Indeed (as we see in Chapter 7), where a charity allows its trading subsidiary use of its data in return for a fee, this is trading income.

5.27 If, having analysed the nature of the fundraising activity, the charity decides that it is trading, the following preliminary issues must be considered (see Chapter 2):

- Is there power to trade?

- Does charity law allow this activity?

- What are the tax and VAT implications?

The answers to these questions will determine whether the charity can carry out the activity directly, or whether it must involve a trading subsidiary.

5.28 In the rest of this chapter we explore particular types of fundraising activity.

PRIMARY PURPOSE TRADING

5.29 As explained in more detail in Chapter 3, primary purpose trading is trading carried out in fulfilment of the charity's main purposes. In many cases, the activity raising funds for the charity will be primary purpose trading. For instance, in the examples at **5.24**(c) and (d), the sale of tickets by a charitable theatre and the sale of publications by a university press is furthering their respective aims of advancing the arts and education. Similarly, in example **5.24**(e), a charity which provides substance misuse support services to its Primary Care Trust may be fulfilling its charitable aims, depending on what they are.

5.30 If the work in connection with the trade is carried out mainly by the beneficiaries of the charity, this is also primary purpose trading. Trading which is ancillary to a primary purpose trade, such as the sale of refreshments to those who have bought tickets to a charitable theatre's performance is treated as primary purpose trading.

5.31 Primary purpose trading may generally be carried out by the charity, and there should be no direct tax implications, although VAT may be an issue: primary purpose trading is covered in detail in Chapter 3.

FUNDRAISING EVENTS

5.32 Events held to raise money for charity may well involve trading activity, with the associated charity law, tax and VAT implications. There is, however, a key exemption from tax and VAT for many fundraising events, which we explore in more detail below.

Is a fundraising event trading?

5.33 A charity which holds regular fundraising events, for which it makes a charge, is likely to be trading. However, where supporters attending an event make a donation to the charity, rather than paying an entry fee, this may not be trading. But the donation must be voluntary. A 'minimum donation' is not voluntary: HMRC has treated an admission fee of £20 plus a 'minimum voluntary contribution' of £10 as an admission fee of £30 for VAT purposes (*Glasgow's Miles Better Mid Summer 5th Anniversary Ball (VTD4460)*). (See also **4.79**.)

Is there power to trade?

5.34 As explained in Chapter 2, the charity should have appropriate constitutional power to hold the event. This may be covered by a general power to trade or to raise funds.

Does charity law allow the activity?

5.35 As explained in detail in Chapter 2, the Charity Commission's position is that non-primary purpose trading which involves significant risk to the resources to the charity should not be carried out by the charity: any such activity could be run through a trading subsidiary. Trustees should be alert to the possibility that a fundraising event may pose a significant risk, meaning that even though the charity might be able to carry out the activity without a tax charge (thanks to the fundraising event exemption), the Charity Commission would insist on involving a trading company (see **2.20–2.32**).

The tax and VAT exemption for 'one-off' fundraising events

5.36 A specific exemption from VAT (VATA 1994, Sch 9, Group 12) applies to events organised and promoted to raise money for charity. By concession (Extra-Statutory Concession C4), direct tax will not be charged on the profits of events organised by voluntary organisations or charities falling within the VAT exemption, provided those profits are transferred to charities or otherwise applied for charitable purposes.

5.37 Given that the exemption from direct tax (ie income tax in the case of a charitable trust and corporation tax in the case of other charities) is dependent on the VAT exemption, the first step is to look at the VAT rules in more detail.

5.38 The exemption applies to the supply of goods and services by a charity in connection with an event that is organised for charitable purposes by a charity, whose primary purpose is the raising of money, and that is promoted as being primarily for the raising of money.

Who does the exemption apply to?

5.39 'Charity' in this context includes a company which is wholly owned by the charity if that company has agreed in writing to transfer all its profits to the charity, or the company's profits are otherwise payable to charity. So events organised by the charity's trading subsidiary will qualify for the VAT exemption, provided a written agreement is in place. They will not, however, qualify for the direct tax exemption (see **5.54**).

5.40 The exemption also applies where the event is organised jointly by more than one charity. (And it applies to certain not-for-profit cultural and recreational bodies, even though they may not be charities.)

What events does it apply to?

5.41 In order to qualify, the event must be clearly organised and promoted primarily to raise money for the charity. Social events which incidentally make a profit, such as networking events for charity members, will not qualify. However, they may amount to primary purpose trading. Similarly, a charity's AGM will not qualify for the exemption.

5.42 Those attending or participating in the event must be aware of its primary fundraising purpose. HMRC's internal guidance V1-9 'Charities', para 9.3.3 reads:

'The main and overriding purpose of holding the event should be to raise funds and people attending should be aware of that. This means that the advertising literature, tickets, programmes, etc make this clear. On occasion you may need to look at background papers, such as minutes of meetings, to confirm that the main reason for holding the event was to raise funds.'

Activities of a semi-regular or continuous nature, such as the frequent operation of a shop or bar, will not be an event.

5.43 HMRC gives the following non-exhaustive list by way of examples of different types of event (see HMRC's 'Detailed guidance notes for charities', Annex IV, para 41):

- A ball, dinner dance, disco or barn dance.

- A performance – such as a concert, a stage production, and any other event which has a paying audience.

- The showing of a film.

- A fete, fair or festival.

- A horticultural show.

- An exhibition – such as art, history or science.

- A bazaar, jumble sale, car boot sale, or a good-as-new sale.

- Sporting participation (including spectators), such as a sponsored walk or swim.

- A sporting performance.

- A game of skill, a contest, or a quiz.

- Participation in an endurance event.

- A fireworks display.

- A dinner, lunch or barbecue.

- An auction of bought-in goods.

Number of events

5.44 The exemption will not apply where there are more than 15 events of the same kind, at the same location, by the charity or its trading subsidiary in any financial year. If there are 16 events the exemption will not apply to any of them. Note that if the charity's financial year is less than 12 months the number of events allowed is pro-rated accordingly. HMRC insisted on this complication because of concerns that the exemption could be abused.

5.45 Events which raise less than £1,000, by way of gross takings, in a week, will not count towards the total of 15. (But note that if small scale events of this kind are held very regularly (eg more than once or twice a week), they may not be regarded as an 'event', but more of an activity of a semi-regular or continuous nature.)

What is a location?

5.46 What constitutes a location is a bit of a moveable feast and will depend on the type of location and kind of event. Balls held for the same charity in different towns would not be regarded as being held in the same location. Where events need to be held in special premises (eg a swimming gala in a swimming pool, or a theatrical event in a theatre), each of these will constitute a separate location. Where an event is held in a complex, such as an arts complex comprising cinemas, theatres or concert halls, the location is the specific cinema, theatre or concert hall in which the event takes place. HMRC regards a charity's entire website as a location for events held over the internet.

5.47 HMRC states that the rules are designed to be generous to charities holding a number of events of the same type in different locations in the same town. But arrangements such as weekly car boot sales in different, but adjacent, fields would not be regarded as being in a separate location unless HMRC was happy that the arrangement was not potentially distorting competition (see **5.50**). Essentially HMRC will consider whether the attendees will be from different catchment areas when considering whether or not there is a different location.

5.48 Where an event such as a concert is repeated on successive evenings, each performance is a separate event. A single event taking place at the same location for more than one day, such as a golf tournament, will be one event, unless it includes more than two nights' accommodation or falls within the Tour Operator's Margin Scheme (see **5.49**).

Accommodation

5.49 The exemption will apply where accommodation is provided, unless:

–   the accommodation is for more than two nights (although the two nights need not be consecutive); or

–   the supply of accommodation falls within the Tour Operator's Margin Scheme (or 'TOMS').

TOMS is a special VAT scheme for businesses involved in organising travel and accommodation services. It applies not only to traditional tour operators but other organisations involved in organising travel services, and may well catch charities operating events.

Distorting competition

5.50 The exemption will not apply where the event is likely to cause distortion of competition and place a commercial enterprise carried on by a taxable person at a disadvantage. This is because the exemption stems from European law and is only intended to apply as a concession to charities, without prejudicing regular businesses which are liable for VAT. But HMRC say that there has to be 'significant and systematic' evidence of commercial distortion, so this is unlikely to be an issue in most cases. For instance, a charity opening a night club next door to a commercial night club and offering a series of different events (eg 15 '70s nights', 15 '50s nights', 15 raves, 15 'heavy metal nights', etc) would probably be regarded as distorting competition.

How is the exemption applied?

5.51 For VAT purposes, all the proceeds of the fundraising event will be exempt from VAT. This includes:

– admission charges;

– the sale of commemorative brochures and the sale of advertising space in those brochures;

– other items usually sold by the charity, eg T-shirts, non-donated auctioned goods;

– sponsorship payments directly connected with the event, eg the fee paid by a local business to cover the costs of the flowers at a ball, in return for publicity for the business.

Commemorative goods and souvenirs sold for a period after the event will not be covered by the exemption.

5.52 Note that since the event is VAT exempt, the charity will not be able to recover VAT which it has paid on goods and services which it has purchased in connection with organising the event. However, if it has incurred VAT on expenses which relate both to an event which qualifies for the exemption and other taxable or non-exempt activities, it may be possible to recover a proportion of the VAT, for instance in relation to the purchase of a computer used partly to make event bookings and partly to manage a charity shop's accounts.

5.53 Note also that if any of the proceeds of the fundraising event come from taxable supplies which are zero rated, such as the sale of printed matter or children's clothing, or the sale of donated goods, they remain zero rated despite the exemption. This means that although the charity need not charge VAT on those items, it can reclaim any VAT incurred by the charity which is directly attributable to those items.

Direct tax

5.54 By virtue of Extra-Statutory Concession C4, where the event is organised by a voluntary organisation or charity, and the profits are transferred to charities or otherwise applied for charitable purposes, no income or corporation tax will be charged on the profits from the event. Note, however, that the direct tax exemption will not apply where the event is organised by a charity's trading subsidiary, although the VAT exemption will apply in these circumstances. However, in such cases it should be possible for the trading subsidiary to escape a tax bill by paying any profits up to the parent charity under the gift aid rules (see **7.233–7.238**).

Other considerations

5.55 Charities organising fundraising events will have other issues to consider, in addition to tax and VAT. A full analysis of these is beyond the scope of this book, but the following checklist may be useful:

- Will the event be organised by and in the name of the charity or by and in the name of an event organiser?
  - If the latter, will the event be run by the event organiser on its own account – passing the proceeds to the charity – or by the event organiser as agent for the charity? The structure will affect whether the tax and VAT exemption for fundraising events applies.
  - If the charity is using an event organiser it should put in place a contract for the services to be provided.
  - Is the event organiser a commercial participator (see **5.106–5.118**) or professional fundraiser within the meaning of the Charities Act 1992? Where professional fundraisers are used, the charity must have an agreement with the fundraiser covering certain minimum terms and the fundraiser must make a statement containing certain information about its remuneration (see **5.81**).

- Have any commercial partners involved in sponsoring the event been properly vetted by the charity (see **5.158–5.160**)?

- Is the charity clear about the costs of the event, and what the likely profits will be? Charity Commission guidance CC20 'Charities and Fundraising', para 5 reads:

'It is essential to spend time before undertaking any fundraising exercise to develop a strategy: some forms of fundraising can be costly and it is important to be sure that the costs will be justified in terms of a realistic return.'

- Trustee approval should be obtained for all types of events, particularly ones involving potentially dangerous or challenging activities.

- Is there a clear contract with the owner of the venue? For example:
    - What is included in the price?
    - Who will be responsible for insurance, and what does the venue owner's cover include?
    - Who is responsible for health and safety, and what health and safety steps will be taken?
    - Can the price be increased? When, why and by how much?
    - What provision is there for cancellation by either party, and associated penalties?
    - Has the venue owner limited its liability in any way?
    - Can the charity obtain an indemnity from the owner in case it is sued by a participant?

- Have a risk assessment, a health and safety, and an emergency plan been prepared? Particular issues might be:
    - Fire precautions: compliance with the Fire Precautions Act 1971.
    - Food safety: compliance with the Food Safety Act 1990 and relevant regulations (see **8.88–8.89**).
    - Product safety: if new or second-hand products are being sold (see **8.64–8.78**).
    - Health and safety: under the Health and Safety at Work Act 1974 an organisation will be responsible for breaches of health and safety at any event it organises, eg failing to ensure that fire escapes are not blocked.
    - First Aid: under the Health and Safety (First Aid) Regulations 1981 first aid must be provided to employees – organisations should also make adequate first aid provision to others involved in the event.
    - Organisations should be aware of the scope for prosecution for the offence of corporate manslaughter under the Corporate Manslaughter and Corporate Homicide Act 2007 in the event of a fatal accident.

- What risks can be insured against? The scope of the insurance should be discussed carefully with the charity's insurers (see Chapter 10).

- Have other relevant regulations been considered? For example:
    - An alcohol licence may be needed if alcohol is being provided or sold.
    - A licence may be required if entertainment is being provided (eg a public entertainment licence from the local authority, a Performing

Rights Society licence for live performances or playing recorded music, or a Phonographic Performance Ltd licence for playing recorded music).

–   If there will be any advertising, the relevant advertising rules must be complied with (see **8.124–8.135**).

–   The rules on public collections must be followed: eg a licence may be needed for a collection outside the venue of an event which people have paid to attend.

–   The rules on lotteries must be observed, where relevant.

–   There are special rules about certain types of aerial display, which require consent from the Civil Aviation Authority.

–   Event organisers should consider whether Criminal Records Bureau checks on employees, contractors and volunteers will be necessary.

–   The requirements of the disability discrimination legislation must be observed.

–   As explained at **2.75–2.77**, a registered charity with an income over £10,000 must state that it is a registered charity on various documents.

–   Data protection law should be complied with. In preference this means that anyone whose data is collected (including participants and others such as their next of kin) should, at the time the data is collected, be given clear information about how it will be used, and sign to confirm that they consent to such use (see Chapter 9).

CHALLENGE EVENTS

5.56   Challenge events have become a popular fundraising tool. Members of the public take part in some physical challenge – the London Marathon, a cycling trip around Vietnam or a sailing challenge around the Isle of Wight, for example – and raise funds for a particular charity in the process. Challenge events are organised in a myriad of ways: in many cases there will be an element of trading. This section illustrates some of the issues which may arise.

Direct tax

5.57   HMRC has accepted that challenge events are not trading for direct tax purposes. In certain circumstances funds raised by a challenge event can be eligible for gift aid (see **5.70–5.73** below).

VAT

5.58   Income from a challenge event may well be within the scope of VAT. There are several issues to consider.

Does the 'one-off' fundraising exemption apply?

5.59 As explained in detail at **5.36–5.53** above, charities and their trading subsidiaries may hold up to 15 fundraising events of the same type in the same location per year and the proceeds will be exempt from both tax and VAT. No more than two nights' accommodation may be provided if the exemption is to apply (see **5.66–5.69**). Neither will the exemption apply if the charity is caught by the TOMS scheme (see **5.49**), although this is unlikely.

5.60 Charities should therefore first consider if this exemption applies to the challenge event; it may in particular be appropriate for some UK events such as parachute jumps, walks, bike rides, etc that take place over a single weekend.

Events run by a commercial operator

5.61 Some challenge events, such as the London Marathon, are organised by an external organiser rather than the charity. Since these events are not organised by a charity (the charity simply buys places in them from the commercial organiser) they are not covered by the fundraising event VAT exemption.

5.62 For example, ABC charity purchases a number of coveted places in the London Marathon. It offers them to supporters, who must pay a registration fee to the charity. Supporters are encouraged to raise sponsorship income over and above the registration fee.

5.63 For VAT purposes the registration fee is effectively an entry fee and will be subject to VAT at the standard rate.

5.64 Note that there are no hard and fast rules about how much the registration fee should be. If a charity charges a low registration fee of £1, for example, and charges VAT on the fee, it will be able to reclaim the VAT it has paid when buying places in the event. So, even though the VAT included in the £1 fee is only 13p (and will be 15p once VAT rates rise from 15% to 17.5% – see **2.61(5)**) the charity can recover all the VAT it has paid on the cost of entry places and other costs associated with the event. But if a low fee is charged, the charity trustees will need to be happy that the event is still likely to raise funds for the charity. There will be no obligation on supporters to raise money over and above the registration fee.

5.65 If the charity tells a supporter they must raise a minimum amount by way of sponsorship in order to participate in the event, HMRC will regard the minimum amount as an entry fee which is subject to VAT. This can be avoided if the charity does not insist on a minimum amount of sponsorship, but asks for a pledge to raise a certain amount, allowing the supporter to take part regardless of the amount raised. Again, the trustees will need to be happy that this does not open up the charity to abuse, as participants will be able to join in, potentially at considerable expense to the charity, without raising a penny. The pledged amount is outside the scope of VAT and potentially eligible for gift aid (see **5.70–5.73**).

Events involving more than two nights' accommodation

5.66 HMRC introduced new rules which took effect on 31 July 2008 for events that involve more than two nights' accommodation (typically overseas events) – ie events not covered by the fundraising event exemption.

5.67 Charities that organise their own events or act as undisclosed agents (so the participant thinks the charity is providing the event, although in reality it is provided by a tour operator) are caught by the HMRC tour operator's margin scheme (TOMS), ie they are regarded for VAT purposes like a travel agent. This means they must charge VAT on their gross profit margin for events held in the EU; no VAT is chargeable on events held outside the EU.

5.68 Charities which act as disclosed agents – ie participants are aware of and contract with the tour operator, which is the usual scenario – must charge VAT on the commission they earn from the tour operator.

5.69 Where the charity has either entered into a contract with a tour operator for a future event before 31 July 2008, or has commenced negotiations with a tour operator before 31 July 2008, or has publicised an event before 31 July 2008, VAT can be accounted for (or not) under whatever method the charity had previously agreed with HMRC.

Gift aid

5.70 Where individuals obtain sponsorship from friends or family for participation in a challenge event, this is typically regarded as a straightforward donation. Charities should therefore seek to bring the payments within the gift aid regime, by including gift aid declarations on the sponsorship forms. However, under the gift aid rules, there are limits on the benefits which donors and those connected to them can receive. These limits are:

Amount of donation	Maximum value of benefits
£0 to £100	25% of the donation
£101 to 1,000	£25
£1,001 +	5% of the donation

5.71 If the benefits received by the participant exceed the relevant limits, no gift aid can be claimed on the sponsorship received by the participant and those connected to him or her. Connected persons are defined in s 993 of the Income Tax Act 2007 and include spouses, relatives (ie siblings, ancestors and lineal descendants) and their spouses and companies under the control of the participant, or of any connected person. If enough sponsorship is raised to match the value of the benefit, additional gifts by the participant and connected persons after the value of the benefit has been raised are potentially subject to gift aid relief. This is because no benefit has been received as a result of the donations.

5.72   In the case of UK events such as the London Marathon, HMRC does not regard there as being a benefit for gift aid purposes where the benefits provided consist of any of the following:

- Free training and health advice.

- A free T-shirt, running vest or similar that clearly portrays the charity the individual is taking part on behalf of.

- Free massages and support for physical wellbeing during the event.

- Free pre-event meeting, which may include free professional advice or support, a simple meal, energy drinks and encouragement from the charity and other participants.

- Free post-event meeting, which may include medical treatment or advice, changing facilities, light refreshments and gives the charity the opportunity to thank participants.

- Prizes for top fundraisers.

But free travel, accommodation or other benefits such as prizes for all are benefits. Overseas events are always seen as providing a benefit; in HMRC's eyes they are akin to a foreign holiday.

5.73   If supporters are expected to pay for the costs of an event themselves, and encouraged to raise sponsorship over and above that payment, then the additional sponsorship income will be a pure donation, and should be eligible for gift aid.

Donation from travel company

5.74   If the charity does not organise the event itself, but receives a donation from a travel company, this will be trading for direct tax purposes if the charity allows the travel company to use its name and logo, or database, in return for the donation (see **5.84–5.152**).

Tax and VAT – conclusion

5.75   Challenge events throw up complicated tax and VAT issues, and specialist advice should always be taken. Small differences in the structure of the event can make a big difference in tax or VAT terms. It may be wise to seek clearance from HMRC on the proposals, although this can take time.

Other issues

5.76 There are many other issues which charities involved in challenge events should be aware of, including many that crop up for fundraising events generally, such as contract problems, data protection, and health and safety (see **5.55**). In addition, the specific issues highlighted below are particularly important for challenge events.

Travel law

5.77 The Civil Aviation Authority (CAA) takes the view that if the arrangements involve flights, the flight bookings must be protected by an ATOL (Air Travel Organisers' Licensing) bond and/or sufficient ATOL protection contributions. The licence holder must lodge a money bond with the CAA and/or pay contributions per person travelling. Failure to comply can lead to criminal offences and fines. An alternative to charities having to arrange this themselves is to buy flights from an ATOL bonded travel agent.

5.78 The Package Travel, Package Holidays and Package Tours Regulations 1992 (SI 1992/3288) (as amended) are broad enough to cover any arrangements which last more than 24 hours or include overnight accommodation, and include two out of the following three services:

–   transport (whether by plane, train, coach, car, etc);

–   accommodation;

–   other tourist services (e g sightseeing services, tour guide services).

Travel within the UK as well as overseas is covered.

5.79 The Regulations place a number of responsibilities on the 'organiser' of the package, including obligations to include certain information in brochures and to provide certain information to the participants before travel. The Regulations also stipulate a number of minimum terms implied into the contract between the organiser and the participant. For each challenge event, it should be clear whether the charity is the 'organiser' or whether (which is preferable) the 'organiser' is a third party tour operator. In the latter case, any contract should make clear that the tour operator is accepting responsibility for complying with the regulations.

5.80 Since 1 January 2009 the sale of 'connected travel insurance' (or 'CTI') has been regulated by the Financial Services Authority. Travel insurance that is sold in connection with a challenge event is CTI: any person offering such insurance will either require authorisation from the FSA or need to be an authorised representative of an authorised person. However, simply providing information about CTI that is available from an FSA-authorised tour operator or other third party, without taking any further steps to arrange or sell CTI, will not generally require authorisation.

Professional fundraisers

5.81 If the event is structured so that the participant effectively receives a 'free' trip (or a partly funded trip), the participant may fall within the definition of 'professional fundraiser' in the Charities Act 1992. There is an exemption that may apply – at the time of writing this applies if the benefit the participant receives in a year is less than £500 (but this is expected to be increased to £1,000 by April 2009). Where a participant is a professional fundraiser, the charity must have an agreement with the participant covering certain minimum terms (under s 59(1) of the 1992 Act) and the participant must make a statement containing certain information about the charity and the benefits to the fundraiser when soliciting donations for the charity (under s 60(1) of the 1992 Act). The Office of the Third Sector has produced detailed guidance on the statements required under s 60(1) – 'Charitable Fundraising: Guidance on Part 2 of the Charities Act 1992'. The appropriate statement is often included as part of the sponsor form.

Commercial participators

5.82 Where a commercial organisation, such as a travel company, is planning an event themselves on the understanding that some level of donation will be paid to charity, they will probably fall within the definition of a 'commercial participator' under the Charities Act 1992, which imposes requirements about the agreement with the charity and statements to be made to the public (these are explained in detail at **5.106–5.148**).

PARTNERSHIPS WITH BUSINESSES

5.83 Charities receive funding from businesses in a variety of ways, from straightforward donations to more complicated arrangements involving using a charity's name and logo in publicity materials. Wherever an arrangement between a charity and a business involves anything other than a simple donation, the charity may well be carrying out trading activity. The most common examples are explored below.

Cause-related marketing – use of a charity's name and logo

5.84 A common fundraising arrangement involves a business representing that a proportion of the sale price from a product will be paid to a charity. Arrangements vary from the simple – '5p from the sale of this tin of baked beans will be paid to ABC Charity' – to more complex arrangements involving charity-branded (or 'affinity') credit cards (see **5.115** and **5.185–5.192**). This type of fundraising is often known as 'cause-related marketing', because as well as selling its products and raising funds for charity, the business is highlighting the cause which the charity represents.

5.85 In legal terms, a cause-related marketing arrangement involves the charity agreeing that the business can use the charity's name and logo for the purposes of the promotion, in return for the share of the promotion's income which will be paid to the charity. The charity is licensing its intellectual property rights in its name and logo to the business in return for a fee.

5.86 This is trading activity. The charity needs to consider whether it is able to enter into the arrangement, and what the tax and VAT consequences might be (see the list of preliminary questions in Chapter 2). The charity also needs to consider the terms of its agreement with the business.

Constitutional powers and charity law considerations

5.87 As with other forms of trading, the charity's constitution should contain an appropriate power to carry out this form of trading.

5.88 Since the activity is non-primary purpose trading, in the Charity Commission's view it should not be carried out directly by the charity if it involves significant risk to the resources of the charity (see **2.20–2.32**). The charity trustees should consider this, although if a fundraising relationship with a commercial partner is likely to involve significant risk (eg reputational risk or a risk stemming from the terms of the agreement with the commercial organisaton), should the charity really be entering into the relationship on those terms in the first place? (See **5.90–5.92**.)

5.89 If the charity cannot carry out the trading activity directly, it may wish to run it through its trading company. There may also be good tax reasons for using a trading subsidiary for these arrangements (see **5.94–5.97**).

5.90 If the charity can enter into the arrangement, it will need to consider whether it is appropriate for it to do so and, if so, on what terms. These considerations apply equally where the charity's trading subsidiary is involved. Charity Commission guidance in this area points out that 'a charity's name is a valuable asset' (Charity Commission publication 'Fund-raising through partnerships with companies', para 1). In allowing a third party to use its name a charity must be sure (a) that it truly wishes to be associated with that business, and has explored any potentially adverse effects this might have on its reputation, and (b) that it has negotiated the best possible deal for the charity. Charity Commission guidance makes it clear that 'such relationships are beneficial to both parties and charities should not be hesitant in negotiating the best possible return for their part in them' ('Fund-raising through partnerships with companies', para 3).

5.91 The Charity Commission recommends that charities should develop written criteria for agreement by the trustees for use in judging the acceptability, in principle, of any proposed joint venture with a commercial organisation. This should involve consideration of whether the company is a suitable partner for the charity, bearing in mind what is known of its products, activities, public image and financial position. How will the charity's association with that company be seen by its supporters, beneficiaries and other stakeholders? What will the charity do to anticipate and answer any complaints or criticisms that might be made of the association? (See 'Fund-raising through partnerships with companies' for further Charity Commission guidance.)

5.92 The Commission's concerns are echoed in the Institute of Fundraising's Code on 'Charities Working with Business'. The Code suggests:

- Charities should undertake careful research on any company they are proposing to enter into an arrangement with, including its associated companies, its motives, values and ethics and its reputation.

- Charities should have a clearly defined policy for working with business, covering:
  - The overall rationale for working with business.
  - The basis and limit on which the charity will work with companies.
  - Which companies it will or will not work with.

- The policy should dovetail with a clear internal system setting out how decisions on working with companies will be made – so that staff know when decisions need to be referred to a more senior level, or indeed when trustees need to be involved.

- The charity should ensure that there are no conflicts of interest between it and the company. A good example would be where a medical charity co-operates with a pharmaceutical company.

- As with other activities, the charity should use a process of risk assessment to establish what risks the relationship will bring, and how they can be managed.

The relationship between the charity and business should be regulated by a contract (see **5.149–5.152**), and the charity should be happy that the business has the resources to comply with its terms.

5.93 Note that not all arrangements between charities and commercial partners will be trading. There may be arrangements which do not generate an income for the charity. For instance, a charity interested in promoting a healthy diet teams up with a supermarket to encourage the public to eat more fresh fruit and vegetables. The charity may allow the supermarket to use its name and logo to promote the sale of fruit and vegetables as part of a '5 portions of fruit and vegetables a day' campaign. This helps the charity to achieve its aims, so it will be justified in allowing the supermarket to use its name and logo for free. But it would still be wise for a written agreement to cover the arrangement for use of the name and logo so as to ensure, in particular, that the name and logo are used in a way which the charity is 100% happy with (see **5.152**).

Tax

5.94 Where a charity allows a business to use its name and logo in return for a fee, it is carrying out taxable trading activity. This has direct tax and VAT implications.

5.95 The starting point is that the profit which the charity makes on the arrangement will be subject to direct tax. It is highly unlikely that it will be possible to argue that the activity is primary purpose trading. There may be situations, however, where the 'one off' fundraising event exemption (see **5.36–5.54**) is relevant – if, for instance, the company is permitted to use the charity's name and logo only in the course of a qualifying fundraising event. And if the charity's total taxable income falls within the small scale exemption (see **2.41–2.50**), tax will not be payable.

5.96 A further exemption is available where all that the charity is doing is allowing the company to use its name and logo and the arrangement lasts for more than one year, ie the payment must be capable of recurring. The payment is pure income profit to the charity without it having to do anything in return. Where the fee is payable under a legal obligation, and recurs each year, and the charity does nothing else at all in return for the payment, the income is exempt from income tax in the case of a charitable trust under ITA 2007, s 536(3)(c), and from corporation tax in the case of a charitable unincorporated association or company under ICTA 1988, s 505(1)(c)(ii). This exemption will be useful in some situations, where all that the charity is doing is offering the use of its name and logo. However, this type of arrangement is fairly uncommon. It is much more likely that the charity will be offering other services to the business, such as use of the charity's publicity and advertising.

5.97 If no exemption is available, the profits from the arrangement will be taxable. The classic method of avoiding tax in these situations is to run the arrangement through a trading subsidiary. The charity licenses the use of its name and logo to a trading subsidiary. The trading subsidiary, in turn, sub-licenses the charity's name and logo to the business for the purposes of the promotion. The fee due is then paid to the trading subsidiary (although it may be split between the charity and the trading subsidiary in some cases – see **5.101–5.104** below). Chapter 7 deals with establishing and running a trading subsidiary.

VAT

5.98 When a charity gives a business the right to use its name and logo, it is making a taxable supply. This is within the scope of VAT. Where the

arrangement forms part of a qualifying 'one off' fundraising event (see
5.36–5.53), the VAT exemption may well apply. But in other cases, where the
charity is registered for VAT, it will need to account for output tax on the fee.

5.99 This means that the charity should ensure that the business paying the
fee is obliged to pay both the fee and any VAT. For instance, ABC Charity
charges XYZ Supermarket a fee of £10,000 plus VAT for the use of its name
and logo. XYZ Supermarket pays £11,500 to ABC Charity, which accounts to
HMRC for output tax of £1,500 and retains £10,000. The business may well be
able to recover the VAT it has paid.

5.100 But some businesses, particularly banks and insurance companies, will
not be able to recover all of the VAT charged in these circumstances, and may
well insist that the charity pays the VAT, which effectively reduces the level of
the fee in the charity's hands. For instance, ABC Charity charges XYZ Bank a
fee of £10,000 including VAT for use of its name and logo. XYZ Bank pays
£10,000 to ABC Charity, which accounts to HMRC for output tax of roughly
£1,300 and retains the balance of around £8,700.

5.101 A tried and tested solution is to split the fee payable into two: part is a
fee for the use of the name and the logo (which will be payable to the charity or
the trading subsidiary, depending on the direct tax treatment – see **5.95–5.97**),
and part is a straightforward donation to the charity. VAT will still be relevant,
but it will only apply to the fee, and not to the donation element. The parties
have to reach agreement on how the total payment will be split: as a rule of
thumb 90% could be treated as a donation to the charity and 10% as a licence
fee. Either the business or the charity will pay the VAT on the 10% fee,
depending on the terms of the agreement. Readers should bear in mind that the
exact percentage will depend on the circumstances, and if a larger degree of PR
is provided, a higher percentage should be considered as a licence fee.

5.102 The fee element of the transaction will attract direct tax (see **5.95–5.97**).
So in most cases a split fee arrangement of this kind will involve the business,
the trading company and the charity. The donation will be paid to the charity
and the fee (inclusive or exclusive of VAT, depending on the deal which has
been negotiated) will be paid to the trading company. Thus, ABC Charity, ABC
Trading Limited (the charity's wholly owned trading subsidiary) and XYZ
Bank will agree as follows. XYZ Bank makes a donation of £9,000 to ABC
Charity. XYZ Bank pays a fee of £1,000 including VAT to ABC Trading
Limited. ABC Trading Limited accounts to HMRC for roughly £130 output
tax on the fee and retains the balance of around £870. Occasionally, more than
10% will need to be agreed as the fee element of the transaction. This will be
when a very high level of advertising is provided by the corporate business
sponsor.

5.103 Note that the agreement between the parties must make it clear that the
payment is a split one – HMRC will not apportion a single payment.

5.104 It is important, however, that the donation is literally a donation, and that the business is not contractually obliged to make it. This means that the agreement has to be carefully drafted. A pledge to make a donation is not legally enforceable, unless it is set out in a deed, which involves using specific wording and a slightly different procedure for executing, or signing, the agreement. This carries risks for the charity: if the arrangement is not confirmed in a deed and the business chooses not to make the donation after all, there is little the charity can do. While using a deed may sound overly cautious, it is a sensible way of protecting the charity.

5.105 Note that the examples given above assume a VAT rate of 15%: this is due to rise again to 17.5% in January 2010 – see **2.61**(5).

Commercial participators

5.106 In the majority of cases, where a charity has agreed that a business can use its name and logo in return for a fee, the business will fall within the definition of 'commercial participator' under the Charities Act 1992. This has two key implications: first, certain statements about the relationship must be made to the public and, secondly, the agreement between the parties must be in writing and contain certain terms.

What is a commercial participator?

5.107 A typical example of a situation where a charity might allow its name and logo to be used by a business is where the business wants to encourage customers to buy its products because part of the sale proceeds will be paid to the charity. For example:

–   'Ten pence from the sale of this packet of cereal will be paid to XYZ charity' – the charity's name and logo will appear on the packet and on any promotional material.

–   'One per cent of the price of any holiday booked to France this month will go to ABC charity' – again, the charity's name and logo will appear on the marketing material.

In these situations, the business will be regarded as a 'commercial participator' under s 58 of the Charities Act 1992.

5.108 Charities Act 1992, s 58(1) defines a 'commercial participator' as:

'in relation to any charitable institution ... any person ... who:

(a)   carries on for gain a business other than a fund-raising business, but
(b)   in the course of that business, engages in any promotional venture in the course of which it is represented that charitable contributions are to be given to or applied for the benefit of the institution'.

5.109   A 'charitable institution' is defined as:

> 'a charity or an institution (other than a charity) which is established for charitable, benevolent or philanthropic purposes.'

This definition includes registered charities and those charities which are exempt from registration under the Charities Act 1993 (such as universities). In addition to charities, the definition also covers 'benevolent and philanthropic' organisations which are not exclusively charitable.

5.110   A 'promotional venture' is defined as:

> 'any advertising or sales campaign or any other venture undertaken for promotional purposes.'

5.111   To 'represent' is defined extraordinarily widely by s 58(6) as meaning to represent:

> '... in any manner whatever, whether expressly or impliedly and whether done ... by speaking directly ... or ... by means of a statement published in any newspaper, film or radio or television programme ... or otherwise.'

5.112   'Charitable contributions':

> '... in relation to any representation made by any commercial participator or other person, means—

> (a)   the whole or part of—
>   (i)   the consideration given for goods or services sold or supplied by him, or
>   (ii) any proceeds (other than such consideration) of a promotional venture undertaken by him, or
> (b)   sums given by him by way of donation in connection with the sale or supply of any such goods or services (whether the amount of such sums is determined by reference to the value of any such goods or services or otherwise)'.

5.113   'Services' is defined by s 58(9) as including facilities and, in particular:

> '(a)   access to any premises or event;
> (b)   membership of any organisation;
> (c)   the provision of advertising space; and
> (d)   the provision of any financial facilities.'

5.114   The upshot of these definitions is that if, as a result of its relationship with the charity, the business is representing that it is paying money to charity, it is likely to be a commercial participator. Further examples of commercial participator relationships are as follows.

Affinity card arrangements

5.115 Banks or financial institutions issue credit cards in conjunction with a charitable institution and donate an agreed percentage of the customer's total expenditure on the card to the charitable institution. In these arrangements, the bank is:

– engaging in a business (running a credit card agency) which is not a fundraising business; and

– in the course of that business, engaging in a promotional venture in which it is representing that a percentage of the consideration paid by the consumer for the services provided by the credit card company will go to a charitable institution.

Hence, the credit card company is a commercial participator. This is made expressly clear by CA 1992, s 58(9)(d), where the definition of 'services' includes 'the provision of any financial facilities'.

Pizza Express

5.116 The restaurant Pizza Express currently advertises that it will give 25p from the sale of its Veneziana pizza to support the charity Venice in Peril and restoration projects throughout the UK. In selling pizzas, the restaurant is:

– engaging in a business (running a restaurant) which is not a fundraising business; and

– in the course of that business, engaging in a promotional venture in which it is representing that part of the price paid by the consumer for the pizza will go to a charitable institution.

Catalogues

5.117 Some commercial organisations distribute catalogues of merchandise coupled with the inducement that part of the profits from the activity or part of the price per item will be passed to a named charity. In this case the catalogue company is running a commercial business (selling goods by mail order) and, in the course of that business, is representing that part of the taxable profit or part of the price paid for each item (the situation will vary) will pass to a named charity. The catalogue company is a commercial participator.

5.118 Each of the above examples is based on the formal negotiated activities of, for example, a credit card company which has an arrangement with a charity to use its logo on the credit card. However, the legislation on commercial participators can also bite on informal arrangements. For example, suppose there is an international emergency (eg an earthquake). Members of the public may feel moved to respond and help. A local newspaper may decide to give, for example, 1p for every newspaper sold on a particular day to the International Red Cross. If the newspaper owner advertises this (which, no doubt, he will do), he immediately will become a form of commercial participator, although he does not have a formal agreement with a charitable institution. He is carrying on a business (selling newspapers), and in the course of that is inducing people to buy his newspapers coupled with the statement that part of the proceeds will pass to a charitable institution (the International Red Cross).

Statements

5.119   If a business is operating as a commercial participator, s 60(3) of the Charities Act 1992, which has been amended by the Charities Act 2006, requires that certain public statements must be made. The legislation reads as follows:

'(3)   Where any representation is made by a commercial participator to the effect that charitable contributions are to be given to or applied for the benefit of one or more particular charitable institutions, the representation shall be accompanied by a statement clearly indicating—
  (a)   the name or names of the institution or institutions concerned;
  (b)   if there is more than one institution concerned, the proportions in which the institutions are respectively to benefit; and
  (c)   the notifiable amount of whichever of the following sums is applicable in the circumstances—
      (i)   the sum representing so much of the consideration given for goods or services sold or supplied by him as is to be given to or applied for the benefit of the institution or institutions concerned,
      (ii)   the sum representing so much of any other proceeds of a promotional venture undertaken by him as is to be so given or applied, or
      (iii)   the sum of the donations by him in connection with the sale or supply of any such goods or services which are to be so given or supplied.'

5.120   Section 60(3A) provides that a reference to the 'notifiable amount' of any remuneration or other sum is a reference—

'(a)   to the actual amount of the remuneration or sum, if that is known at the time when the statement is made; and
  (b)   otherwise to the estimated amount of the remuneration or sum, calculated as accurately as is reasonably possible in the circumstances.'

5.121   Prior to its amendment by the 2006 Charities Act, s 60 allowed a commercial participator to state 'in general terms' the method by which it would be determined how much of a contribution to charity they would make. This meant that, theoretically, a commercial participator did not need to give any specifics at all, but Home Office guidance on the legislation made it clear that commercial participators should, in practice, make more precise statements.

5.122 The changes to s 60, which took effect in April 2008, mean that a commercial participator is now obliged either to state the actual amount which it intends to give to charity or to calculate an accurate (in so far as that is reasonably possible) estimate of such amount and give that estimate in its statement. Commercial participators are therefore now required to be far more transparent in their dealings with charities.

5.123 In December 2008, the Office of the Third Sector published guidance on the professional fundraiser and commercial participator requirements in the Charities Act 1992 – 'Charitable Fundraising: Guidance on Part 2 of the Charities Act 1992'. The guidance includes the following commentary on the content of the statement required by a commercial participator under the amended law (para 3.8.2):

> 'In our view, the requirement to provide the notifiable amount means that in practice any representation made by any commercial participator will be accompanied by a statement setting out:
>
> – the amount of the price paid for each product or service by consumers which will be given to or applied for the benefit of the charitable institution(s) concerned. This might be a percentage or a precise amount, such as 10 pence, depending on the particular promotional venture;
> – the actual amount, or an estimate of the amount, of any other proceeds from a promotional venture that will be given to or applied for the benefit of the charitable institution(s) concerned; or
> – the actual amount, or an estimate of the amount, of the donations to be given by the commercial participator to the charitable institution in connection with the sale or supply of the relevant goods or services. The amount required to be stated will be determined by the particular venture. For example, if a commercial participator intends to donate 50p to charity 1 for every customer that spends £20 or more in his shop in a particular month, it would be sufficient for the commercial participator to state the donation to be made per customer. However, if the commercial participator intended to donate 2% of his profits for a particular month, he should give an estimate of the amount that he will actually donate at the end of the month.
>
> The amount actually stated will of course depend on the particular promotional venture being undertaken by the commercial participator.'

5.124 The guidance gives the following examples of compliant commercial participator statements:

'1.   <<X%>> of the purchase price will be donated to <<charity>>.
2.   For each item sold, <<£X>> will be donated to <<charity>>.

3. <<Company>> will donate <<X%>> of profits from this promotional venture to <<charity>>. This is expected to be at least <<£YYY>>.
4. <<Company>> will donate <<£XXX>>> to <<charity>> as a result of this promotion for the first <<YYY>> items sold, and a further <<£YYY>>> for each additional item sold.'

The guidance makes it clear that, provided the requirements of the legislation are complied with, commercial participators are not prevented from including any additional information.

5.125 Regrettably, the guidance does not include any examples of how a statement should be worded if, as is common, the relationship between the charity and the business is a tripartite one, involving the business, the charity and the charity's trading subsidiary. This lack of guidance means there are likely to be a range of different style statements made by commercial participators in these situations and until there is further guidance, or there are any prosecutions, there will continue to be debate about whether the trading subsidiary should be mentioned.

5.126 The Office of the Third Sector is expected to update the guidance over time.

5.127 As we explain below, failure to comply with the requirement to make a statement under s 60 can result in criminal prosecution of the commercial participator. There is no risk of prosecution for the charity. However, in practice charities are more likely to be familiar with the requirements of the legislation than their commercial partners, and the Charity Commission will expect a charity to ensure compliance. Fundraising relationships which do not comply with the law have prompted the Charity Commission to exercise its investigative powers under the Charities Act 1993, which gives rise to disruption, and reputational damage for the charity.

5.128 It is therefore prudent for a charity entering into an arrangement with a commercial participator to agree the form of statement which will be made to the public, and to set this out in the written agreement.

When should the statement be made?

5.129 The statement must accompany any representation made by a commercial participator within the meaning of s 60(3). A representation, as we have already seen, can be made expressly or impliedly and can be made by speaking directly or by means of a statement published in a newspaper, film, radio or television programme or otherwise. In the case of an oral representation, this means that the statement has to be made at the same time or be clearly visible at the same time. In the case of a newspaper advertisement, this means the advertisement must contain the statement. In shops it should be sufficient that the statement is made by a clear and legible sign, provided it is readily visible when the representation is made (eg it is near the point of sale of the goods concerned, if not printed on the goods themselves).

General fundraising

5.130 Strangely, the controls on commercial participators in the Charities Act 1992 only apply if the commercial participator claims that part of the proceeds of sale of goods or services will go to a named charitable institution. There is no control on a commercial party which seeks to sell goods or services coupled with the inducement that part of the proceeds of sale will go to a general charitable cause (eg 'to relieve poverty in the Third world', 'to help earthquake victims', or 'to benefit children'). However, despite this oversight in the primary legislation, the Charitable Institutions (Fund-Raising) Regulations 1994 (SI 1994/3024) contain controls on such activities. Under reg 7 such persons have to make a statement to the public. At the time of writing, the Office of the Third Sector is proposing to amend the Regulations to ensure that they are consistent with the recent amendments to the 1992 Act.

Telephone and broadcast communications

5.131 If a commercial participator makes 'a representation' (as defined in s 58(6)) by telephone, then within seven days of any payment of £50 or more being made to the commercial participator in response to the representation, the commercial participator (under s 60(5)) has to give to the purchaser a written statement complying with s 60(3) and including full details of the right of the purchaser to cancel under s 61(2). The payment can be made by whatever means, including a credit or debit card.

5.132 The purchaser then has 7 days from the date he is given the written statement (s 61(2)(b)) to exercise, if he so wishes, the right to cancel the purchase, but this is conditional, in the case of the sale of goods, on the restitution of the goods in question by him (s 61(4)).

5.133 If a commercial participator makes a solicitation in the course of a television or radio programme and states that payment can be made by credit or debit card, the commercial participator must (under s 60(4)), in addition to the statement required under s 60(3), make it clear that the consumer has the right to cancel if he makes a payment of £50 or more.

5.134 The £50 threshold mentioned at **5.131** and **5.133** is likely to increase to £100 from April 2009.

Breach of section 60 – criminal sanction

5.135 Section 60(7) of the Charities Act 1992 imposes a strict criminal liability on a commercial participator who is in breach of s 60 (ie a commercial participator who fails to make the statements required under s 60(3), (4) or (5)). The maximum fine is currently £5,000. It should be noted that the liability will arise on the commercial participator and not the charitable institution.

5.136 It is a defence for a person charged with any offence under s 60:

'to prove that he took all reasonable precautions and exercised all due diligence to avoid the commission of the offence' (s 60(8)).

This is similar to a phrase used in the Trade Descriptions Act 1968, s 24. It shifts the burden of proof from the prosecution, who would, under normal rules of criminal law, have to prove that the defendant had mens rea and committed the offence, onto the defendant, who has to show that he took all reasonable precautions, etc. That is a heavy burden. However, in one case under the Trade Descriptions Act 1968 (*Tesco Supermarkets v Nattrass* [1972] AC 153), the House of Lords ruled that the defendant's employer had exercised all due diligence by devising a proper system for the operation of its supermarkets and securing implementation as far as was reasonably practicable.

5.137 Under s 60(9), where there is a breach of s 60 which is due to the act or default of some other person, that other person (eg an employee) shall be guilty of the offence. The same defence of having taken all reasonable precautions, etc can be pleaded. The subsection is principally designed to allow criminal charges to be brought against employees who break the requirements of the Act in breach, for example, of their employer's rulebook.

5.138 To date there have been few, if any, prosecutions under s 60. This stems more from an apparent unwillingness on the part of the authorities to prosecute than from widespread compliance with the law. In discussions prior to the passing of the Charities Act 2006, the Government indicated its willingness to explore the potential for enforcement and prosecuting authorities to give greater priority to fundraising crime, but whether this will result in more prosecutions under the 1992 Act remains to be seen.

Written agreements

5.139 A further key implication of the business being a commercial participator is that there must be a written agreement in place between the commercial participator and the charity which deals with certain defined issues. Section 59(2) of the Charities Act 1992 provides that:

'It shall be unlawful for a commercial participator to represent that charitable contributions are to be given to or applied for the benefit of a charitable institution unless [it] does so in accordance with an agreement with the institution satisfying the prescribed requirements.'

5.140 The prescribed requirements are laid down in the Charitable Institutions (Fund-Raising) Regulations 1994. The agreement must include the following:

(a)   the names and addresses of the parties;

(b)   the date when the agreement was signed by or on behalf of each party;

(c)   the duration of the agreement;

(d)   arrangements for early termination;

(e)   any terms relating to the variation of the agreement;

(f)   a statement of the agreement's principal objectives and the methods to be used in pursuance of those objectives;

(h)   provision as to the manner in which the following are to be determined:
   (i)   if there is more than one charitable institution party to the agreement, the proportion in which the institutions which are so party are respectively to benefit under the agreement;
   (ii)   the proportion of the consideration given for any goods or services sold or supplied by the commercial participator or of any other proceeds of a promotional venture undertaken by him, which is to be given to or applied for the benefit of the charitable institution; or
   (iii) the sums by way of donations by the commercial participator in connection with the sale or supply of any goods or services sold or supplied by him which are to be so given or applied.

5.141 If there is no written agreement between the charity and the commercial participator that complies with these requirements, the agreement can only be enforced by the commercial participator to such extent (if any) as may be provided by an order of the court. This will mean that the commercial participator will not be able to continue to use the charitable institution's name until the court has ordered that it can. This could mean that, for example, a commercial participator must stop using stock which bears the charitable institution's logo until the agreement satisfies the prescribed requirements.

5.142 Equally, the commercial participator will not be entitled to receive any remuneration under a defective agreement until the agreement satisfies the prescribed requirements or a court orders that the commercial participator may be paid. It is unlikely that this provision will be of much use to charities. This is because money will normally pass from the commercial participator to the charity, rather than the other way round.

5.143 In addition, if the court is satisfied that a commercial participator has been, or is, representing that funds will be paid to a charity without an appropriate agreement in place, it has powers to grant an injunction preventing this activity from taking place.

5.144 In strict legal terms, therefore, the party most likely to be at a disadvantage if there is no written agreement in place is the business. However, the Charity Commission has criticised charities which have failed to ensure that a proper agreement is in place, so there is a reputational risk as far as the charity is concerned.

Other provisions

5.145 The Charitable Institutions (Fund-Raising) Regulations 1994 contain other rules which have an impact on the agreement between the business and the charity.

5.146 Under reg 5, a commercial participator must, on request and at all reasonable times, make available to any charitable institution which is party to an agreement with the commercial participator any books, documents or other records, however kept, which relate to the institution and are kept for the purposes of the agreement. It is sensible to underline this by including a specific clause to this effect in the written agreement.

5.147 Under reg 6, any money due to the charitable institution from the commercial participator must be paid over as soon as is reasonably practicable after its receipt, and:

> 'in any event not later than the expiration of 28 days after that receipt or such other period as may be agreed with the institution'.

Payment has to be made to the charitable institution or into a bank account controlled by it. In practice, it may be almost impossible for the commercial participator to comply with the 28-day requirement. For example, once a promotion appearing on a packet had been going for 28 days, the retailer might well have to account to the charitable institution on a daily basis! The agreement between the parties should therefore replace the 28-day requirement with something more commercially sensible, but which still protects the charity.

5.148 It is a criminal offence not to comply with regs 5 and 6, giving rise to a maximum fine of £500. The authors are not aware of any prosecutions having been made.

Terms of the arrangement

5.149 The charity needs to think carefully about the terms on which it is prepared to allow its name and logo to be used. As explained at **5.139–5.140** above, if the business is regarded as a commercial participator, it is a legal requirement to have a written agreement, which must contain certain terms. It is good practice, in any event, for the agreement between the charity and the business to be in writing. The charity's trustees have a duty to ensure that the agreement works in a way which is as beneficial to the charity as possible, and this involves making sure that the charity's interests are properly protected in legal terms.

5.150 Note, however, that it is possible to create an enforceable contract without having a formal agreement in place, so care should be taken to avoid creating a contract – for instance via a series of telephone calls, or in an exchange of correspondence – before the charity is ready. This can be avoided by ensuring that all pre-contractual negotiations are expressly made 'subject to contract', by simply using those words in correspondence and on the telephone. It is always a good idea to start negotiations in good time to avoid last minute panics.

5.151 The charity should ensure that it has done its research into the business, and complied with any internal policy on working with businesses (see **5.90–5.92**).

5.152 It is a good idea for the agreement to cover the following areas, some of which may be legally required (in writing) where the arrangement involves a commercial participator (see **5.140**):

- Who will be a party to the agreement? Will the arrangement be run through the charity and/or its trading subsidiary? If the business has a group of companies, which company is entering into the legal obligations?

- What does the charity (or trading subsidiary) stand to gain under the agreement?
  - How much will it charge for use of its name and logo? Some charities have a standard charge for allowing the name and logo to be used – and there may be different levels of charge depending on whether use is to be local or national. Charities may wish to take professional advice on the value of their brand. Bear in mind the Charity Commission's advice that charities should negotiate the best possible return from the arrangement.
  - How will the sums due to the charity be calculated? It is always preferable for the charity to receive a fixed amount, rather than a proportion of the profits, because the charity often has no way of controlling the business's expenses and, therefore, cannot be sure how much profit the venture will make. It is better to receive, for instance, a fixed amount from the sale of each product – such as £1 from the sale of every ticket for an event, or an overall fixed sum, regardless of how much money the business makes from the venture.
  - Will the fee be split between a payment to the trading subsidiary and a donation to the charity (see **5.101–5.104**)? In the interests of clarity the fee and donation should be paid to separate accounts.
  - Who will bear any VAT (see **5.98–5.105**)?
  - What are the mechanisms for payment, including timing?
  - Will there be interest on late payments?

- What will the charity be doing for the business?
  - If it is licensing its name and logo, how wide will the licence be? What geographical area will it cover, and what activities? It is usually sensible for the licence to be drafted as narrowly as possible. Is the charity prepared to agree to exclusivity, ie that it will not enter into a similar arrangement with any other business operating in the same

field as the contracting business? This is a matter for the charity to decide, depending on the circumstances.

- How will the charity allow its name and logo to be used? Many charities have brand guidelines which must be complied with by any third party business using their name and logo – these are often attached to the agreement. It is sensible for the charity to insist on the right to approve material with the name and logo on it before it is mass-produced. See **9.67** for further issues to be considered in a licence of a name and logo.
- If the charity is to carry out other work, this should be clearly set out in the agreement, or a mechanism for agreement to extra activities should be included. Clearly, the charity should make sure that it does not have to agree to do anything else without being given an opportunity to renegotiate the fee.

• How long will the arrangement last? Under what circumstances should it be possible to terminate the agreement early? The charity will certainly want an opportunity to terminate the agreement immediately if the business does anything which might damage its reputation, or which conflicts with its charitable objects.

• What obligations will the business have?
- The business should be expected to agree not to do anything which might damage the charity's reputation.
- If the business is required under the commercial participator rules to make a statement to the public, it may be sensible to refer to this in the agreement, and agree a form of statement to be used (see **5.119–5.138**).
- Where the business will be selling a product, the business should comply with any statutory requirements relating to health and safety and consumer protection, for instance.
- The business should be required to give reasonable access to its financial records in relation to the promotion, particularly where the amount passing to the charity or trading subsidiary is based on sales and/or profits.

• How will potentially uncertain areas be dealt with? For example:
- Who will have the rights to any new intellectual property created as a result of the relationship?
- What will happen to unsold stock once the arrangement comes to an end?
- Which elements of the agreement are confidential?
- How will any disputes be dealt with?

See Chapter 8 for more detail on contracts.

Sponsorship

5.153 'Sponsorship' is a term much used in the voluntary sector, often with different meanings. There are 'sponsored' walks and 'sponsored' swims. Runners in the London Marathon seek 'sponsorship' from 'sponsors'. In all these cases the sponsor is merely a giver or donor. Such sponsorship does not amount to trading.

5.154 But a sponsor can also be someone who supports an event in return for publicity, eg the official sponsor of the London Marathon or a sponsor of an opera at Covent Garden. Here there is a supply of a service, and this is trading.

5.155 The sponsorship may only really be a straight cash donation to the charity. The term 'sponsorship' might have been used to make the application to the business for financial support seem more important, and there may have been nothing offered in return other than reasonable recognition of the support. But frequently 'sponsors' are looking for something extra in return for their 'donation', which raises important issues for charities.

5.156 The most common type of arrangement is where a sponsor makes a contribution to a charity, for example, to underwrite a concert of classical music, on condition that the sponsor's name or logo is advertised or promoted at the event (eg as a backdrop to the concert orchestra or on the back of the conductor's jacket). It is this element of advertising which turns what would otherwise be a straightforward donation into a transaction involving trading on the part of the charity. The charity is carrying out a service – advertising – for the sponsor.

5.157 Note that where it is the sponsor, rather than the charity, which is taking steps to publicise or exploit its affinity with the charity, this may not be trading, as the charity may not be doing anything in return for the donation. If, however, the charity is allowing the business to use its name and logo, some of the issues discussed at **5.84–5.152** above may be relevant.

Constitutional powers and charity law considerations

5.158 As with all trading activity, the charity trustees must consider whether the charity has power under the constitution to enter into the arrangement (see Chapter 2). Sponsorship is unlikely to be primary purpose trading (although see **5.164–5.168**): if it is non-primary purpose trading, in the Charity Commission's view it should not be carried out directly by the charity if it involves significant risk to the resources of the charity (see Chapter 2), but provided the trustees are happy that the relationship with the sponsor is an appropriate one, and the terms of the arrangement are sufficiently favourable, this is unlikely to be a problem in practice. If the trustees are not happy about these issues, should the charity be associating with the sponsor in the first place? Tax reasons, rather than reasons of risk, are more likely to dictate use of a trading company in a sponsorship context.

5.159 The charity must consider whether the arrangement is in its best interests. As discussed above in relation to licensing of the charity's name and logo, is the charity really happy to be involved with this particular company? The considerations described at **5.90–5.92** above apply equally here.

5.160 Some charities have an ethical policy requiring that details of corporate sponsors giving over a certain amount to the charity must be made public.

Tax

5.161 The sponsorship money paid over by the business is essentially a fee in return for the performance of advertising services by the charity. It is thus potentially subject to income or corporation tax, unless any specific exemptions apply.

5.162 However, HMRC accepts that where the charity's acknowledgement of the business's support is within certain limits, the 'sponsorship' income will not be regarded as trading income for tax purposes. HMRC's 'Detailed guidance note for charities', Annex IV, para 29 reads:

> 'Provided that [references to the sponsor in publications, posters, etc and at events organised by the charity] amount to no more than acknowledgements of the sponsor's contributions they will not cause the payments to be regarded as trading income. However, references to a sponsor which amount to advertisements will cause the payments to be treated as trading income. HMRC Charities will regard a reference to a sponsor as an advertisement if it incorporates any of the following:
>
> • large and prominent displays of the sponsor's logo,
> • large and prominent displays of the sponsor's corporate colours, or
> • a description of the sponsor's products or services.
>
> For example, if a project organised by a charity is sponsored by a well-known company, and acknowledgement of the support of this company is in the form of its name and logo inserted in the corner of a project report, this would not be considered to be advertising. However, if the name and logo was substantially and widely displayed throughout the report, this might be considered to be advertising in return for the sponsorship payment.'

It will therefore sometimes be a question of judgment as to whether the income from the sponsorship will be treated as taxable. Charities may wish to err on the side of caution and, in cases of doubt, treat the payments as taxable. Alternatively, they may wish to seek prior clearance from HMRC.

5.163 If the income from the sponsorship activity is potentially taxable, other exemptions may apply.

Primary purpose trading

5.164 It is possible that where the sponsorship is linked to the charity's primary purposes it may be regarded as primary purpose trading (see Chapter 3). In this case the scale of the advertising of the sponsor's support will be relevant. HMRC's guidance comments on this as follows ('Detailed guidance note for charities', Annex IV, para 30):

> '... any arrangement in which the charity's response [to the sponsor's funding] is on such a scale that it appears to be a main purpose of the donation may be challenged. In such a case, HMRC will want to consider the possibility of non-primary purpose trading by the charity and whether there has been a breach of the donor's benefits limits.

Examples

Example 1

> A charitable theatre group's production is sponsored by a local business "X". X's logo is placed discreetly within the event programme. An executive of X appears on stage on the final night and is thanked. One sign of moderate size is positioned prominently in the hall stating that the event is sponsored by X.
>
> In this case it could not reasonably be argued that a main purpose of the production is advertising X, and there would be no loss of direct tax reliefs for charity or donor.

Example 2

> An arts organisation's broadcast national awards ceremony is sponsored by a nationally well-known brand "Y". The event is named "The Y Awards", which brings Y's name up on television frequently in trailers and programme breaks. Y's logo features prominently in the programme. An executive of Y appears on stage and thus on television and is thanked. There are many prominent signs advertising Y in the venue.
>
> In this case it could reasonably be argued that a main purpose of the event is advertising Y, and there is the possibility of a loss of direct tax reliefs for charity and donor.'

5.165 In both HMRC's examples, the event is, on the face of it, furthering the primary purposes of the charity. HMRC seems to be saying that the scale of the support given to the sponsor can convert the event from an event designed to further the charity's purposes into an event designed to promote the sponsor.

5.166 Perhaps a more sensible approach would be to consider whether the sponsorship covers all or part of the cost of the event, or whether, after taking account of the cost of the event, the charity makes a profit. If the charity makes a profit, then HMRC has a point. However, if the charity does not profit, then their stance is less sound (see also **5.171**).

5.167 Aside from this, given that HMRC has published its view in its 'Detailed guidance notes for charities', any charity which wishes to challenge this should do so in writing – with the understanding that they will face an uphill struggle to persuade HMRC otherwise.

5.168 A further possible example of primary purpose trading in a sponsorship context is where a medical research charity sells a report which has been sponsored by a pharmaceutical company.

'One-off' fundraising exemption

5.169 Where the sponsorship activity is associated with an event which falls within the scope of the tax exemption for fundraising events, the sponsorship income should fall within the exemption. See **5.36–5.54** above for more detail.

Small scale trading

5.170 Equally, where the income from sponsorship, and from other non-exempt trading, forms a small proportion of the charity's incoming resources, the small scale exemption may apply. See **2.41–2.50** for more detail.

Is there a profit?

5.171 If none of the exemptions mentioned above are of assistance, the charity will need to assess whether a profit has been made on the activity (see **2.52–2.55**). This is, in fact, not always the case. Sponsorship income is often obtained to underwrite the costs of a particular service or event, in which case it would be unlikely for a charity to make a surplus on sponsorship, although this is, of course, possible. Take HMRC's Example 2 from **5.164** above as an example. While the main purpose of the event may, in HMRC's eyes, be to advertise Y, if the charity does not make a surplus on the event, there will be no profit to tax.

Trading subsidiary

5.172 Where sponsorship activity is likely to give rise to profits which do not fall within any tax exemption, a tax bill can be avoided by running the arrangement though a subsidiary trading company (see Chapter 7).

Charitable foundations

5.173 It is increasingly common for commercial organisations to set up their 'own' charitable foundation. The charity will typically be funded by donations from the company, and from the proceeds of staff fundraising activity. Care should be taken to ensure that any grants from the company to the charity are not regarded as sponsorship payments, in return for advertising. The issue will be particularly acute where, as is often the case, the company and charity share a name. Problems may be avoided if the charity's logo is different from that of the company, and if the company's donation is clearly accounted for as a charitable donation, rather than as a business expense.

Additional services

5.174 A sponsorship arrangement may involve the charity providing the sponsor with more than just publicity for its support, such as use of the charity's mailing list or logo, endorsement of products or services, and website links. These more complicated arrangements are discussed at **5.184**.

VAT

5.175 Where a charity advertises a sponsor's support in return for a sponsorship payment, this also has VAT implications. HMRC's 'Detailed guidance for charities', Annex IV, para 32 reads:

> 'Where a sponsor receives any benefits in return for a sponsorship payment all of the payment for the sponsorship is consideration for a taxable business supply for VAT purposes.
>
> However it is recognised that there will be situations where the "benefit" amounts to no more than a mere acknowledgement of support, given gratuitously by the charity to the sponsor and is not directly linked to the payment made by the sponsor. Where this is the case the payments are considered to be a donation and therefore outside the scope of VAT. Some examples of such benefits are:
>
> - a flag, or sticker received in return for a donation
> - the sponsor's name being included in a list of supporters in a programme, or on a notice
> - naming a building or university chair after a donor
> - putting the donor's name on the back of a seat in a theatre.
>
> The granting of the right for a sponsor's logo or name to appear in a charity's publication or on their website is a supply of services for VAT purposes. It is the granting of the right that triggers the taxable event for VAT purposes rather than any activity (or lack of it) undertaken by the charity or the size and/or prominence of the logo.'

5.176 Thus, the tax and VAT treatment of sponsorship income are different. If a sponsor's name and logo are included, say in a research publication, there will be a taxable supply for VAT purposes, but if they only appear once in the corner of a page, they may escape a direct tax charge.

5.177 This can be confusing and, for simplicity, charities may wish to keep the VAT and tax treatment the same; ie if the sponsorship payments are liable to VAT, the charity may wish to assume that there will also be liability for income or corporation tax and so run the sponsorship through a subsidiary trading company.

5.178 If the sponsorship fee is within the scope of VAT, the charity should ask the sponsor to pay VAT on top of the fee. In many cases, this will not be a problem, as the sponsor should be able to recover any VAT paid. But where the sponsor carries out VAT-exempt activities, such as banking or insurance services, it may be reluctant to pay VAT on top of its sponsorship fee, as it will not be in a position to recover all the VAT paid. In this situation, it is common to split the sponsorship fee into two elements: part is a fee for the advertising services and part is a straight donation to the charity. This is similar to the approach adopted in relation to payments for use of the charity's name and logo, described at **5.98–5.105** above. The parties have to agree on how to split the payment: in this case, as a rule of thumb the split could also be 90% donation and 10% fee. While the fee could be paid to the charity, if there is a risk of direct tax it may be sensible to pay it to a trading subsidiary, with the donation passing directly to the charity. Readers should bear in mind that the exact percentages will depend on the circumstances.

5.179 As described in relation to licensing of the charity's name and logo (see **5.104**), the agreement between the charity (including any trading subsidiary) and the sponsor must be carefully drafted to ensure the donation is not regarded as part of the fee.

The agreement

5.180 If the arrangement is a straightforward sponsorship deal – a charity receives £5,000 towards the costs of a performance and publicises this in the programme – it is not always the case that the sponsor will be regarded as a commercial participator (see **5.107–5.114**). In order to be a commercial participator the sponsor must be representing, in the course of its own business, that contributions will be made to charity: where it is not advertising its relationship with the charity at all, then that may not be the case.

5.181 Despite this, it is always sensible to have a written agreement with the sponsor, even if this is recorded in a simple exchange of letters, in order to make sure that each party is clear about the other's expectations, and to give a point of reference in the case of disputes.

5.182 As mentioned at **5.158–5.160**, the charity must be clear about the implications of a relationship with the sponsor, and must have done its research. The considerations mentioned at **5.90–5.92** in the context of a charity considering a joint working relationship with a commercial organisation apply equally here.

5.183 As with an agreement about use of a charity's name and logo (see **5.152**), a useful checklist for an agreement is:

- Who will the parties be? Will the charity's trading company be involved? Tax and VAT considerations will affect this. Where is the sponsorship payment coming from? This will be particularly relevant where the sponsor is one of a group of companies.

- What will the sponsorship payment be? How will it be paid, and when? Who will be responsible for any VAT on the payment (see **5.175–5.179**)? Will it be split between a fee and a donation (see **5.178**)? Will there be interest on late payment and, if so, at what rate?

- What will the charity be doing in return for the payment? Remember the tax and VAT implications if this goes beyond a simple acknowledgement.

- What procedures are in place for the approval of any material bearing the charity's name and/or logo?

- If this is a commercial participator arrangement, what statement must be made by the commercial organisation?

- How long will the arrangement last, and what are the mechanisms for early termination? The charity should certainly be able to terminate the agreement early in the event of the business doing anything which might damage the charity's reputation, or which conflicts with its charitable objects.

- Will the business have any additional obligations, eg publicising any events?

- How will any disputes be settled?

More complicated arrangements

5.184 It is often the case that a charity's relationship with a business may not be as straightforward as a simple licence of the charity's name and logo, or acknowledgement of a sponsor's support. The relationship may involve a package of benefits. For example, a major supermarket may 'adopt' a charity as its charity of the year. The agreement might involve:

- The supermarket will pay the charity a lump sum of £250,000 over the year.

- The supermarket will print the charity's name and logo on its carrier bags. It will also advertise its support of the charity in the stores, in publications, on its website, etc.

- The supermarket will have collecting tins on its tills for the charity.

- As well as the £250,000 lump sum, the charity will also receive a proportion of the sale price of some of the supermarket's own branded goods.

−   The supermarket will support its staff in fundraising efforts for the charity, and will match anything that they raise.

−   The charity will advertise the supermarket's support on its website and in other publications. It will offer the supermarket's executives visits to some of its charitable projects. It will offer the supermarket three free tables at its annual fundraising dinner.

Each aspect of this arrangement must be looked at individually. It is likely that many aspects of the arrangement will be trading, with the tax and VAT implications referred to above. It is therefore likely to be sensible to run such an arrangement through a subsidiary trading company.

Affinity cards

5.185   Many charities have entered into arrangements with banks and other financial institutions, whereby the financial institution issues a credit card which bears the name and/or logo of the charity. Such cards are known as affinity cards. Supporters of the charity are encouraged to take out such cards because a fee for every card issued plus a percentage of the total expenditure on the card is paid to the charity by the bank. The bank will be given access to the names and addresses of the charities' supporters/donors for the purposes of marketing the card. This is a joint promotional arrangement which benefits both parties. This section explores the issues charities contemplating such arrangements should be aware of.

Charity law

5.186   The licensing by a charity of access to its database of members or supporters and the use of its name and logo on the credit card and promotional literature to a financial institution constitutes a form of for-profit trading. If the 'badges of trade' are applied, it is clear there is a profit motive, there will be repetition (details of new members/supporters will almost certainly be supplied to the financial institution), there may be a selling organisation (the charity might establish a campaign) and the arrangement is clearly a commercial one. Moreover, the charity may undertake to market the affinity cards directly to its members. Such activities will constitute for-profit trading and will not be primary purpose trading. It will be advisable for such activities to be run through a trading subsidiary.

5.187   As with all arrangements with commercial organisations, a charity should ensure that it negotiates the agreement with the card provider on favourable terms (see **5.149–5.152**). Charities should be particularly careful in ensuring that they have the right to access all the data about customers and that they can disclose this to other potential partners so that they are not 'locked into' the deal and can negotiate a replacement with an alternative supplier.

VAT

5.188 HMRC operates a special concession in relation to income from affinity cards, which means that most of the income from such arrangements may be treated as outside the scope of VAT. Its guidance (Notice 701/1, para 8) reads as follows:

'A typical qualifying agreement between the charity and the card provider will provide for the supply by the former (or its trading subsidiary) to the latter of the following services:

- access to the charity's membership or mailing lists and/or mailing of the card provider's promotional literature to members.
- endorsement of the card and marketing of the card by the charity to its members/supporters.
- the right to use the charity's name and logo on the card and on the card provider's promotional literature.

Subject to the agreements between the charity and card provider being structured in a qualifying manner, the bulk of the monies received by a charity from the card provider can be treated as outside the scope of VAT.

Typically a card provider will pay an agreed amount to the charity (or its trading subsidiary) on the issue of each new card. Thereafter the card provider pays the charity a percentage of the turnover (value of purchases) on the card.

How the relief works

The basis of the relief is that payments by card providers to a charity, made solely in respect of the use of the charity's name and logo, can be treated as contributions for which the charity is not obliged to do anything in return.

To benefit from this treatment there must be two separate agreements:

- One agreement, between the charity (or its trading subsidiary) and the card provider should provide for the supply by the charity (or its trading subsidiary) of the necessary marketing and publicity services, access to membership lists and other promotional activity for the card (marketing services). These supplies are taxable at the standard rate.
- A second and separate agreement between the charity and the card provider should provide for contributions to be made by the card provider in respect of the use only of the charity's name and/or logo. Contributions made under this agreement can be treated as outside the scope.

This being the case, part (at least 20%) of the initial payment can be treated as the consideration for the standard-rated business supplies by the charity. The remaining 80% or less of the initial payment, and **all** subsequent payments based on turnover will be outside the scope of VAT.'

5.189 This treatment will not be available where the charity acts as an intermediary between the card provider and the applicant, although the authors are not aware of this happening in practice. In any event, in such a case any payment made for acting as an intermediary would be exempt from VAT. Notice 701/1, para 5.3 states:

> 'A charity will be acting as an intermediary in arranging a contract between its members and a credit card provider where it:
>
> • stands between the parties to a contract in the performance of a distinct act of negotiation, without having any interest of its own in the terms of the contract;
> • brings the two parties to the contract together; and
> • undertakes preparatory work, such as completing or assisting with completion of application forms, forwarding forms to the credit card company, and making representations on behalf of either party.
>
> We do not see clerical tasks, such as providing a list of names or access to a database as intermediary services.'

Tax

5.190   HMRC states in its 'Detailed guidance notes for charities' (Annex IV, para 35) that the direct tax treatment of the income is likely to be similar to that for VAT purposes:

> 'Any payment accepted as a true donation for VAT purposes would normally be accepted as such for tax purposes. Anything else paid to the charity in relation to the affinity card is likely to be taxable non-primary purpose trading income. It is recommended that separate payments are made under carefully drafted legal agreements, in order to make the position clear. The commercial payment should be at a market rate.'

Strictly, it is likely that payment to the charity for use of its name and logo may be an annual payment rather than a donation, but as explained at **5.86**, income from annual payments may be received tax-free by the charity.

Charities Act 1993

5.191   Once again issues arise under the Charities Act 1993 (see **2.75–2.77**). Is an affinity card an 'advertisement' for the purposes of s 5? The affinity card will bear the charity's name and logo. Section 5 applies to any advertisement issued 'by or on behalf of the charity'. It is considered that an affinity card could constitute an advertisement. It is issued by the bank and not by the charity, but nonetheless pursuant to an agreement with the charity. Hence, it is reasonable to conclude that the card is issued 'on behalf of' the charity. But does the card 'solicit money ... for the benefit of the charity'? Under the usual arrangements the charity has a continuing financial interest in the use of the card. Each time the card holder uses it, the charity gets its cut. It would be different if the charity only received a one-off payment (as a fee for access to its list of supporters) before the promotion was begun.

5.192 A card holder may have more than one credit card. As the card holder flips through his or her wallet, he or she has a choice whether to use one of the cards, write a cheque or use cash. The charity's logo on the affinity card might induce him or her to use that card. Hence, he or she would be solicited to use that card. Moreover, s 5(3) states that a solicitation can be express or implied. At the very least, the fact that the affinity card bears the charity's name or logo must amount to an implied solicitation, with the result that s 5 must be considered as applying to an affinity card. This means that the words 'a registered charity' must appear on the card, possibly on the back. The words do not have to be adjacent or close to the charity's name.

LOTTERIES

5.193 Charities which sell lottery (or raffle) tickets in order to raise money are, strictly speaking, carrying out a trade. However, special rules apply.

5.194 As with all trading activity, the trustees will need to consider whether they have constitutional power to run the lottery. It is likely that they will: running a lottery is clearly fundraising activity and a power to fundraise will generally be sufficient.

5.195 The activity does not qualify as primary purpose trading. Generally, in the Charity Commission's view, non-primary purpose trading should be carried out only if it does not involve significant risk to the resources of the charity. But the Commission accepts that lotteries can be carried out directly by the charity (CC35 'Trustees, trading and tax', para C11):

> 'The promotion and conduct of a lottery in accordance with [the relevant gambling legislation] is not regarded as contravening the charity law restrictions on carrying on non-primary purpose trading, since any risk to the charity's assets from carrying on this sort of trading is negligible.'

5.196 In addition, the profits from a lottery should qualify for an exemption from tax, set out in ICTA 1988, s 505(1)(f). The exemption applies to:

> 'profits accruing to a charitable company from a lottery if the profits are applied solely to the charitable company's purposes and—
>
> (i) the lottery is an exempt lottery within the meaning of the Gambling Act 2005 by virtue of Part 1 or 4 of Schedule 11 to that Act; [or]
> (ii) the lottery is promoted in accordance with a lottery operating licence within the meaning of Part 5 of that Act'.

There are similar exemptions for lottery income in Northern Ireland. There is an equivalent exemption in ITA 2007, s 503 for charitable trusts.

5.197 Lotteries are illegal unless they are conducted within the scope of the Gambling Act 2005. A full discussion of the lottery rules is outside the scope of this book: the Gambling Commission can provide further information (www.gamblingcommission.gov.uk). However, the arrangements covered by the tax exemption are described in broad terms below:

- So-called 'incidental non-commercial lotteries' (exempt under GA 2005, Sch 11, Pt 1), which are incidental to an event which is not held for private gain, where the tickets are sold on the premises at the event (and certain other conditions are complied with).

- Small society lotteries (exempt under GA 2005, Sch 11, Pt 4), which are run by a non-commercial society which is registered with the local authority, where the ticket sales are less than £20,000 in a single lottery and less than £250,000 per year. (Certain other conditions set out in the legislation also apply.)

- A large society lottery, which falls outside the income limits which apply to small society lotteries, which is run by a non-commercial society or an external lottery manager acting on its behalf, under the terms of an operating licence from the Gambling Commission.

Lotteries run by charities should fall within these categories: if they do not, they will probably be illegal under the Gambling Act 2005.

5.198   If a lottery is run by a trading subsidiary rather than the charity itself, the tax exemption will not apply. However, to the extent that the trading subsidiary's profits are passed to the parent charity under the gift aid regime, they will not be subject to tax (see Chapter 7).

5.199   The sale of lottery tickets is exempt from VAT: see Value Added Tax Act 1994, Sch 9, Group 4. Games of chance are generally exempted from VAT.

5.200   Note that lotteries run in connection with a fundraising event which qualifies for the tax and VAT exemption (see **5.36–5.54**) should be exempt from tax and VAT in an event under the terms of that exemption.

5.201   Many charities will have arrangements with commercial organisations (external lottery managers or 'ELMs') to run lotteries on their behalf. In most cases the ELMs will be carrying on a 'fundraising business' (within the meaning of the 1992 Act) because they will be carrying on a commercial business (for gain) which involves soliciting and collecting money for the charitable, benevolent or philanthropic purposes of their charity clients. Accordingly these ELMs will be professional fundraisers under the Charities Act 1992 (see **5.81**). In a small minority of cases, ELMs may be commercial participators (see **5.106 5.148**).

CONCLUSION

5.202 Charity fundraisers are often surprised to learn that fundraising can be regarded as trading. It is very important that charities are aware of the 'trading trap' so that they can structure their fundraising activities to avoid difficulties under tax and charity law. Failure to do so could be a breach of the charity trustees' duties to act in the best interests of the charity.

Chapter 6

INCOME FROM CHARITY PROPERTY

6.1 *This chapter deals with the implications of charities using their property to earn additional income. This may not necessarily be trading, but if it is there may be tax and VAT implications.*

INTRODUCTION

6.2 Some charities have assets which they do not utilise to the full in fulfilment of their charitable purposes. School facilities stand empty during holidays; a Women's Institute hall may be used only once a week by the Women's Institute; a historic building may be the perfect venue for a 'dream function'. If the trustees cannot fully use the charity's assets to fulfil its purposes, trustees should consider whether or not they should exploit *commercially* the charity's under-used assets so as to generate more income, which could be applied in fulfilling the charity's objects or in meeting the charity's costs.

6.3 What are the legal consequences if trustees do decide to exploit such surplus assets?

IS THIS TRADING?

6.4 The first step is to establish whether the activity is trading. It may well not be. Where a charity rents out its property, and does not provide any additional services, the income is regarded as rental income rather than trading income.

6.5 The distinction is important because charities are exempt from tax on rental income. Section 505(1)(a) of the Income and Corporation Taxes Act 1988 provides an exemption from corporation tax:

> 'in respect of any profits or gains arising in respect of rents or other receipts from an estate, interest or right in or over any land (whether situated in the United Kingdom or elsewhere) to the extent that the profits or gains—
>
> (i) arise in respect of rents or receipts from an estate, interest or right vested in any person for charitable purposes; and
> (ii) are applied to charitable purposes only'.

There is a similar exemption for the income of charitable trusts set out in the Income Tax Act 2007, s 531.

6.6   HMRC appears to accept that the exemption applies to furnished lettings ('Detailed guidance notes for charities', Annex I, para I.3.2). However, if services are provided along with the use of land or buildings, these services might amount to trading. HMRC's 'Detailed guidance notes for charities', Annex IV, para 25 reads:

> 'Letting activity will itself constitute a trade where the owner remains in occupation of the property and provides services over and above those usually provided by a landlord. Essentially the distinction lies between the hotelier (who is carrying on a trade) and the provider of furnished accommodation (who is not). An important difference is that in a hotel etc the occupier of the room does not acquire any legal interest in the property. Each case must be considered on its own facts.'

6.7   This point is illustrated by *Coman v Governors of the Rotunda Hospital, Dublin* [1921] AC 1. The governors of the hospital let out certain rooms for entertainments for periods varying from one night to six months at charges which included the use of heating and seating, and applied the profits from the lettings to the support of the hospital. The House of Lords ruled that the hospital was carrying on a trade, and that the profits derived from that trade were taxable and not within any of the exemptions from income tax.

WHERE THE ACTIVITY IS TRADING

6.8   Where the charity is carrying out a trading activity, the general principles apply. Is this permitted by the constitution and by charity law, and what are the tax implications?

Is this primary purpose trading?

6.9   In many cases, such activity will be primary purpose trading (see Chapter 3). If, for example, Charity A owns a hall and allows Charity B to use it, in circumstances where Charities A and B share common objectives, any income paid by Charity B for the use of the hall will be primary purpose trading. In allowing Charity B to use the hall, Charity A will, albeit indirectly, be fulfilling its own objectives. If A and B have some overlapping objects, the same principles will apply, provided that B's use of the premises is solely in accordance with those parts of its objects shared with A. In both situations it will be open to Charity A to charge less than the full commercial rate, or indeed nothing at all, as this will be fulfilling its objects.

6.10   There may be circumstances where a charity rents out its property to individuals in furtherance of its charitable purposes. For example, The Landmark Trust is a charity established to protect and promote the enjoyment of places of historic interest or natural beauty. The Trust owns a range of historic properties throughout the United Kingdom which it lets to the paying public. In so doing, it is furthering its charitable objectives by promoting the public's enjoyment of the locations. To the extent that this is regarded as trading activity, it will be primary purpose trading.

6.11 Similarly, where a community hall provides facilities to a local community group in return for a fee, this is likely to be primary purpose trading.

6.12 As explained in detail in Chapter 3, there are few charity law restrictions on primary purpose trading, and the profits from such activity are not taxable. There may, however, be VAT implications.

Is there a profit?

6.13 If, however, the trading activity is not primary purpose, the profits are potentially taxable. The charity should therefore consider whether or not it is making a profit from the activity (see **2.52–2.55**). It should attribute a proper proportion of overheads and expenses against the income derived from the exploitation of its surplus assets. It may be that when this is done there will be no taxable profits.

6.14 For example, an Oxford College might hire out the college for non-educational courses (eg an 'Inspector Morse Murder Weekend'). Can the college charge a fair and reasonable proportion of its overheads against the income derived from that activity, including items such as maintenance of the grounds and upkeep of the fabric of the building, which it would incur in any event? Or can it only charge against those profits the marginal costs of running the commercial weekend event (the costs of staff, meals, heat, light, etc)?

6.15 To try to answer these questions, HMRC conducted an inquiry into the trading activities of five universities in 1992 and considered, in particular, the question of vacation lettings. HMRC concluded that in most cases the vacation lettings of universities do not amount to trade because the activity was not being conducted on a truly commercial basis and none of the sample universities had yet made any taxable profits from vacation lettings. HMRC further advised that unless a university is recovering at least 75% of the direct and *attributable* costs of vacation lettings, it will not regard such activity as conducted on a commercial basis and as trade.

6.16

Example

UNIVERSITY OF RUTLAND

Income from vacation lettings		**£20,000**
Cost of lettings		
Direct costs attributable to activity	£10.000	
Indirect costs attributable (9% of gardening, maintenance & central services)	£20,000	**£30,000**
Loss on lettings (after expenses)		**£10,000**

The University only recovered 66% of the direct and attributable costs, and hence there was no tax liability.

6.17 The 75% rule is somewhat strange. Why not 100%? The answer is probably that HMRC was under pressure to come up with a solution satisfactory to all parties at a time when the universities' income from exploitation was increasing and where it was public (government) policy to encourage such exploitation.

6.18 If the activity does show a profit, and is therefore likely to give rise to a tax bill, it may be appropriate for the charity to establish a separate trading company (if it does not already have one) to act as its agent for exploiting the surplus assets. The trading company should pay a fee to the charity in return for the grant of this right, as the charity cannot give away its assets, nor can it give the right to exploit them to a non-charity for nothing (even where that body is its own wholly-owned trading subsidiary) (see Chapter 7). That fee should be structured as an annual payment and should represent a proper fee for use of the assets. The fee will attract VAT.

Charity law considerations

6.19 In deciding to utilise the charity's assets in this way, the trustees must be sensitive to the charity's reputation and not do anything which could damage it. This is illustrated by the case of *Re All Saint's Church at Harborough Magna* [1992] 1 WLR 1235, which provides an interesting example of a charity exploiting an asset for commercial purposes. In this case the church had to go to a local consistory court for consent to put two aerials and a communications dish on the tower of a church and appropriate power and radio units in the church porch. The church had been asked to provide these services to a national communications company. The court gave its consent and laid down useful guidelines as to how the licence by the church to the communications company should be structured: in particular, it dealt with the need to bar the use of certain telephone numbers which could be used for pornographic purposes.

6.20 This case vividly illustrates the point that, in exploiting surplus assets, charities should *not* hire them out for activities which are inimical to the charity's own purposes.

6.21 Moreover, trustees should always examine first how they might use such surplus assets to fulfil the charity's own primary purposes *before* deciding whether to exploit them for commercial purposes. They should consider whether the need to generate additional income is distorting their judgment as to whether the assets could be further used for the charity's charitable purposes.

Chapter 7

THE TRADING SUBSIDIARY

7.1   *A common solution to the charity law and tax issues thrown up by charity trading is to route the trading activity via a subsidiary company. In this chapter we explore when a trading subsidiary might be used, and what the disadvantages are. We examine the duties of charity trustees when deciding to invest funds in a trading company, and how the relationship between the charity and its subsidiary should be structured.*

INTRODUCTION

7.2   In Chapter 2, we showed that there are limits on the extent to which a charity can carry on trade directly. There are legal constraints, depending on whether the trading activity is a permitted activity in the context of the organisation's charitable status. There are also practical considerations such as liability to taxation on any profits earned, VAT and risk. The classic, widely used solution to these issues is for the charity to set up a separate trading company.

7.3   We will elaborate on the issues for charities setting up a trading company in much more detail in this chapter, but the basic mechanism works in the following way:

(1)   The charity sets up and funds a company limited by shares. All the shares are owned by the charity.

(2)   The trading company carries out the trading activity. Since it is not itself a charity, there are no restrictions on its ability to trade. Since it is an independent legal entity, its activities should not present a risk to the charity's assets.

(3)   Since it is not a charity, the trading company will be liable to corporation tax. But the profits which the trading company makes are paid up to the parent charity under the gift aid scheme. This reduces the trading company's taxable profits – in many cases – to zero, which means that it has no tax to pay.

(4)   Thus, the charity has undertaken its trading activity, but via a mechanism which is largely tax efficient.

But the trading company route is not without its disadvantages and complications. This chapter explores the reasons for setting up a trading company, and how to go about establishing and running one.

7.4   Note that although the expression 'trading subsidiary' is widely used to refer to a charity's wholly owned trading company, strictly this is only accurate where the parent charity is a limited company. In all other cases, for instance where the parent charity is a trust or an unincorporated association, the company cannot be called a subsidiary but only a 'trading company'. However, in this book we have bowed to modern practice and use the two expressions interchangeably.

WHEN SHOULD A CHARITY ESTABLISH A TRADING COMPANY?

Charity law

7.5   A charity has to consider first whether it can carry on the trade directly:

- Is the activity allowed under the terms of the charity's constitution (see **2.5–2.18**)?

- Is it allowed as a matter of charity law? As explained at **2.20–2.33**, the Charity Commission's current view is that charities may only carry out trading activity directly in the following cases:
  - where the trading is primary purpose or ancillary trading (see Chapter 3); or
  - where the trading is non-primary purpose trading that does not involve significant risk to the resources of the charity.

7.6   Note that it will not always be obvious whether the activity in question is trading:

- Do the 'badges of trade', when applied to the activity, suggest that trading is involved (see **5.10–5.23**)?

- The sale of donated goods is not generally trading: it is simply regarded as converting donations to the charity into cash (see Chapter 4).

- Some methods of fundraising (for instance, by entering into a relationship with a commercial organisation) may be regarded as trading (see **5.83–5.192**).

7.7   If the charity cannot carry out the trading activity directly, it should consider establishing a trading company.

Tax

7.8 Another critical consideration is whether it would be more advantageous from a tax perspective to organise the trading through a trading company. A charity should not pay tax on the profits of trading activity in the following circumstances (see Chapter 2 for more detail):

- Where the activity is primary purpose trading.

- Where the trading is ancillary to a primary purpose trade.

- Where the tax exemption for fundraising events applies.

- Where the activity is the sale of goods donated to the charity: HMRC does not regard this as trading.

- Where the payments to the charity qualify as 'annual payments'.

- Where the trading falls within the small scale exemption from tax.

7.9 If the activity is subject to tax, are there any taxable profits (after making proper allowance for all charges, etc) (see **2.52–2.55**)?

7.10 If the trading activity is potentially taxable, the charity should consider establishing a trading company.

7.11 There may be situations where the charity is not 100% sure that a tax exemption will apply. Or the trading activity in question may involve a combination of taxable and non-taxable trades (see, for example, **4.58–4.68**). In such cases it may be simpler to run the combined activity through a trading subsidiary.

7.12 Note that the Charity Commission concedes that if the tax bill is likely to be small, it may not be appropriate to use a trading subsidiary (CC35 'Trustees, trading and tax', para D2):

> 'where the use of a trading subsidiary is primarily tax-driven, the tax benefits may be insufficient to justify the additional costs associated with establishing and operating a trading subsidiary.'

This begs the question, however, of whether trading in these circumstances would be permitted by the charity's constitution. Some constitutions allow trading only in circumstances where they would not give rise to a tax liability, however small.

Risk

7.13 If the trade involves risk, the charity may wish to consider isolating the risk of that particular activity within a separate company. The Charity

Commission's view is that non-primary purpose trading activity which involves significant risk to the resources of the charity should be carried out via a trading subsidiary (see **2.20–2.33**). But there may be risk associated with primary purpose or ancillary trading too: in such cases, even though there may be no charity law or tax reason for using a trading subsidiary, the trustees may wish to protect the other assets of the charity from the risks associated with the trading activity.

Premises

7.14   One example of risk relates to taking on premises. Unless the trading activity is carried out from the charity's premises, it will need its own space. This will depend on the nature of the charity, and the trade. Trading carried out by a charity's fundraising department (arranging fundraising events, for example, or relationships with commercial partners) can be carried out from the charity's offices. But a charity shop selling donated and/or bought-in goods will probably need its own premises. This would involve buying property, or (which is more likely) taking on a lease.

7.15   Where a new lease is taken, the terms of the lease will be negotiated at the outset; the prevailing state of the commercial property market at the time the lease is negotiated will dictate whether they favour the landlord or the tenant. Otherwise an existing lease will be taken over. Due to a strange quirk of English law a tenant can remain liable to fulfil the obligations under a lease until the lease has expired, even if the tenant has transferred the lease to another occupier. In the case of leases predating 1996 the original tenant can remain ultimately liable to the landlord. For more recent leases, or new ones, a tenant will have to provide a guarantee to the landlord (under a so-called 'authorised guarantee agreement') in relation to the person to whom a lease is transferred, but is otherwise off the hook after the transfer. If the transferee goes out of business or is otherwise unable to meet the obligations under the lease, the landlord can claim any outstanding rent and/or service charge and/or the continuing liabilities under the lease from the previous tenant (until the expiry of the lease or its transfer to a subsequent transferee) and, in the case of pre-1996 leases, also from the original tenant and any subsequent transferee. This can mean that a tenant has ongoing contingent liabilities under a lease which might materialise years after it has been transferred. Clearly, if the lease is in the name of a separate trading company, then claims made under that lease will not be made against the charity which controls the trading company, unless the charity has guaranteed the obligations of the trading company under the lease. (It is worth remembering that landlords will be extremely reluctant to grant a lease to a company with no assets.)

7.16   If a charity is asked to give such a guarantee, this should be strenuously resisted by the charity on the basis that it does not have the constitutional capacity to guarantee the obligations of a commercial entity, albeit one which it owns (see **7.155–7.164** for further details). If the charity does give a guarantee, and it is unincorporated, the liability under the guarantee should be limited to the charity's assets and it should provide that the trustees shall not incur any personal liability under the guarantee. An alternative to a guarantee may be for the trading subsidiary to offer a rent deposit, for example 6 months' rent, but that ties up capital.

7.17 It might, therefore, be prudent for a charity to establish a separate company to take on leases and protect the charity from any risks arising. However, as explained at **2.69–2.73** and in Chapter 4, where the trading subsidiary, rather than the charity, occupies the premises, the right to 80% mandatory relief from non-domestic rates will be lost.

7.18 If the trading activity could be carried out by the charity directly, as in the case of the sale of donated goods, and the only reason for establishing the trading subsidiary is to avoid the risks associated with taking on a lease, this company could simply be a property holding company, which would then sublet the premises to the charity on a short-term basis with much less onerous conditions attached to the sublease. This would ensure that the right to 80% mandatory business rates relief was maintained. A potential flaw in this apparently attractive arrangement is that landlords usually insist that any subtenant covenants directly with the landlord to honour all the tenant's covenants in the lease. If so, the charity will end up in a direct contractual relationship with the landlord. Nonetheless, a merit of this scheme is that it might reduce the period of the charity's exposure under the lease to the length of the sublease (if that is shorter than the lease itself).

Sale of goods and consumer protection

7.19 Any sale or supply of goods or services invokes the sale of goods and consumer protection legislation, which is described in more detail in Chapter 8. The charity trustees will need to consider the risks involved, what insurance cover could be obtained, and whether, in the light of that analysis, they are willing for the charity's resources to be exposed.

Other risks

7.20 Other risks will flow from the nature of the trading activity. Is there a risk of injury to the public at a fundraising event? Might a publishing business involve a risk of defamation claims? Will the business involve particularly onerous contracts with third party suppliers? To what extent are the risks fully covered by insurance?

Risk management

7.21 Charity trustees are well advised to consider the potential risks of any activity the charity undertakes. They should identify the risks and decide how to manage them. Charity trustees of charities whose accounts are required by statute to be audited must include in their annual reports a statement confirming that the major risks to which the charity is exposed have been reviewed, and that systems or procedures have been established to manage them. The Charity Commission encourages smaller charities below the audit threshold to make a similar statement as a matter of best practice. Often a way of managing risk may be to run the activity through a trading company.

Limited liability

7.22   Note that, even where a trading subsidiary is used, the charity's assets will continue to be at risk to the extent that they have been committed to the trading company. This will include an initial equity investment in the company, any loans or grants made to the company and any guarantees given on the company's behalf. But over and above these commitments, the charity's resources should be safe.

7.23   For example, a charity invests £10,000 in a trading company set up to run a new trading enterprise developing computer software in partnership with commercial organisations. After a year's trading, a disagreement breaks out between the trading company and one of the commercial partners: the trading company finds itself on the receiving end of a legal claim for £70,000 for breach of intellectual property rights. The trading company does not have the resources to meet the claim, so it faces insolvency. While the charity will lose its original £10,000 investment, it should not be liable for any further costs, providing the trading company's activities have been conducted at arm's length from the charity (see **7.220–7.221**) and the charity has not inadvertently assumed any additional liabilities.

7.24   Many commercial organisations – and indeed some charities – spread risk by having a large number of separate subsidiary companies, each undertaking a different activity. If one business fails, this will not jeopardise the financial position of the whole group (unless guarantees have been given). For example, a charity owning a centre in a deprived area may carry out a range of activities: training, running a community café, holding exercise classes. Each of these activities may be run through a separate company, all owned by the parent charity, in order to isolate the risks of any particular activity.

Administration

7.25   There may be administrative reasons for setting up a trading company. A trading company is a completely separate legal entity from the charity. It will have its own board, its own employees (although these may be shared with the charity in some cases: see **7.210–7.212**), and its own resources and operations. And the trading subsidiary must file its own set of accounts with Companies House (see **7.218**), although its operations will often be consolidated with those of the charity in the charity's accounts (see **7.265**).

7.26   Some aspects of a charity's business may be reasonably self-contained. For instance, a charity working with the homeless may have a division which is devoted entirely to public service delivery contracts (see **3.103–3.134**). It may be administratively convenient for these contracts to be run via a trading subsidiary, even though the activity is likely to be primary purpose trading which could be carried out by the charity itself. If a trading company is used, not only will any risk associated with that particular aspect of the charity's work be ring-fenced, but managing the contract may be more straightforward.

Management

7.27   There may be reasons why using a trading company with its separate board of directors could be attractive to a charity. The charity may wish to become involved in a new, innovative project designed to help the charity's beneficiaries. It may have identified a key individual to help with the strategic management of the project. If a trading subsidiary is used, that individual can sit on the board of the trading company, and be paid for doing so, and for any other work he or she does for the trading subsidiary, out of the trading subsidiary's funds. That would not be possible if the project were run by the charity, as it is generally not possible for charity trustees to be paid.

7.28   Equally, the trustees may feel that they lack the commercial expertise to manage a particular venture. If a trading subsidiary is established to run the project, a more experienced board can be appointed to the trading company: they will have strategic responsibility for the project.

7.29   In all cases, the board of the trading subsidiary is accountable to the parent charity. And the trustees of the charity have a responsibility to ensure that the trading subsidiary, in which the charity's funds are invested, is properly run. So, while it is perfectly appropriate to delegate management of an enterprise to the board of the trading subsidiary, the trustees must make sure that they monitor the trading company's activities properly.

7.30   Issues about the make-up of the trading subsidiary's board are dealt with below at **7.167–7.176**.

Branding

7.31   The legal separation of a charity and its trading subsidiary may also be an advantage where the charity wishes to set up a new, separately branded project. Although there are some cases where the advertisement of a trading subsidiary's links with its parent charity may be an advantage, or even a legal requirement (see **5.125**), this is not always the case.

7.32   For example, a charity working with the homeless decides to set up a project providing employment opportunities for those who have moved out of hostel accommodation. These beneficiaries will be offered training and employment with a catering business run by a trading company owned by the charity. Many of the charity's beneficiaries are uncomfortable with the concept of 'charity'. Involvement with an organisation which is not a charity, as a way of helping them rebuild their lives, is an immensely valuable form of rehabilitation. The trading company can help the charity's beneficiaries in a way which does not emphasise the links between the charity and the business. Yet when the trading subsidiary wishes to take advantage of the connection (eg contacting the charity's supporters with business proposals), it is free to do so.

7.33 A charity may develop a new project with a view to its ultimate separation into an independent enterprise. If the project is initiated via a separate trading company, its branding can develop independently of the charity. And the ultimate transfer of the business elsewhere will be much simpler from an administrative perspective than having to separate its strands from that of the charity. For instance, in 2008 the charity Ealing Community Transport transferred ownership of its subsidiary trading company, ECT Recycling CIC, to the AIM listed company May Gurney.

VAT

7.34 A charity may also consider establishing a trading company to improve VAT efficiency. For example, certain educational services are VAT exempt if provided by the charity – if the same services are run through a trading company they are VAT taxable, which enables the recovery of input VAT on costs. Note that the charity should have commercial reasons for running the activity through the trading subsidiary.

7.35 Some charities also use trading companies to run a design and build scheme when undertaking construction of a new building at the zero rate of VAT. The company engages the builders and surveyors, architects and other professionals and sells the completed building at the zero rate of VAT to the charity, in the process recovering all the VAT incurred on its costs. If the charity engaged the builders and professionals direct, the building would be constructed at the zero rate of VAT, but VAT would be incurred on the professionals' costs.

Working jointly

7.36 Where charities, or indeed charities and commercial organisations, wish to work together in a particular area, it may be appropriate for this to be orchestrated through a trading company. In this case, the shares of the company will be owned by the various parties to the project.

7.37 Particular issues which spring from joint ownership of a trading company are dealt with in more detail at **7.239–7.250**.

WHAT ARE THE DISADVANTAGES?

Costs and administration

7.38 The main disadvantage of establishing a trading company is the extra administration, and associated expense, which is involved. As we explore in this chapter, the charity needs to go through the process of setting up the trading company, deciding how it should be funded, and maintaining it as a separate legal entity at arm's length from the charity. This is complicated, time consuming and costly. The Cabinet Office Strategy Unit report on charity law in 2002, *Private Action Public Benefit*, concluded that the difficulty with the trading company route 'is that it is administratively complex, expensive for individual charities, and can inhibit them from diversifying their income streams'. As mentioned at **2.31**, the Charity Commission recognises (CC35 'Trustees, trading and tax') that where the use of a trading subsidiary is mainly tax driven, the tax benefits may be insufficient to justify the additional costs associated with establishing and operating a trading subsidiary.

VAT

7.39 There are VAT issues involved in establishing a trading company which need to be considered. Supplies made between the trading company and the charity may be VATable, so the charity should consider establishing a VAT group. This is explored in more detail at **7.165–7.166**. In addition, the trading company will not qualify for all of the VAT reliefs available to charities.

7.40 The VAT issues are complex, and professional advice will need to be taken.

Rating and other reliefs

7.41 As explained at **2.69–2.73**, where a ratepayer is a charity and occupies property which is wholly or mainly used for charitable purposes (whether by one or more charities), the charity is entitled to 80% mandatory relief from non-domestic rates under s 43(5) of the Local Government Finance Act 1988. Section 47 of the same Act allows local authorities discretion to award up to a further 20% relief, but this is rare and so should not be relied on.

7.42 If the trading operation is run by a trading company and not by the charity, the trading company is not eligible for rate relief. Occupation by a trading company, even if wholly owned by a charity, is not occupation 'by a charity' for the purposes of rating law. Trading subsidiaries are therefore reliant on the discretion of the local rating authority, which may decide to grant relief. This is a particular concern in the case of charity shops not run directly through the charity(see **4.58–4.68**).

7.43 Equally, while charities do not pay stamp duty land tax on the purchase or leasing of land, trading subsidiaries do not enjoy a similar exemption.

ESTABLISHING A TRADING COMPANY

Forming a company

7.44 A trading company is formed by filing the memorandum and articles of association (see **7.51–7.72**) and all the necessary ancillary documents with the Registrar of Companies and paying a registration fee. There are various methods of filing documents: hard copy documents can be filed for a registration fee of £20 (registration takes around eight to ten days) or for a fee of £50, which allows for registration within 24 hours. The documents can also be filed electronically with Companies House, but only via an intermediary, such as a company formation agent, which has an electronic account with Companies House. The fees for electronic formation will be charged by the intermediary, and do vary.

7.45 Even if filing the forms personally, or using a company formation agent, it is wise to take professional advice. Company law is complex and it is easy to make a mistake. Fines for breaking company law can be high – for example, the fine for filing accounts more than 6 months late is £1,500. It is worth paying some money initially to get the structure right and to have the structure you need.

What is a trading company?

7.46 A trading company will normally be established as a *company limited by shares*. Most charitable companies are constituted as *companies limited by guarantee*, and many people in the voluntary sector are accustomed to operating such companies. A charity might therefore be tempted to stick with the devil it knows and establish its trading company as a company limited by guarantee. That would not be prudent, but to understand why it is necessary to understand the nature of a company limited by shares.

7.47 A company limited by shares has what is called 'a share capital'. For example, a company may have a share capital of £100 divided into £100 shares of £1. Each £1 share gives the owner of that share a stake in the company's wealth. If 100 shares are issued, the holder of one share owns 1% of the company's wealth. By owning a share a shareholder 'shares' in the wealth of the company with the other shareholders – hence the term.

7.48 The shareholder has to purchase the right to share in the company's wealth; he or she receives this entitlement in return for investing money in the company. The ability to issue shares is a very useful method of financing a company. The shareholder gets a return through sharing in the profits of the company by receiving dividends. Dividends will be paid out when the company has profits available to distribute. If the company is running at a loss or has accumulated losses, the shareholders will get nothing. From the company's point of view, to issue shares is a cheap source of finance. In contrast, if it borrows money, it will normally have to pay interest on the loan from the start, and these interest charges will continue until the loan has been repaid. The company will commit itself to the interest payments and loan repayments regardless of profitability. By contrast, shares are rarely repaid – they can be only if the company issues redeemable shares or resolves to buy back its own shares.

7.49 The position is different with a company limited by guarantee. It can only borrow money. It cannot issue shares. Hence, one of the possible methods of financing a trading company – issuing shares – is lost if a company limited by guarantee is used.

7.50 At present, the constitution of a trading company will have two parts: a memorandum of association and articles of association (see **7.72** for the position post October 2009).

Memorandum of association

7.51 The memorandum of association sets out what the company can do.

The objects clause

7.52 Under s 3A of the Companies Act 1985, a company can have general trading objects such as:

'(a) The object of the company is to carry on any trade or business whatsoever; and
(b) The company has power to do all such things as are incidental or conducive to the carrying on of any trade or business by it.'

It is also sensible to include a statement such as:

'The company is established to procure profits and gains for the purpose of paying the same to the charity called .... (registered charity no ....).'

in order to show the close relationship between the charity and the trading company.

7.53 To amend the main objects clause requires a special resolution passed by 75% majority vote of the members (ie the shareholders) of the company. The resolution can either be passed at a meeting of which appropriate notice has been given, by members representing 75% of the voting rights of those who vote (the shareholders in a company limited by shares usually have one vote per share, so some shareholders may have more voting rights than others) or in writing, by members representing 75% of the total voting rights.

The capital clause

7.54 The memorandum of association will also contain the capital clause stating the authorised or nominal share capital. Companies usually start off with an authorised share capital of £100. The authorised share capital does not mean that £100 worth of shares have been issued: it merely means the company has the *capacity* to issue those shares. If the company wishes to increase the authorised share capital, it has to pass an ordinary resolution, which must be passed by a simple majority of the members. The resolution can either be passed at a meeting of which appropriate notice has been given, by members representing a simple majority of the voting rights of those who vote, or in writing, by members representing a simple majority of the voting rights. Note that the concept of an authorised share capital is due to be abolished from October 2009 (see **7.72**).

Types of shares

7.55   A company limited by shares can issue a number of different types of shares if the memorandum and articles of association give it the capacity to do so. If they do not, its constitution can be changed by a special resolution (see **7.53** above) to empower the company to issue other types of share. The principal types of shares are as follows.

Preference shares

7.56   As the name implies, preference shares carry some preferential rights over ordinary shares. They are designed to get around some of the risks attached to ordinary shares. The principal features are as follows.

Type of dividend

7.57   Preference shares are usually described as, for example, 8% preference shares. This means that for each £1 invested, a dividend of 8% per annum is due. Hence the dividend is fixed, rather like an interest rate. However, unlike a loan, the dividend on preference shares will only be paid where there are profits available for distribution.

Preferential dividend

7.58   The dividends on preference shares are paid before the dividends on ordinary shares. If there are accumulated arrears of the preferential dividends, those too must be paid off prior to paying a dividend on the ordinary shares.

Preferential rights in a winding up

7.59   If a limited company is wound up, the ordinary shareholders will get paid out last (if there is any surplus after paying off the creditors). The preference shares are paid off before the ordinary shares, but after the confusingly named preferential, secured and unsecured creditors (see **11.77**).

7.60   There is little point in a charity investing in its trading company by way of preference shares.

Redeemable preference shares

7.61 These are normal preference shares but with the additional feature that the company has to redeem the shares at a stated date, say after ten years. A trading company could issue redeemable preference shares to a charity, but it should be borne in mind that, if this is done, the money for the redemption of the shares will have to come from company profits. This will mean that the trading company will have to retain profits and pay corporation tax on them in order to build up a fund to redeem the shares. This conflicts with the policy of many trading companies of paying 100% of the taxable profits of the trading company to the charity (see **7.233–7.238**).

Ordinary shares

7.62 These are by far the most common form of shares. Ordinary shares (except in complicated share structures) give the holder of each share one vote per share (whereas a preference shareholder normally only has a vote if the dividends are in arrears). Hence, the ordinary shareholders control the affairs of the company. For a charity's trading company, all ordinary shares will normally be issued to the parent charity (in the case of a corporate charity), or held by the trustees on the charity's behalf (in the case of an unincorporated charity).

Dividends

7.63 It is normal for a conventional commercial company to reward its ordinary shareholders by paying dividends, when there are profits available for distribution. However, in the case of a trading company owned by a charity, it is normal for the profits to be paid to the charity by way of gift aid (see **7.233–7.238**).

7.64 It is possible for a company to have only one shareholder: so a charity can own all the shares in its trading subsidiary. Prior to 1992 two members were required, so for historic reasons some charities may own one share via a nominee.

Name

7.65 The memorandum of association states the trading company's name. It is worth pausing for thought, before giving the trading company a name which includes the charity's name in its title (which is the normal practice), and consider first the *purpose* of establishing the trading company. If the trading company is expected to be a permanent contributor to the charity's funds working alongside it, then it may well be appropriate for it to *share* the charity's name. But it may be that the particular activities of the trading company can be built up and after a few years the charity may be able to cash in its investment by selling the trading company to a commercial purchaser. At that point, the name and goodwill of the trading company may be too intimately connected with the charity's name to be disentangled from it. Allowing a third party to own a company which includes the charity's name in its title could bring the reputation of the charity into disrepute, or at the very least cause public confusion.

7.66 An example of this is the charity Beauty Without Cruelty. The charity set up a cosmetics firm with the same name in 1963, but sold it in 1980. By 1993 public confusion about the purpose of the two organisations – which still had identical names – forced the charity to review its name. This could be a very expensive business – the launch of 'a new corporate image' for some major charities has cost over £200,000. Hence, trustees would be well advised, if they consider there is a chance that the trading company might be sold off, to give it a name which does not incorporate the charity's name.

7.67 Another problem occurs if the trading company intends to undertake high-risk activities which could lead to it becoming insolvent. Here it would be advisable to give the trading company a name which did not include the charity's, so as to lessen the damage to the charity's reputation if the trading company were to fail.

Articles of association

7.68 The articles of association set out the rules for the running of the company. Most companies use standard articles based on a model contained in the Companies (Tables A to F) Regulations 1985 (SI 1985/805), which were issued pursuant to the Companies Act 1985. This model has served its function well, having been used (albeit amended from time to time) since 1862. It is due to be amended again in October 2009 to take account of the Companies Act 2006 (see **7.72**). For a charity establishing a trading company the following points need to be considered.

What is the authorised share capital?

7.69 See **7.54**: both the memorandum and the articles of association refer to the authorised share capital.

What is the share structure?

7.70 Will the company issue preference shares, redeemable shares or ordinary shares?

How are the directors to be appointed?

7.71 Do one third have to retire by rotation each year and submit themselves to re-election? Does the charity want to have a provision put into the articles that it may dismiss any person from serving as a director by giving written notice to that effect? This would give the charity far greater control over the directors of the trading company than under company law. The Companies

Act 2006 does provide a mechanism for the dismissal of a director, but it is a somewhat protracted process requiring a meeting for which 28 days' notice has to be given.

Company law reform

7.72 The Companies Act 2006 makes some major changes to company law. At the time of writing, not all of the Act is in force, but the following changes are due to come in from October 2009:

- The memorandum of association for new companies will only contain the details of those subscribing for the initial shares. Most of the other provisions currently found in the memorandum will be found in the articles.

- Companies will no longer need to have an objects clause. The objects of a company will be unrestricted unless the articles state otherwise.

- The concept of authorised share capital will be abolished. New companies will simply need to provide a statement of capital and initial shareholdings. There will be no need to obtain the shareholder's approval before issuing new shares. Any change in the number of shares will be reported to Companies House.

- Table A will be replaced by new model articles.

INVESTMENT BY A CHARITY IN A TRADING COMPANY

7.73 The rules which apply to a charity's investment in its trading company will be slightly different depending on the purpose for which the trading company has been established. In very broad terms there are two motives for establishing a trading company:

- to carry out non-primary purpose fundraising activities, where they would involve a significant risk to the charity's assets if they were carried out by the charity directly, or where there would be a tax risk (see **7.5–7.12**);

- as a vehicle for carrying out primary purpose trading, which could be carried out by the charity directly, but which the charity wishes to run through a trading subsidiary, for risk or other reasons (see **7.13–7.37**).

7.74 To the extent that the trading subsidiary is carrying out primary purpose trading activity, the position is relatively straightforward. If the trustees are satisfied that the funds they are proposing to invest in the trading subsidiary will be used for the charitable purposes of the charity, they have complied with their duties under charity law. They may wish to ensure that the funds are used in this way, by imposing some restriction on their use, and funding of trading companies in these circumstances is explored in more detail at **7.142–7.148** below. But, in broad terms, in this situation the funding of a trading company will be regarded as a charitable application of funds, not a true 'investment', so the trustees have much more flexibility.

7.75 To the extent that the trading company is not carrying out primary purpose trading, very different considerations apply. The charity is not supporting the trading company's activities because they further the charity's charitable purposes, but because it is hoping that those activities will make a profit for the charity, whether by way of income or capital return.

7.76 This means that in these circumstances the charity's funding of its trading company is treated, in the eyes of the law, in exactly the same way as any other type of investment by the charity, eg in a share or property portfolio. Before a charity can decide to invest, whether by purchasing shares in the trading company, or by lending money to it, the charity trustees must check that the charity has the necessary constitutional capacity to do so and ensure that they comply with the appropriate duties regarding investment.

Power to invest

7.77 Charitable companies are likely to have powers to invest set out in their constitution. If there are no express powers, the charity may well wish to change its constitution to include them (see **2.14–2.16**). The charity should check whether Charity Commission consent will be required: this will depend on the terms of the constitution (see **2.15–2.16**).

7.78 Charitable trusts and unincorporated associations may also have express investment powers in their constitutions. If they do not, the trustees will probably be able to rely on the statutory power of investment conferred by the Trustee Act 2000. This allows trustees to make any kind of investment they could make if they were absolutely entitled to the charity's assets. This essentially gives the trustees free reign, subject to the scope of the term 'investment' and to the trustees' duties to act prudently, take appropriate criteria into account and take advice – which are explored at **7.80–7.95**. While the Charity Commission takes a narrow view of what constitutes an 'investment', it does accept that investment in shares or loans qualifies as an investment.

7.79 The statutory power is subject to any restrictions or exclusions in the charity's constitution, except where the constitution is dated before 3 August 1961 (when the Trustee Investment Act 1961, which previously provided a limited statutory power of investment, came into force).

Trustees' duties when investing

7.80 The Trustee Act 2000 sets out a general duty of care which applies to the trustees of charitable trusts and unincorporated associations in relation to investment. The Charity Commission's view is that although the Trustee Act 2000 does not apply to charitable companies, trustees of charitable companies would be well advised to comply with all duties imposed by the Trustee Act 2000 in any event, as they are likely to have comparable duties under the general law. These duties will apply to a proposed investment in a trading company in exactly the same way as they apply to other types of investment by the charity.

The general duty of care

7.81 The general duty of care is a duty to exercise such care and skill as is reasonable in the circumstances, having regard in particular:

(a) to any special knowledge or experience that the trustee has or holds himself or herself out as having; and

(b) if the trustee acts as trustee in the course of a business or profession, to any special knowledge or experience that it is reasonable to expect of a person acting in the course of that kind of business or profession.

This means that a trustee who works with investments, for instance, will have a higher standard of care imposed on him or her when it comes to making investment decisions for the charity.

7.82 Unless it appears from the constitution that it is not meant to apply, the statutory duty of care will apply to the exercise of any power of investment (including a power in the constitution), any review of the charity's investments, consideration of the standard investment criteria (see **7.83** below) when reviewing investments, and obtaining and considering advice (see **7.84–7.87**).

Standard investment criteria

7.83 When exercising any power of investment (whether in the constitution or conferred by the Trustee Act 2000), and when reviewing the charity's investments, the trustees must have regard to the so-called 'standard investment criteria' in that Act. These are:

(a) the suitability to the charity of investments of the same kind as any particular investment proposed to be made or retained and of that particular investment as an investment of that kind; and

(b) the need for diversification of investments of the charity, in so far as is appropriate to the circumstances of the trust.

If the proposed investment in the trading company is likely to be the charity's only significant investment, there will be little diversification of investments. This does not mean that the trustees should not make the investment, but it is a factor they should take into account.

Advice

7.84   Charity trustees must generally obtain advice about investments. Under the Trustee Act 2000, before exercising any power of investment, whether in the Act or in the constitution, and when reviewing the investments of the charity, a trustee must obtain and consider proper advice about the way in which, having regard to the standard investment criteria, the investment power should be exercised or the investments varied. Proper advice is the advice of a person who is reasonably believed by the trustee to be qualified to give it, by his ability in and practical experience of financial and other matters relating to the proposed investment.

7.85   There is an exception from this rule where the trustee 'reasonably concludes that in all the circumstances it is unnecessary or inappropriate to do so'. This gives the trustees some flexibility, perhaps where they consider that they have appropriate investment experience themselves, or where it would not be cost effective to seek advice.

7.86   The Charity Commission recommends that the trustees 'ordinarily take appropriate advice on the investment and the financial viability of the trading subsidiary' (CC35 'Trustees, trading and tax', para D8). In the Commission's view, 'what is "appropriate" will depend on the circumstances: the cost of taking the advice is a relevant factor, and cost should be commensurate to the size of the proposed investment' (CC35, para D8).

7.87   The most obvious source of advice is a suitably experienced accountant.

Review

7.88   The Trustee Act 2000 requires the trustees to review the investments of the charity from time to time and consider whether they should be varied, having regard to the standard investment criteria. This applies equally to investment in a trading subsidiary, although, in practice, if a charity has made an investment in a trading subsidiary, it will probably find it difficult to withdraw its investment.

Trading subsidiary

7.89   While it may seem surprising, charities which are investing in their trading companies in the hope of an investment return must comply with the rules explained above. In practical terms this means the following:

- The trustees must reasonably consider that it is in the charity's interest to make the investment.

- The trustees should compare the return the investment is expected to generate with other similar forms of investment. For example, would an investment of £10,000 in a company set up to exploit the charity's name and logo by selling branded products produce more than if a similar sum were invested in the stock market? It is legitimate for the charity to take account of the fringe benefits of investing in its own trading company – see **7.107–7.114** below – but it is still important to compare it with other possible investments.

- The trustees must request that they be provided with sufficiently detailed information to allow them to make a sound and proper decision. Such information may well include:
  - market research (unless it is a question of the charity hiving off to a separate trading company a business which it has already built up);
  - a proposed budget showing projected capital and on-going expenditure and income;
  - a cash flow forecast for at least 2 years;
  - a business plan, showing how it is proposed to develop and market the business;
  - an analysis of working capital requirements.

- An important factor will be the period of time for which the investment will be tied up in the trading subsidiary. Is this something which can be justified?

- Investment in the trading subsidiary should be considered in the overall context of the charity's investment policy. Does this represent a significant investment of the charity's funds, or only a small part? Are the charity's investments sufficiently diversified?

- The trustees should consider whether they need to seek appropriate advice on the investment.

- The trustees should review the charity's investment in the trading subsidiary on a regular basis.

These duties will apply not only to the charity's initial investment in the company, but also to any subsequent injection of funds.

7.90 Charity Commission guidance at the time of writing (CC35 'Trustees, trading and tax', para D1) notes that trading subsidiaries should become financially viable within two years:

> 'A trading subsidiary should become financially viable as soon as possible. It is therefore important to have a business plan in place that clearly identifies the point at which trading is expected to be profitable and to assess progress against the business plan. Where financial viability is not anticipated within two years of operation, careful consideration should be given to the appropriateness of undertaking the planned trading activity.'

7.91 The trustees should consider the information provided to them carefully and in detail, mindful of their duty to act in accordance with their various obligations listed above. The minutes of the trustees' meeting should record the terms of any resolution to invest in a trading company, or the results of any review of the investment, and should refer to the documents which the trustees have reviewed in reaching their decision. Those documents should be annexed to the minutes, so that if the trustees' decision is ever challenged, evidence will be available to justify the trustees' action. The wording of the resolution should be carefully drawn up – it should not commit the charity to an open-ended commitment to finance the trading company and should address the duties mentioned above. It is advisable to consider taking advice from a suitably qualified professional adviser.

7.92 The Charity Commission's detailed guidance on investment generally ('Investment of Charitable Funds: Detailed guidance') highlights the trustees' obligations under the investment rules in the following terms (paras 72 and 73):

> 'The making of investments in companies which are owned wholly or substantially by the charity is within the scope of the general power of investment. But the suitability and diversification considerations apply as much to this form of investment as to any other. So does the duty to take "proper advice".

> Experience suggests that some trustees lose sight of this, and become committed to the support of the connected company, regardless of whether, considered objectively, it is in the interests of the charity to make or retain an investment in that company. Investing in a company which is not economically viable, and has no real prospect of becoming so, involves a failure on the part of the trustees to discharge their duties with regard to investment. This applies more strongly where the only object in making the investment is to prevent the company from going into insolvent liquidation.'

Similar views are expressed in CC35 'Trustees, trading and tax', para D16.

7.93 The Charity Commission actively monitors the relationship between charities and their trading companies. In 2004, the Charity Commission published the results of several formal inquiries into charities' relationships with their trading subsidiaries. The inquiries were prompted by the Commission's monitoring of annual returns, which had highlighted concerns relating to charities making loans to their trading subsidiaries. These concerns centred around a number of recurring themes, namely that the loans were unsecured, interest-free and not repayable over a specified period.

7.94 One charity, for example, ran a number of local community sites. Each site comprised a meeting room and a drop-in café. A shop, which would help to cover the running costs, was located on each site, and run through a separate subsidiary trading company. The retail activity was not as successful as the original business plan had assumed. This meant that the charity needed to support the ongoing trading activity of the subsidiary. The Charity Commission reminded the trustees of their obligations as regards ongoing investment. Although no action was apparently taken against the trustees at the time, the Commission undertook to review the position after 12 months to monitor whether the trading company's debt to the charity had reduced.

7.95 This example illustrates the consequence of a breach by the trustees of their duty to invest prudently. In the first place, the charity may be put to the cost and expense of investigation by the Charity Commission. Secondly, charities have a responsibility to look after their charity's funds: failure to do so may be regarded as a breach of trust, and it is possible for trustees to be made personally liable for any loss to the charity flowing from their breach of duty. If this is the case, the protections of limited liability (if the charity is a limited liability company, charitable incorporated organisation, industrial and provident society or corporation established by Royal Charter) are of no avail. The veil of incorporation is lifted and the trustees can be made personally liable for the loss.

Tax considerations

7.96 Before making an investment in a trading company, charity trustees also have to consider whether or not the loan constitutes 'charitable expenditure' for the purposes of ss 505 and 506 of the Income and Corporation Taxes Act 1988 in the case of corporate charities, or s 540 onwards of the Income Tax Act 2007 for charitable trusts. These provisions contain curbs on charities which would otherwise be entitled to tax relief on their income.

7.97 If such charities incur 'non-charitable expenditure', they will lose tax relief (and hence pay tax) on the amount of their income and gains which equals their non-qualifying expenditure in the relevant accounting period in the case of charitable companies, or tax year in the case of charitable trusts. For example:

– XYZ Charity (a charitable company) has tax-free income and gains of £1,000,000 in year ended 31 December 2008.

– It spends £875,000 of this income.

– £800,000 is spent by way of 'charitable expenditure'.

– £75,000 is 'non-charitable' expenditure.

– The charity retains £125,000 as a surplus.

– The charity will pay corporation tax at the appropriate rate on £75,000 (the amount of its 'non-charitable' expenditure).

7.98 Thus, if a charity makes an investment in a trading company which is regarded as 'non-charitable' expenditure, there is a significant risk that it will incur a tax bill.

7.99 'Charitable expenditure' means expenditure which is exclusively for charitable purposes. By virtue of ICTA 1988, s 506(4), a loan or other investment by a charity will only be regarded as charitable expenditure if it is a 'qualifying loan' or 'investment'. A 'qualifying investment' is defined in ICTA 1988, Sch 20, Pt I. Investment in shares in private companies will only be regarded as a qualifying investment if HMRC is satisfied that the investment is made for the benefit of the charity and not for the avoidance of tax. A 'qualifying loan' is defined in Sch 20, Pt II as:

(a)   a loan made to another charity for charitable purposes only; or

(b)   a loan to a beneficiary of the charity which is made in the course of carrying out the purposes of the charity; or

(c)   money placed on current account with most banking institutions recognised under the Financial Services and Markets Act 2000; or

(d)   any other loan (which would include a loan to a trading subsidiary) as to which HMRC are satisfied, on a claim made to it in that behalf, that the loan is made for the benefit of the charity and not for the avoidance of tax.

7.100 The definitions quoted above relate to charitable companies and unincorporated associations: there are similar definitions for charitable trusts in ITA 2007, ss 543 and 558 onwards (although the terminology is slightly different: the expression used is 'approved charitable investment', rather than 'qualifying loan' or 'investment').

7.101 Thus, any investment in a trading company, whether by way of loan or share capital, will be regarded as 'non-charitable expenditure' by the charity unless it can be shown to be made other than for the avoidance of tax. At first glance this seems unlikely. After all, the very purpose of the charity making the investment is to provide working capital to the trading company which will allow it to generate taxable profits which will be gift-aided to the charity, thus avoiding tax! In practice, HMRC does not appear to apply this argument and it does accept that a charity's investment in its trading company may be a qualifying investment or a qualifying loan (or an approved charitable investment).

7.102 HMRC may require the charity to make a formal claim for the investment to be regarded as a qualifying loan or investment. Annex IV of HMRC's 'Detailed guidance notes for charities' explains (at para 62) that:

> 'Investments will be regarded as made for charitable purposes and the benefit of the charity if they are commercially sound. Usually, charities should ensure that investments are secure, carry a fair rate of return (actually paid) and, in the case of loans, provide for recovery of the amount invested in due course.'

The Charity Commission guidance (CC35 'Trustees, trading and tax', para D12) elaborates on this:

> 'An investment would not be considered to be "for the benefit of the parent charity", if, for example, the investment was speculative, or driven by a desire to keep the trading subsidiary going, regardless of the prospects of economic return to the parent charity.'

Further details about HMRC's approach to loans are included at **7.118–7.137** below.

7.103 Although there is no mechanism for seeking prior approval of investments from HMRC, it will give an opinion if asked. In the authors' view it would certainly be advisable to seek an opinion in the case of all large loans or investments.

7.104 HMRC will also be interested in ensuring that the investment duties described at **7.80-7.95** above have been complied with. In the authors' experience, if the charity complies with the Charity Commission guidance in making an investment in a trading subsidiary, HMRC will accept this as charitable expenditure.

7.105 The possibility of challenge by HMRC highlights the importance of minuting investment decisions (including the factors on which the decisions were based) carefully. Both HMRC and the Charity Commission guidance stress the need to keep records (see **7.91**).

7.106 Tax rules designed to discourage abuse of charitable tax reliefs by so-called 'substantial donors' were introduced in 2006. These do not affect the relationship between charities and trading companies wholly owned by them, but they may be relevant where a charity is investing in a company which is not owned by it, or which is only partly owned by it, and is wholly or partly owned by a substantial donor.

Non-financial considerations

Complementary activities

7.107 One other relevant factor for some charity trustees in considering an investment in a trading company is the fact that the trading company itself may be undertaking activities which complement those of the charity.

7.108 There will be many cases where the activities of the trading company overlap with the aims of the charity. As explained at **7.142–7.148**, if the trading company's activities could be carried out perfectly properly by the charity as primary purpose trading, but the trustees have decided for reasons of risk, for example, to run them through a separate trading company, the funding of a company of this nature is not regarded as an investment in the conventional sense.

7.109 There may be situations, however, where the trading company's activities do complement those of the charity, but could not be carried out by the charity itself. For example, a charitable theatre will need a bar to offer sustenance to its customers but may improve its financial viability by opening the bar to the general public. Such a bar will need to be run by a separate trading company in line with the decision in *Grove v Young Men's Christian Association* (1903) 4 TC 613 (see **3.40**). But the bar will enhance the theatre even if it is not a great financial success. Can the trustees take this into account when investing? The question is easily answered. If the bar enhances the theatre so that more tickets are sold, then even if the bar is not a great financial success in its own right, the enhanced revenue of the charity (via ticket sales) will justify the trustees' decision.

Goodwill

7.110 Where the charity's association with the trading company is obvious to the public – which will clearly be the case where the two entities share a name – the charity will benefit indirectly from the goodwill and favourable publicity generated by the trading company's work. This, too, is something the trustees may take into account.

Ethical considerations

7.111 What if the trading company is run along ethical lines? To what extent can the trustees take this into account? There will be some situations where ethical issues overlap with considerations of primary purpose trading. For example, Oxfam Activities Limited is a trading company owned by Oxfam. It sells many products which have been manufactured in developing countries and, hence, are complementary to Oxfam's own charitable activities in seeking to relieve poverty in such countries. The Charity Commission has now recognised that promoting fair trade is a proper way of relieving poverty (see **4.10**). So there is an argument that to the extent that Oxfam Activities Limited's activities promote fair trade, it is carrying out primary purpose trading, and the considerations mentioned at **7.142–7.148** apply.

7.112 There will be cases, however, where ethical considerations, though laudable, do not actively promote a charity's objects. For instance, an educational charity works to advance education, not to relieve poverty. It has a trading subsidiary which sells manufactured goods: to what extent can it take account of the fact that the trading subsidiary only deals in fairly traded goods or, equally, only works with suppliers which actively promote the environment?

7.113 Although the basic rule is that the trustees' powers of investment must be used to further the charity's purposes, and that those purposes will normally be served by seeking the maximum investment return which is consistent with commercial prudence, Charity Commission guidance at the time of writing recognises that an ethical investment policy can be consistent with the principle of seeking the best returns. There are three cases where trustees are able to allow their investment strategy to be governed by considerations other than the level of investment return:

- Charities can avoid investing in a business which would conflict with the aims of the charity. Thus, an environmental protection charity might feel it inappropriate to invest in a business which pollutes the environment.

- Charities can avoid investments that might hamper their work. For instance, some investments may alienate the charity's beneficiaries or supporters, although the trustees must always balance the difficulties which this might involve with any corresponding financial risk of poorly performing investments.

- Trustees can accommodate the views of those who consider the investment to be inappropriate on moral grounds, but only if this does not involve 'a risk of significant financial detriment'.

7.114 So trustees may, in considering a proposed investment, have some regard to ethical issues. The educational charity in the example could seek to justify investment in a trading company which operates along fair trade or environmental lines on the grounds that to do otherwise might alienate its supporters. However, the trustees need to be alert to the fact that there is a limited extent to which ethical considerations can be taken into account when investing, which applies equally to investments in a trading company.

HOW TO INVEST

7.115 Once the trustees have decided that they will sanction an investment in a trading company, the next issue to be resolved is how that investment is to be structured. The investment can be by way of loan or share capital.

7.116 Traditionally, the preferred approach has been for the investment to be made by way of loan. The Charity Commission's 2001 guidance on trading by charities recommended that 'normally, investment in a subsidiary trading company should take the form of secured loans by the charity on market terms' (CC35 – Charities and trading, July 2001 edn). Investment by way of loan was, in the authors' experience, far less likely to give rise to a challenge from HMRC.

7.117 More recent Charity Commission guidance (CC35 'Trustees, trading and tax', April 2007) makes no concrete recommendation either way; nor do the HMRC 'Detailed guidance notes for charities', Annex III. But investment by way of loan, on appropriate terms, still remains the usual way for the arrangement to satisfy HMRC. Both forms of investment are explored more fully below.

Loans by the charity

7.118 The main advantage of investment by way of loan rather than share capital is that as a creditor, the parent charity has a contractual right to payment of interest, and repayment of the capital. This ranks ahead of any payment of dividends to shareholders, or any rights of the shareholders to repayment of their capital investment on an insolvency or dissolution of the company. It is for this reason that loans have traditionally been regarded as the best form of investment by a charity in its trading subsidiary.

7.119 When investing in a subsidiary by way of loan, the charity must have an eye to the insolvency rules (see Chapter 11). Companies must not trade whilst insolvent, and loans owed by the company will be taken into account when determining solvency. Charity Commission guidance (CC35 'Trustees, trading and tax', para D11) recommends that:

> 'Trustees should not, therefore, invest loan capital in a trading subsidiary, if it is reasonably foreseeable that the subsidiary may not be able to service the loan or repay it when the term expires'.

The Commission goes on to point out that where finance is provided by way of loan, the insolvency rules will also be a factor when the trading subsidiary is deciding whether to pay its profits up to the parent charity by way of gift aid (see **7.233–7.238**). If all the profits are paid to the charity:

> 'the trading subsidiary may retain insufficient recourses for it to repay loans made by the charity as and when due. That would render the trading subsidiary insolvent, in that it would be incapable of paying its debts.'

Strictly, the company should retain sufficient profits to enable the loan to be repaid, although this may result in a corporation tax charge. See **7.132–7.137**.

7.120 The terms of the loan are also important. The main driver in this respect is HMRC, which will generally regard a loan as non-charitable expenditure (see **7.96–7.105** above) unless it provides for a proper rate of interest, is secured and includes proper provision for repayment, as follows.

A proper rate of interest

7.121 Some charities make interest-free loans to their trading companies, but then receive the trading companies' profits by way of gift aid donation (see **7.233–7.238**). It could be argued that the sums donated are not 'pure income profit' in the hands of the charity, but a payment in lieu of interest forgone. Thus, if a charity makes an interest-free loan to its trading company, it runs the risk that tax deducted by the trading company on sums paid via gift aid to the charity will not be recoverable, on the basis that HMRC will claim that the donation by the trading company under gift aid to the charity is, in reality, in return for the loan.

7.122 In addition, it is unlikely that HMRC would regard an interest-free loan to a trading subsidiary as a 'qualifying loan' (see **7.99–7.102**). Charity Commission guidance (CC35 'Trustees, trading and tax', para D11) advises that it is unlikely that such loans could be justified as an investment, unless the amount of the loan was small.

7.123 So far as the trading company is concerned, it does not matter if the charity charges interest, as it is tax-deductible. It merely means that the charity receives the money from the trading company in two forms, as interest and as the reduced taxable profits (if any) under gift aid.

7.124 What is a proper rate of interest? When considering making a loan to a trading company, the trustees should weigh up a number of factors:

(a) *Risk*: commercial lenders charge higher rates of interest to riskier customers and charity trustees should bear this in mind. Charity Commission guidance (CC35 'Trustees, trading and tax', para D12) specifically notes that HMRC may regard a loan as non-charitable expenditure 'if the loan agreement provides for a rate of return that does not reflect the level of risk'.

(b) *Rate*: what rate could the trustees obtain by depositing surplus cash with a conventional commercial borrower?

(c) *Additional benefits to the charity*: for example, will the loan enable the company to maximise profits which will be donated to the charity?

7.125 It should be noted that the interest should be physically paid by actually transferring funds from the trading company's bank account and clearing it through the charity's bank account, by cheque or bank transfer. The case of *Minsham Properties Ltd v Price (Inspector Of Taxes)* [1990] STC 718 involved the administration of a loan of £270,000 by a charity to its wholly owned trading company. A loan account was opened in the books of each company; a charge for interest was periodically entered in the account. The subsidiary claimed relief from corporation tax in respect of the interest charges. In order to qualify for relief the interest must have been paid out of the company's profits. It was held that the periodic journal entries, in which the interest charges were credited to the charity's account and debited to the subsidiary's account, did not amount to evidence that the interest had been paid. The entries merely amounted to evidence that the interest had not been paid. Thus the relief from corporation tax was not available.

7.126 The Charity Commission could allege that operating in this manner, whereby corporation tax relief was lost, with the result that the charity received less money from the trading company, amounted to a breach of trust by the trustees for which the trustees could be made personally liable.

7.127 If the loan stipulates interest is payable and it is not recovered, the Commission may step in. In one case a charity had lent moneys to three non-charitable associated trading companies. The Charity Commission noted in its report on the situation that:

'We have been able to secure a repayment of £139,711 to the charity which represents unpaid interest on these loans.'

Security for a loan

7.128 Equally, the investment should usually be secured by way of a charge or mortgage in favour of the charity. Charity Commission guidance (CC35 'Trustees, trading and tax', para D11) comments that:

'whilst the creation of a charge over property of the trading subsidiary to secure a loan involves expense, it is unlikely that a loan secured only by the contractual undertaking of the trading subsidiary could be justified as an investment, unless the amount of the loan is small, or the value of the security which is available in the subsidiary is limited.'

7.129 The charge will be over all the trading company's assets – thus, it should be a fixed charge over, for example, any land, buildings, plant, machinery, etc, and a floating charge over stock and other items which change in the course of trade. This is, of course, subject to the assumption that no charge has been given to any other party (eg a bank), in which case the prior lender's consent will almost certainly be required.

7.130 By having a charge the charity will have priority over the assets of the company in the event of a liquidation of the trading company (see Chapter 11 for more details). However, this security may be more apparent than real, as in many cases the assets of a trading company may amount to very little, other than some unsold stock (eg last year's Christmas cards) and debts due. This is because the trading company will, despite Charity Commission recommendations, often pay over all its taxable profits each year to the charity, hence having no retained earnings with which to purchase fixed assets, plant or machinery, or to build up reserves (see **7.233–7.238**).

7.131 Note that to be effective, details of the charge must be submitted to Companies House on Form 395. There is a strict 21-day time limit for registering the charge, otherwise it will not bind a liquidator of the company. A fee of £13 (at present) is payable. If land held by the trading company is charged, then the charge may also need to be registered with the Land Registry. Trading companies rarely hold land of value, only leases, and so it will be necessary to check whether a landlord's consent is needed to charge the lease.

Repayment of the loan

7.132 The repayment of loans made by charities to trading companies is fraught with difficulties. The Charity Commission (perfectly reasonably) expects that when a loan is sanctioned, the trustees should stipulate repayment terms. Usually the loan is repayable on demand, but repayment is rarely demanded.

7.133 The problem with the repayment of a loan is that it comes out of taxable profits. The payment of interest is a tax-deductible item for the purposes of calculating taxable profits which will be subject to corporation tax, but the repayment of the capital element of a loan is not. The only way in which the loan can normally be repaid is out of the trading company's profits. But if the trading company retains profits in order to repay the loan, it will incur a tax bill. For example:

XYZ Trading Limited borrows £50,000 from XYZ Charity (a charitable company) @ 10% per annum interest.

Trading company's taxable profits after all deductions (other than interest)	£45,000
Less interest	£5,000
Taxable profit	£40,000

If XYZ Trading Limited pays all its profits to XYZ charity under gift aid, it will reduce its taxable profits to nil (see **7.233–7.238**). But equally it will have no retained profits from which it could repay the loan. If it retained some of the profits in order to be able to repay the loan, it would have to pay corporation tax on that part of the profits it retained.

7.134 Between April 2002 and March 2006 there was a corporation tax band of 0% on the first £10,000 of a company group's profits. In a typical two-member group involving a charity and a trading subsidiary, this meant that the trading subsidiary could retain up to £5,000 each year, for the purpose of repaying the loan, or simply to use as working capital, without incurring a tax bill. Unfortunately this 0% band was abolished from April 2006 onwards.

7.135 Can these problems be avoided if the loan to the trading company is repaid within the trading company's financial year so that the loan is not on the books of the trading company at its year end? For example:

– XYZ Trading Limited borrows £20,000 from XYZ Charity on 1 January 2009.

– It repays it on 30 October 2009.

– Its financial year end is 31 December 2009.

– Its taxable profits are £100,000.

The receipt of the loan will appear as a form of income in the profit and loss account whilst the repayment of the loan should appear as one of the items of expenditure in the profit and loss account, or alternatively as an extraordinary item. The repayment of the loan will not reduce the taxable profits. XYZ Trading Limited can pay all its taxable profits to XYZ Charity under gift aid, assuming it has sufficient cash to do so, having repaid the £20,000 loan.

7.136 Trading subsidiaries that are wholly owned by charities now have 9 months following the end of a financial year to make gift aid payments that will be tax relievable in that earlier year (see **7.236**). So, using the above example, the trading subsidiary could make a gift aid payment of £80,000 by 31 December 2009, and use cash available in the subsequent year (ie to 31 December 2010) to make the additional £20,000 gift aid payment, provided this is made by 30 September 2010, and claim for this to be treated as paid for tax purposes in the year to 31 December 2009. In this way the trading subsidiary has effectively retained £20,000 out of its profits to repay the loan, and has not had to pay tax in the process.

7.137 However, note that this route may ultimately require tax to be paid in some future year, as the gift-aided profits (using the above example) will be continually £20,000 ahead of the taxable profits, so that, for example, in the final year of trade the company will be £20,000 short of gift aid to set against the taxable profits of that final year.

Shares purchased by the charity

7.138 If a charity has the appropriate investment powers, it may consider purchasing shares in the trading company rather than making a loan. Traditionally, an investment by way of loan has been the preferred option. This is for a number of reasons:

(a)   There is unlikely to be a market for the shares.

(b)   Shareholders are paid out last on a liquidation of a company. If a charity takes a charge to secure a loan, it will gain priority in the payment of debts in an insolvency situation (see Chapter 11). But, as a shareholder, the charity will be paid out last, after the preferential creditors, and after the secured and the unsecured creditors. The chances of the charity recovering its money in an insolvent liquidation will be very small.

(c)   In the authors' experience, HMRC is less likely to question an investment by way of loan.

7.139

The Charity Commission has also traditionally preferred the use of loan finance (see **7.116**). But the Charity Commission's most recent guidance (CC35 'Trustees, trading and tax', para D10) accepts that:

'there are valid reasons why a parent charity might choose to capitalise a trading subsidiary by means of share capital rather than loan capital. For example:

- the subscription by a parent charity of substantial share capital in its trading subsidiary can give confidence to suppliers, customers, creditors, prospective creditors and others with whom the trading subsidiary has a business relationship; or
- where a trading subsidiary would be exposed to the risk or actuality of insolvency if it were to be capitalised by loan, trustees will have little choice but to invest share capital (subject to the [trustees' usual investment duties]).'

Converting loan finance into shares

7.140 It may be that the trustees' attitude to investment in the trading subsidiary changes over time. It might be sensible for trustees to consider making a loan to the trading company when financing a start-up. When the risk is at its greatest in the early years, the charity thereby stands a better chance of getting its money back in the event of failure. The loan will appear as a liability on the trading company's balance sheet.

7.141 But once the trading company has built up a track record, and perhaps even paid money to the charity by way of gift aid, the trustees can consider converting the loan into shares in the trading company. They must consider any such proposal in accordance with their investment duties (outlined at **7.80–7.95** above). If they decide to do so, this will strengthen the trading company's balance sheet. Creditors will be reduced by an amount equal to the loan and will be matched by an increase in shareholders' funds. The charity's balance sheet will no longer show the trading company as a debtor; instead, its investments will have increased. The trading company's strengthened balance sheet and the fact that the charge in favour of the charity will have been removed (as the loan which the charge secured will have been converted into shares) will mean that the trading company may be able to borrow money from a commercial source, hence diversifying the financing of the trading company and removing some of the charity's risk. There will be a price to be paid, namely the interest that will be paid to the bank which had hitherto gone to the charity (see **7.154**).

PRIMARY PURPOSE TRADING

7.142 As mentioned at **7.74**, there may be situations where a trading company's activities could be carried out directly by the charity, as they represent primary purpose trading. The trustees have decided that they would prefer the trading to be carried out by a separate trading subsidiary for reasons of risk, for example, or of branding.

7.143 Funding a trading company in these circumstances is not 'investment' in the traditional sense. While there is no harm in the trustees having regard to the investment considerations set out at **7.73–7.106**, they are not obliged to do so. Trustees considering establishing a trading company in these circumstances should consider the following issues.

7.144 What are the pros and cons of using a separate trading subsidiary? Do the factors which have caused the trustees to consider a trading subsidiary (eg management, risk and branding) justify the administrative and financial costs of setting up and running a separate legal vehicle?

7.145 Does the charity's constitution allow it to set up and fund a trading subsidiary? Power to set up a trading subsidiary may be implied in these circumstances, possibly, under a general sweep-up power to do anything which furthers the charity's objects. Funding the subsidiary is likely to be allowed, as the charity is simply using its funds to further its charitable purposes.

7.146 There are unlikely to be any constraints under charity law. Charity Commission guidance (CC35 'Trustees, trading and tax', para D1) says:

> 'If primary purpose trading is conducted through a trading subsidiary, much of [the Commission's guidance on trading subsidiaries] does not apply: the funding of the trading subsidiary would be a charitable application of funds, rather than an investment of funds for profit.'

7.147 How should the trading subsidiary be funded? The charity may choose to fund the trading subsidiary by way of loan. The loan may be on favourable, rather than commercial, terms: as this is a charitable application of funds, the considerations set out at **7.118–7.131** do not apply. Equally, the charity may decide to fund the subsidiary by way of grant, which could avoid the problems associated with repayment described at **7.132–7.137**. Since the subsidiary is a separate legal entity, a grant agreement would be required, allowing the charity to claw back funds in certain circumstances (eg if the funds were inappropriately applied by the subsidiary).

7.148 It should be easy to satisfy HMRC that a loan to a trading subsidiary which carries out primary purpose trading is made for the benefit of the charity and not for the avoidance of tax (see **7.99–7.100**). The injection of funds would therefore be regarded as a 'qualifying loan' (or 'approved charitable investment'), which is in turn proper 'charitable expenditure' under the rules of ICTA 1988 and ITA 2007.

THIRD PARTY FINANCE

7.149 The Charity Commission advises (CC35 'Trustees, trading and tax', para D9) that:

'It is good practice for trustees of a parent charity to consider the desirability of obtaining investment from others in its trading subsidiary. This would spread the risks of the trade, and it may contribute positively to the charity's liquidity.'

However, the Commission acknowledges that 'it may be difficult to attract such investment at reasonable cost'.

7.150 The Commission's recommendation assumes that a trading company will be able to raise funds from a commercial source. This may be difficult. Traditionally, high street banks and other commercial lenders have been reluctant to assist, often because they do not fully understand the nature of the voluntary sector. However, while to a certain extent this remains the case, in recent years the growth of the social enterprise sector has given rise to a corresponding growth in the number of lenders prepared to support charities' trading enterprises. These include specialist arms of well-known banks, banks with a particular interest in the voluntary and community sector (often called social banks), community development finance institutions or 'CDFIs' (which receive special tax breaks), special community venture capital funds, and government sponsored loan funds. The types of support offered by these organisations vary: many will offer loans, some may assist with equity finance and others may provide grant funding, or a combination of all three. In some cases, members of the public may be encouraged to offer support.

7.151 The following list gives an idea of the types of support which might be available:

(1)   A long-term loan from a mainstream bank, social bank or CDFI.

(2)   A subordinated term loan, which will generally rank behind the other debts of the business. Such support is unlikely to be provided by a commercial or social bank, but may be available from a community fund or so-called 'patient capital' provider.

(3)   A short-term bridging loan to cover a temporary cash shortfall, which may be available from a social bank or CDFI.

(4)   Overdraft facilities, which may be available from a social bank, for example.

(5)   A bond issue, which is a method of raising debt capital from private investors. In 1998 mental health charity Mencap established Golden Lane Housing, a company limited by guarantee and a registered charity. Golden Lane Housing buys and leases homes, and rents them to people with learning disabilities. Golden Lane Housing was financed by a bond issue: 10-year bonds were issued to private investors, providing a return of inflation plus 1 per cent.

(6) A share issue. This may be public or private and small or large scale. A social entrepreneur may be interested in taking a stake in a charity's trading enterprise (see **7.239–7.250** for more detail). Public share issues are rare, but in 2004 Cafédirect, a fair-trade company founded by four charities in 1991, famously raised £5 million from 4,500 investors in a public share issue, with sponsorship from a social bank.

(7) A loan on favourable terms, or a capital investment, from a charity. This is now known as 'programme-related' or social investment. The charitable supporter provides financial assistance by way of loan or share investment, in the hope that it can recover its investment at the end of the day and 'recycle' the funds to help other charities.

This list has been complied with the help of the Social Enterprise Coalition publication *Unlocking the Potential: A guide to finance for social enterprise*, which contains further information on sources of funding (see www. socialenterprise.org.uk).

7.152 The requirements of the supporter will vary. In evaluating whether or not to lend money, for example, third party lenders (even those with a full understanding of the voluntary and community sector) will look for:

(a) A proper rate of interest which can be met by the borrower.

(b) Reasonable certainty that the borrower will repay the loan.

(c) Security.

So far as repayment of the capital is concerned, this will require the trading company to retain profits (which will be taxed) in order to give it enough cash to repay the borrowing.

7.153 Equity investors will seek a return on their investment commensurate with the risk they take which is, as indicated above, higher than for those investing by way of loan. Some investors may seek a social return as well as a financial return.

7.154 If the charity is considering using third party finance rather than investing its own funds to the trading subsidiary, the implications need to be considered carefully. If a trading company has a good track record or prospects (based on realistic appraisals), it may well be sensible for the charity to provide the financial backing, as the profits will stay with the charity rather than being paid away to a third party investor! The charity can also take advantage of the tax benefits of the gift aid regime (see **7.233–7.238**).

Guarantees

7.155   When seeking loan finance for a trading subsidiary, charities should be alert to the fact that lenders may well seek guarantees from the parent charity. As indicated above (see **7.130**), the assets of a trading company are often very few and inadequate to secure a charge in favour of the lender. In such circumstances the lender may request that the charity give it a guarantee in respect of the trading company's borrowings. This is absolutely standard practice in the commercial world, where holding companies give guarantees in respect of the borrowings of subsidiary companies. This guarantee might, in turn, be backed up by a charge over the holding company's assets. Unfortunately, it is outside a charity's powers to do this. A charity *does not have the legal capacity* to guarantee the debts of a non-charitable organisation.

7.156   The case of *Rosemary Simmons Memorial Housing Association Limited v United Dominions Trust Limited* [1986] WLR 1440 is a good example. The Rosemary Simmons Memorial Housing Association was an incorporated charitable housing association. Its rules stated that its objects were the provision of housing for the needy and aged, and that it was empowered to borrow and 'to do all things necessary for the fulfilment of its objects'. So as to carry out a housing development in pursuance of its objects, it negotiated with United Dominions Trust ('UDT') for a loan by UDT to a company ('R Limited') which was to carry out the project on behalf of the housing association. R Limited was not a subsidiary of the housing association and was not a charity. The housing association guaranteed to UDT to pay on demand all moneys due to UDT from R Limited, and backed this up by charging certain land to UDT.

7.157   In this case, decided in 1986, the court ruled that the housing association did not have the legal capacity to give a gratuitous guarantee in respect of the liabilities of a non-charitable body in which it was not associated in any legal sense, notwithstanding that the purpose of the transaction was to promote the housing association's objects, so both the guarantee and charge were void and could not be enforced by UDT. The judge did suggest that the position might have been different if R Limited had been a subsidiary of the housing association, but in the authors' view this is unlikely.

7.158   The case may well have been decided differently today. Section 65 of the Charities Act 1993 gives protection to anyone dealing with a charitable company acting outside its powers, where full consideration is given, and the third party did not know that the act was outside the charity's powers. The Rosemary Simmons Housing Association was a charitable industrial and provident society: similar protections were given to third parties dealing with industrial and provident societies in 2004, by s 7D of the Industrial and Provident Societies Act 1965.

7.159   If the guarantee had been enforced by UDT, however, there may have been charity law problems. In referring to guarantees given by a parent charity in relation to a trading subsidiary's liabilities, Charity Commission guidance (CC35 'Trustees, trading and tax', para D19) makes it clear that:

> 'if liability under the guarantee **is** enforceable, and is enforced by the creditors of the trading subsidiary, the trustees may be personally liable to make good the corporate charity's liability under the guarantee, where:
>
> - the liability arises out of a failure of a trade carried on by a trading subsidiary; and
> - the parent charity could not itself properly have carried on that trade.'

Liability under a guarantee of this nature may also cause tax problems, as it may be regarded as non-charitable expenditure (see **7.96–7.97**).

7.160   Given the emphasis on gratuitous guarantees in this case, there might be grounds for arguing that a charity with sufficiently wide investment powers could give a guarantee *in return for* a fee (eg 3% per annum of the amount guaranteed). The fee payable by the trading company would mean that the charity was making its assets work twice – both in connection with its normal activities *and* through charging the guarantee fee. But the fee payable would have to be calculated at a reasonable level so as to be justifiable as a prudent investment by the trustees (see **7.73–7.106**). If not, if the guarantee was called and the charity paid up under it, the trustees could find themselves criticised for breach of their duty as trustees and exposed to the risk of being held personally liable for the loss suffered by the charity in honouring the guarantee.

7.161   A charity may also be asked to give a comfort letter to a lender who is advancing money to the charity's trading company: such a comfort letter may or may not be legally enforceable – it all depends on the wording. Such a letter might mention that the charity is aware of the trading company's borrowings and that the charity would not wish to see it go into liquidation.

7.162   If it is legally enforceable, then it constitutes a guarantee, with all the implications analysed above. If it is not legally enforceable it may still cause the charity considerable moral difficulties. The practice was criticised in the Charity Commission's Report on The Royal British Legion:

> 'A letter of comfort is what it says. It is a document which, whilst it does not bind the writer legally, gives to the recipient the assurance that a third party has the backing and support of the writer. There is no doubt that without such a letter Legion Leasehold Housing Association would have found it difficult to borrow from financial institutions. It also has the effect of confusing the boundary between the charity and its non-charitable associates.'

7.163   Some lenders may also ask trustees to give personal guarantees. If the charity would not be in a position to provide the guarantee itself, it is unlikely to be able to reimburse the trustees for any liability they incur under the guarantee. This would leave the trustees out of pocket. Personal guarantees should not be given lightly.

7.164 If an unincorporated charity is asked to give a guarantee, the trustees should ensure that the liability under it is limited to the charity's assets, and that it provides that the trustees will not incur any personal liability (see **11.117–11.118**).

VAT AND VAT GROUPS

7.165 A charity may wish to set up a 'VAT group' with its trading company. This has the great advantage that all transactions (eg management charges) within the VAT group are VAT-free. Only bodies corporate are eligible to be treated as members of a VAT group. Hence, an unincorporated association or a trust and its trading company cannot be members of the same VAT group, as the former are not bodies corporate. For these purposes a body corporate includes limited or unlimited companies (whether limited by shares or guarantee), industrial and provident societies and bodies incorporated by Royal Charter.

7.166 The big problem for charities with VAT groups is that all members of the VAT group are, in effect, jointly and severally liable for any VAT due from the other members of the group (Value Added Tax Act 1994, s 43(1)). Primary liability for VAT rests with the 'representative member', who is named as such on the application for VAT group status. But if the representative member fails to pay the VAT due, each other member of the VAT group is liable for the VAT owed by the members of the group. This is perfectly normal for a commercial group of companies. But in the case of a charity, the VAT group registration confronts the problems of guarantees set out at **7.155–7.164** above, as the charity could be made liable for VAT incurred by the trading company. The Charity Commission advises (CC35 'Trustees, trading and tax', para D19) that:

> 'There is no objection in principle to the registration of a charity as part of a VAT group. But before doing so, the trustees need to satisfy themselves that the overall benefits of group registration outweigh the risk of loss to the charity's assets, if those assets have to be used to settle a VAT liability of a trading subsidiary.'

THE BOARD

Make-up of the board

7.167 As a separate legal entity from the charity, the trading subsidiary will need its own board of directors. Since the trading company has a different purpose from the charity (ie to carry out for-profit trading) its board will require persons with some different skills and backgrounds from the charity trustees.

7.168 It is advisable to ensure that there is not a complete overlap, with only charity trustees serving as directors of the trading company. However, some trustees (perhaps two or three, possibly including the chairman and treasurer) should be on its board. It may also be appropriate for employees of the charity, who are not trustees, to be on the trading company's board. There should be at least some independent company directors. This ensures that there is an independent element among the directors, and gives scope for directors with specific expertise and enthusiasms related to the trading company's activities to be recruited. And some trustees of the charity should be independent of the company: they will be in a position to evaluate the relationship between the company and the charity, and the company's performance, properly. This will be particularly important when the charity is considering its investment in the subsidiary (see **7.73–7.141** above and **7.170–7.172** below).

7.169 Those trustees who serve as directors of an associated trading company should not usually find that their duty to act in the best interests of the charity (when acting as trustee) will conflict with their duty to act in the best interests of the trading company (when acting as a director), or indeed their own personal interests. However, they can occasionally find themselves faced with difficult choices and conflicts, particularly if the trading company is undergoing financial problems. There may be similar issues for charity employees serving on the trading subsidiary's board. Examples of situations where conflicts might arise are as follows.

7.170 First, say a charity's trading company is experiencing cash flow difficulties. It has insufficient cash to meet its obligations and there is, in consequence, concern over its financial viability. HMRC is owed considerable sums and is pressing for payment. The board of the trading company requests the charity to lend it a sufficient sum to pay off the pressing creditors and give it some working capital.

7.171 The directors of the trading company will be concerned, from their own personal point of view that the charity backs the trading company. If the charity does not, it will be clear that the company is insolvent, as it cannot pay its debts as they fall due. This means the company will have to be placed in insolvent liquidation, which raises the possibility that aggrieved creditors might petition the liquidator of the trading company to initiate wrongful trading proceedings against the directors of the insolvent trading company (see **11.93–11.98**). If a court held that any of the directors had been guilty of wrongful trading, it could order that the directors concerned should make a contribution from their personal assets towards paying the creditors of the insolvent company. Hence, the directors of the trading company will have a direct financial interest in seeing that the charity gives financial support to the trading company. However, this may not be in the best interests of the charity. For individuals who are both trustees of the charity and directors of the trading subsidiary, this is a situation where their personal wishes may conflict with their duties as trustees. In such circumstances trustees who play such a dual role should be advised to declare their interest at any charity trustees' meeting in any proposal for the charity to give financial support to the trading company. They should not vote on any such proposal.

7.172 This illustrates why it is advisable not to have all the trustees serving as directors of the trading company, since, if they do, it will not be possible for independent trustees to consider a request for financial support to the trading company in such circumstances.

7.173 Secondly, a trading company's wish to maximise its income may affect the charity's reputation, although in some circumstances this will be prohibited by the terms of the charity's investment in the trading subsidiary. In addition, as we see at **7.181**, the directors of the trading subsidiary have a statutory duty to promote the success of the company for the benefit of the members as a whole, so where the charity is the sole shareholder, which is usually the case, the directors of the trading company must not act in a way which harms the charity's interests in any event. Nevertheless, there may be situations where such circumstances give rise to a potential conflict between the interests of the trustees of the charity and those of the trading company directors.

7.174 Thirdly, there may be an argument that a director of the trading subsidiary who is also an employee of the charity is in a position of potential conflict simply by virtue of the fact that the subsidiary is raising funds for the charity and some of those funds may end up being used to pay the employee's salary. However, the authors' view is that potential conflicts along these lines should not give rise to concerns.

7.175 The Companies Act 2006 has introduced a statutory regime for dealing with conflicts of interest: this may be relevant in the situations described above. The rules are outlined at **7.182–7.187**.

7.176 Current Charity Commission guidance (CC35 'Trustees, trading and tax', para D15) recommends that:

'As a matter of good governance, there should be both:

- at least one person who is a trustee, but not a director or employee of the trading subsidiary; and
- at least one person who is a director of the trading subsidiary, but not a trustee or employee of the charity.

These people are described as "unconflicted" as they have no conflict of interest in their roles. These unconflicted trustees and directors should advise their colleagues as to the proper course of action where the duties of those with dual responsibilities are in conflict. This reduces the risk of any transaction between the parent charity and the trading subsidiary being challenged or questioned.'

The authors recommend that at least three charity trustees should not serve on the board of the trading company. They should then be in a position to hold a quorate board meeting of the charity without worrying about conflicts of interest. If, however, the charity's constitution requires more than three trustees for a quorate board meeting, a greater number of 'unconflicted' charity trustees, who do not serve on the board of the trading company, will be required.

Payment of charity trustees

7.177 It should be borne in mind that trustees of the charity cannot be paid for serving as directors of the trading company, unless the constitution of the charity specifically provides for this, there is statutory authority, or the Charity Commission has given its consent. This is based on the fundamental provision of trust law that a trustee should not benefit from his or her trust, which is linked to the notion that trustees must avoid conflicts of interest.

7.178 The Charity Commission guidance (CC35 'Trustees, trading and tax', para D15) states that:

> 'The establishment of a trading subsidiary, where the directors of that subsidiary are the same people as the trustees of the parent charity, cannot be used as a means of paying the charity's trustees "by the back door".'

7.179 In March 2008 the Charities Act 2006 introduced ss 73A–73C into the Charities Act 1993. These provisions give charities a statutory power to pay trustees for services provided to the charity. The power does not extend to payment for acting as a trustee, nor to payment for services provided under a contract of employment. It does not apply where the charity's constitution contains any express provision that prohibits the payment of the remuneration: this is, perhaps surprisingly, quite likely to be the case, so the charity's constitution may need to be changed in order to take advantage of the statutory power. The power is also subject to certain safeguards, including a requirement that the remuneration be reasonable, that it be set out in a written agreement, and that only a minority of trustees receive remuneration from the charity (whether under the statutory power or via any other route) at any one time.

7.180 The authors' view is that there is scope for the statutory power, in principle, to cover payments made to a trustee for serving on the board of a trading subsidiary.

Companies Act 2006 – duties of trading subsidiary directors

7.181 The Companies Act 2006 imposes various duties on company directors. These will apply to the directors of the trading subsidiary. The duties include a duty to act in a way the director considers, in good faith, would be most likely to promote the success of the company for the benefit of the members as a whole (s 172): in the case of a trading subsidiary this will usually mean for the benefit of the parent charity as the sole shareholder. The directors must also exercise independent judgment (s 173) and exercise reasonable care, skill and diligence (s 174): a higher standard of care will be expected of a director who has, or might be expected to have, particular knowledge, skill and experience.

7.182 The Companies Act 2006 also contains various provisions which impose duties to deal properly with conflicts of interest, which came into force in October 2008. Directors must avoid a situation in which they have or could have, 'a direct or indirect interest that conflicts, or possibly may conflict, with the interests of the company' (s 175). They must not accept benefits from third parties (s 176) and must declare an interest in proposed transactions or arrangements (s 177). They must declare interests in existing transactions or arrangements (s 182): failure to comply with this particular obligation is an offence.

7.183 The Companies Act 2006 duties are very widely drafted. The wording of s 175 does not just cover situations where a company director has a personal financial interest in his or her company's affairs – as will be the case where a director is paid by the trading subsidiary. But a trading subsidiary director who is a trustee or employee of the parent charity may, on the face of it, also fall within the scope of s 175, as he may be regarded as having an interest which 'possibly may conflict' with that of the company (see **7.169–7.175**)! Yet it is clearly desirable that charity trustees and employees should be able to sit on the trading subsidiary's board!

7.184 There are, in the authors' view, several ways of dealing with this potential problem. It is worth bearing in mind that the duties are not, in fact, new: they are for the most part a restatement of existing principles which had emerged from case law over the years and which are now written down in statute for the first time. This has provided renewed focus on the desirability of avoiding potentially conflicting situations, so the Companies Act 2006 provisions can in fact be regarded as an opportunity to ensure that any conflicts of interest are identified and properly dealt with. For the most part, the Companies Act can be complied with by ensuring that certain simple procedures are observed.

7.185 Note that the provisions of the Companies Act 2006 are complicated, and a full analysis is beyond the scope of this book, but various suggested ways of dealing with the provisions are:

(1) Section 175(4)(a) provides that the duty to avoid conflicts is not infringed 'if the situation cannot reasonably be regarded as likely to give rise to a conflict of interest'. This will be helpful. As explained at **7.181**, in most situations the directors of the trading subsidiary will have an obligation to act in the best interests of the charity, as sole shareholder, so the interests of the trading subsidiary directors will coincide with those of the charity and there may not be a conflict at all.

(2)   In the case of a non-charitable trading subsidiary, the s 175 duty does not apply to interests in proposed transactions or arrangements: these simply need to be declared under s 177.

(3)   Section 180(4)(b) provides that the duty to avoid conflicts of interest will not be infringed if the company's articles contain appropriate conflicts of interest procedures, and they are followed (note that the procedures must be sufficiently fair to have been considered valid under the pre-Companies Act 2006 law). A procedure which ensures that 'conflicted' directors do not take part in decisions which affect them should be sufficient.

(4)   Section 175(4)(b) provides that in the case of non-charitable companies the duty is not infringed if the matter has been authorised by the directors under provisions set out in s 175(5) and (6): this mechanism is available to directors of companies formed after 1 October 2008, and to older companies if their members agree.

(5)   However, both the 'conflicts of interest procedures' (see para (3)) and 'authorisation' (see para (4)) processes require decisions to be taken by enough 'unconflicted' directors to make up a quorum. In many cases the board of trading subsidiaries may include very few directors who have no relationship with the charity, so there may not be enough 'unconflicted' directors to make up a quorum which can deal with possible conflicts arising from the relationship between the charity and trading subsidiary! However, conflicts can generally be authorised by members' resolution, so if this situation looks likely, a resolution by the parent charity authorising the conflict, and authorising directors with a relationship with the charity to take part in (ie to vote and be counted in the quorum for) decisions which do not affect them personally from a financial point of view may be a way round the problem. In the authors' experience, this may be the most practical way of avoiding potential problems with the Companies Act provisions.

7.186   When considering conflicts of interest it is good practice, at the very least, for trading subsidiary directors to disclose any interest in any actual or potential transaction with which the subsidiary is or may be involved: this would include those who are trustees or employees of the charity making a note of their relationship with the charity. It is sensible to keep a register of directors' interests. It is also appropriate to decide how different types of conflict should be dealt with: charities may be happy for trustees or employees of the charity to vote and be counted in the quorum despite any potential conflict of interest, but require those with a personal financial interest to withdraw from the vote and not be counted in the quorum.

7.187   While the Companies Act duties in relation to conflicts of interest may appear alarming, and at the time of writing are the subject of debate in the charity press, in the authors' view they are unlikely to cause many real problems in practice, provided that trustees and directors are aware of the need to look out for conflicts, and that when conflicts arise they are appropriately dealt with. Charities and their trading subsidiaries simply need to ensure that proper procedures are in place to identify and manage potential conflicts.

Administration

7.188 As a separate legal entity, the trading company will need to have separate board meetings, which are separately minuted. It is important that the boards of the charity and trading company do meet separately, although meetings can clearly be arranged consecutively if this is more convenient, in order to demonstrate that the relationship between the two is indeed on arm's length terms (see **7.190**). The trading company will need to maintain its own set of company books and make its own filings with Companies House (see **7.217–7.218** below).

7.189 Systems must be established to ensure that the charity monitors the trading company's performance and activities. For instance, copies of the minutes of the trading company's board meetings, and its management accounts, should be considered at the trustees' meetings of the charity as a matter of routine. A director of the trading company who is also a charity trustee or employee should have responsibility for reporting on the activities of the trading company at each board meeting, or more regularly to the chief executive of the charity.

THE RELATIONSHIP BETWEEN CHARITY AND TRADING COMPANY

7.190 Charities must bear in mind at all times that trading companies are separate legal entities distinct from the charity, and the relationship between the two organisations should be at arm's length.

Cost sharing

7.191 This has a significant practical implication which is often difficult to understand, namely that there should be no subsidy whatsoever by the charity of the trading company.

7.192 It is more than likely that the charity and its trading company will share facilities in some way. This may be shared office space, shared equipment or shared staff. The charity must ensure that it recovers the proper costs of any of its assets used by the trading company. This should include not only direct costs (eg staff salaries), but indirect costs as well (eg a proper attribution of overheads). The charity should render this management charge to the trading company on a regular basis. This may well demand sophisticated apportionments of employees' time (where an employee works for both organisations) and of overheads (probably based on square footage) and for use of equipment (eg monitoring how much each organisation uses the photocopier). Any subsidy of the trading company could be improper expenditure under charity law, and may be non-charitable expenditure in the eyes of HMRC, which could give rise to tax problems for the charity (see **7.96–7.98**).

7.193 Note that where the trading company is established purely as a vehicle for carrying out primary purpose trading activity which could be carried out by the charity directly, strictly the question of subsidy by the charity will be less of a concern from a charity law and tax law perspective, but the authors would still recommend that costs be shared appropriately in order to avoid potential problems with HMRC (see **7.214**).

7.194 Although the charity must ensure that it does not subsidise the trading company in any way, equally this management charge should not be structured in such a way as to result in the charity making a profit. This is because if it were to make a profit as a result of supplying equipment, staff, etc, this profit would potentially be taxable, since it would not have been generated by primary purpose trading. Providing a management service to a commercial company cannot be a primary purpose of a charity. The charity may not be permitted, under the terms of its constitution, or under charity law (see **2.5–2.33**) to carry out this type of trade! This may seem strange to anyone used to the commercial sector, who will be accustomed to the practice of holding companies (especially in transnational groups) making management charges to subsidiaries designed to strip out profits. But the position is very different with charities. (The position may be different if the charity is in the business of providing these services: the promotion of the efficiency and effectiveness of charities and the effective use of charitable resources is recognised as charitable, and some charities provide office and other facilities with a charitable or social purpose. In such cases, if it can be argued that providing the services to the trading company furthers this charitable purpose (note that this will not always be the case!), there may be a primary purpose trade and the charity may wish to charge a mark-up in order to make a profit.)

7.195 The Charity Commission emphasises (CC35 'Trustees, trading and tax', para D22) that 'Cost-sharing arrangements could be subject to challenge by HMRC Charities, if the costs are not calculated in an acceptable way or shared appropriately'. It is the authors' experience that this is indeed the case.

7.196 It may be necessary to charge VAT on the management charge. This will depend upon the level of VATable turnover of the charity, whether or not it is registered for VAT, and whether or not the charity and the trading company are members of the same VAT group. There can be circumstances in which charging a management fee plus VAT is beneficial to the charity. It is not always fully appreciated that the irrecoverable element of VAT may decrease proportionally as VATable supplies increase. Some charities can consequently benefit by trying to increase their VATable outputs. By charging VAT on management charges, a charity may indirectly increase the amount of input VAT it can recover. This can be an advantage of not putting the charity and the trading company into the same VAT group. Naturally, the trading company should be able to recover all the input VAT on the management charge. Whether or not this is appropriate will depend upon the particular circumstances of individual charities, and specialist VAT advice should be considered.

7.197 Note that the management charge should actually be paid. The Charity Commission notes (CC35 'Trustees, trading and tax', para D22) that:

> 'Such charges must be paid within a reasonable period of time. Unpaid charges can become a significant form of long-term financing, and amount to a form of subsidy of the trading subsidiary by the charity.'

This could prove to be a problem, in cash flow terms, if the trading company is not making money. But if it is making a profit, the management charge is effectively tax-neutral, as it is another way of paying profits to the parent charity (see **7.229–7.231**).

Name and logo

7.198 In many cases, particularly where the trading company is established for pure fundraising purposes, the trading company will be making use of the charity's name and logo, although this may not always be prudent or appropriate (see **7.65–7.67** above). Where the name and logo are to be used by the trading company, the charity must grant the trading company a non-exclusive licence to use its name and logo. (See also **9.79** on granting a licence of a registered trade mark.) In order to avoid any element of subsidy between the charity and the trading company, a reasonable fee should be charged. This could be 1 per cent of the total turnover or a set fee of £1,000 – or more, depending on the size of the organisation.

7.199 It is advisable for the fee to be structured as an 'annual payment' because the income received by the charity will then be exempt from corporation tax under s 505 of ICTA 1988 and exempt from income tax under ITA 2007, s 536. In order to qualify as an annual payment, the agreement between the charity and trading company must be capable of lasting more than a year. This should not cause any great problems in practice. The trading company has to deduct tax from the payment and pay this to HMRC. This income tax can then be recovered by the charity. The trading company should complete Form R185 for each payment and pass this on to the charity as a certificate of payment. The charity will then need to include this payment on its standard claim form R68. The charity should ensure that a staff member takes responsibility for ensuring that the payments of the licence fee, the deduction of income tax and the recovery of that tax are properly dealt with.

7.200 It is sensible for the charity to impose conditions on the use of the name and logo, particularly an obligation to avoid damaging the good name and reputation of the charity, alienating its supporters or conflicting with its objects. The charity should consider whether to impose any additional restrictions on the use of the name and logo by the trading company, for instance seeking prior clearance from the trading company before any sublicensing deals. The charity may use such conditions as a further way of monitoring the activity of the trading company, for instance, by requiring that material bearing the name and/or logo is approved by the charity in advance, or by requiring the trading company to provide it with information about its activities on demand.

Data

7.201   Equally, the trading company may well need access to the charity's data, particularly the names and addresses of its donors, supporters or customers. Where this is the case, the charity should licence the use of this data to the trading company.

7.202   In order to avoid any element of subsidy, a fee should be charged for use of the data. This may well be a nominal fee, unless the data is particularly valuable. The supply of such data for a fee is a VATable supply. Income from the supply will also be taxable in the hands of the charity: HMRC does not accept that such a payment can qualify as an 'annual payment'.

7.203   The supply of the database from a charity to its trading subsidiary must also comply with data protection legislation. Names and addresses of individuals will be regarded as personal data under the Data Protection Act 1998 (see Chapter 9). This has a number of implications including the following three requirements:

- When personal data is collected from individuals they must be informed about the uses to which their data will be put (including, if appropriate, whether it will be shared with others).

- They must also be told the identity of the 'data controller' – ie the person or organisation that will determine how the data is used.

- In some circumstances they will also have to give their consent to the proposed uses of their data.

In deciding how to comply with these requirements, the charity must consider whether the trading company is going to be a separate data controller or whether it will only use the information on behalf of/for the benefit of the charity (in the 1998 Act this is called a 'data processor').

7.204   If the trading company is only a data processor, then individuals do not need to be informed that a separate entity will be processing their data. However, the charity must ensure, in a written agreement with the trading company, that the trading company uses the data only in accordance with the charity's instructions, and has in place adequate security measures in place to prevent misuse of the data.

7.205 If, however, the trading company is to use the database for activities which might be outside the charity's control – for instance, if it enters into a joint venture with other organisations in which the database is used, or because it is carrying out some activities requiring the database which are not charitable – then it may be a 'data controller'. In these circumstances each individual whose data is shared will need to be given the trading subsidiary's identity and information about how it will be using the individual's data, and how it can be contacted. The easiest way to achieve this is to ensure that, at the time an individual's data is collected, they are given a simple statement informing them about the two entities. At the same time, if consent for the use of the data is required, the individual's consent can be obtained.

Premises

7.206 There are special considerations where the charity and trading subsidiary share premises. The trading subsidiary will clearly need to reimburse the charity for use of its premises, to avoid any question of subsidy. The Charity Commission advises (CC35 'Trustees, trading and tax', para D21) that:

> 'Any use of the parent charity's land and buildings by a trading subsidiary should be covered by a formal lease or licence of the property concerned from the charity to the subsidiary.'

This rarely takes place in practice, unless the charity only has a lease itself and has to establish and/or document the trading subsidiary's occupation to the satisfaction of the landlord – otherwise the charity will be in breach of its lease (see below). However, the reality is that the trading company will generally not have exclusive use of any part of the building owned by the charity, so will be a licensee and, more specifically, a charity can control the actions of the trading company and resolve any possible property holding issue. The trading company should therefore only need to reimburse the charity for its share of the cost of using the building, e g utilities, rent, etc. Given that the income received will be offset by the expenses incurred by the charity, there should be no tax charge from this reimbursement. Note that where a charity and trading company share premises, the charity's entitlement to relief from business rates will be affected (see **2.69–2.73** and **4.61–4.68**).

7.207 Where the property is leasehold, it is more than likely that the landlord's consent will be needed to the sharing of occupation by the trading subsidiary, even if this is done by means of an informal licence rather than a lease. Under s 36 of the Charities Act 1993, a charity may not dispose of its property unless certain conditions are met, so a sublease to a trading subsidiary will need to comply. Arguably, a licence is not such a disposal and Charity Commission guidance is unclear on this. The disposition to the trading company is a disposal of land to a connected person, in respect of which special provisions apply.

7.208 Where the trading subsidiary has sole use of premises, there are two options. The charity can take on the premises, and let them on arm's length terms to the trading subsidiary. This will generally be allowed as an investment by the charity, provided the charity has power to make the investment in the premises and the trustees have complied with the relevant investment duties (see **7.80–7.88**). The income should not be taxable in the hands of the charity (see Chapter 6). The advantage of this is that the charity will not pay stamp duty land tax on the purchase. It also ensures that ownership and control of the premises remains in the hands of the charity. Note, however, the Charity Commission's warning (CC35 'Trustees, trading and tax', para D21) that:

> '[the] exemption from stamp duty land tax ... will be lost if the purchase of the land and buildings cannot be justified as an investment of the charity's resources; or is made in order to avoid tax by the trading subsidiary.'

7.209 Alternatively, the trading subsidiary can take on the premises itself. There is no exemption from stamp duty land tax, so this may be a significant cost. Where the value is over £500,000, stamp duty land tax is at 4%. However, if a charity cannot recover all its VAT and a property has to have VAT charged on a sale to the charity, it may be better for the trading company to purchase the property, as it may be able to recover the VAT. The charity will have no responsibility for the premises and associated costs, provided it has given no guarantees in respect of them (as to which see **7.14–7.18** and **7.155–7.164**).

Employees

7.210 Where the charity and trading subsidiary share employees, there are two possible approaches. The employees could remain employed by the charity, with the relevant portion of their salaries being charged to the trading subsidiary under the management charge. Another route is for the employees to be jointly employed by the charity and the trading subsidiary. Joint contracts of employment would need to be in place, ensuring that it is clear which organisation will have responsibility for grievance and disciplinary action. The employees will clearly need to be happy with the arrangement. It is possible that the provisions of the Transfer of Undertakings (Protection of Employment) Regulations 2006 (commonly known as 'TUPE') may apply, depending on the circumstances, which would require, amongst other things, compliance with certain procedures. The advantage of joint contracts is VAT: the charity and trading company will each pay the appropriate part of the employee's salary directly under the terms of the joint contract of employment. The relevant staff costs will, therefore, not form part of the management charge – there is no 'supply' for VAT purposes, and so they will not be liable to

VAT. In practice it is likely that the employees will be paid in full through the charity's payroll and the trading company will reimburse the charity for its share of the staff costs.

7.211 Where the trading subsidiary has sole use of employees, they should be employed in the trading subsidiary's name. The charity does not need to be involved.

7.212 Note that where individuals are employed by the trading subsidiary, and also sit on the trading subsidiary's board of directors, there will be conflict of interest issues under the Companies Act 2006 which need to be addressed (see **7.182–7.187** above).

Agreement

7.213 In order to ensure that the relationship between a charity and its trading company is clear, some charities have a master agreement between the two to regulate their dealings. The topics which an agreement should cover will vary for each case but, broadly speaking, it would be sensible to consider such items as:

(1) Use of the name and logo, and an appropriate fee (see **7.198–7.200**).

(2) Use of the charity's data, and an appropriate fee (see **7.201–7.205**).

(3) Terms for use of the charity's facilities (eg premises, computers, machinery, equipment and staff).

(4) Accounting – production of management accounts and keeping the company's accounting records.

(5) Termination. How much notice should either party have to give in order to terminate the agreement? This may seem somewhat unnecessary in an agreement between a charity and its trading company, but the two are separate entities, and are likely to have different boards of directors. It is important to maintain the distinction in all parties' minds.

Transfer pricing

7.214 Some charity groups may also need to consider the implications of transfer pricing legislation. This can apply when one member of a group charges the other an artificially high or low price in order to obtain a tax advantage. Where applicable, this requires 'arm's-length' pricing of transactions within the charity group for tax purposes, regardless of the terms of the actual agreement between the parent charity and the trading subsidiary. The substitution of an arm's length price for the actual price (for tax purposes) may increase the receipts of a trade, increasing the profits of the trade, and so give rise to a tax liability. It should be noted that this will not be an issue to most charity/trading company relationships, where management charges and staff recharges are made at cost because there is as a result no tax advantage. Also, HMRC does not normally expect charities to commission expensive transfer pricing reports. But nevertheless charities should otherwise be in a position to demonstrate that arrangements are on commercial (ie arm's length) terms.

Bank accounts

7.215   In the authors' view, the charity and trading company should have separate bank accounts. The Charity Commission takes a more relaxed view, saying in its updated guidance (CC35 'Trustees, trading and tax', para D20) that:

> 'The bank accounts of a charity and its trading subsidiary or subsidiaries may be consolidated so long as:
>
> • a proper record is kept of the state of the balances on the individual accounts which have been consolidated;
> • the benefits and burdens of the consolidated account are fairly apportioned between the parent charity and the trading subsidiary or subsidiaries, having regard to the state of the individual accounts; and
> • the consolidation does not result in the charity incurring non-charitable expenditure, creating in turn a potential tax effect, or otherwise suffering a tax disadvantage.'

Notwithstanding this, the authors have real concerns about the practicality and control of a single account, and the risk of charity money being lost if the trading subsidiary is sued. HMRC may also be unhappy about whether a payment of money has been made to the charity under gift aid, if this arrangement is used. All in all, in our view it is better to keep two separate accounts.

7.216   If the trading company receives money on behalf of the charity (eg donations given at the same time as purchases are made through a catalogue), the money should be paid over to the charity immediately.

Minutes

7.217   As mentioned at **7.188** above, separate minutes of the meetings of the board of directors of the trading company should be kept and maintained in separate statutory books as required by company law.

Accounts and company filings

7.218   The trading company will need to prepare its own accounts, although these may also be consolidated with those of the charity (see **7.265**). Separate filings will need to be made to Companies House, including the annual return, report and accounts, details of changes to the memorandum and articles of association, and alterations to the registered office, directors and secretary (if any) on the appropriate forms.

Company information

7.219 The proper information must appear on the trading company's business letters (including emails) and order forms, and on its website, namely:

(1) its registered name (not the charity's) – eg XYZ Limited;

(2) its registered office;

(3) its place of incorporation (ie England and Wales or Scotland);

(4) its registered company number (not the charity's);

(5) the names of all its directors or none of them. You cannot be selective and only put the chairman's name.

The trading company's name must also be displayed at its registered office, any other place of business and any other place where it keeps company records available for inspection under company law. The name must be positioned in a way which means it can be easily seen by any visitors.

Separate identity

7.220 It is very important to ensure that in dealings with the outside world a distinction is maintained between the two organisations. This is particularly important where the trading company is carrying out fundraising activity in close collaboration with the charity. As ever, problems can arise most acutely when there is insolvency. Where funds have been raised by the trading company, but supporters were under the impression that they would be passed straight to the charity, there will, not unnaturally, be disquiet if they subsequently realise that the funds are being used to meet claims against the trading company. Equally, there could be problems for the charity if creditors claim that they thought they were dealing with the parent charity rather than the subsidiary trading company. For example, in the early 1990s a national healthcare charity encountered difficulties when its trading company's creditors claimed that they thought they had been contracting with the parent charity.

7.221 It is therefore vital that staff are aware of the difference between the two organisations. Fundraising teams, in particular, should be briefed on when arrangements with corporate sponsors or fundraising events, for instance, will be run through the charity, and when the trading subsidiary will be involved. It is worth considering 'colour coding' the two organisations so that members of staff are constantly aware of the distinction – for example, the charity could have buff notepaper and the trading company white paper. All purchase orders, invoices, internal memos, letters, etc would be printed on the appropriate paper. Equally, there should be separate and distinct pages on any website. Many charities set up structures which are understood by the chief executive and finance director, but not always fully understood by members of staff lower down in the organisation, which can result in confusion and problems. There can also be difficulties if knowledge on the detail of the charity and trading company relationships rests with only one or two individuals. If they subsequently leave the organisation without briefing their remaining colleagues, problems often arise.

Employee shareholdings/profit bonuses

7.222 Many commercial organisations over the last two decades have taken advantage of legal and tax changes to set up schemes to encourage employee motivation through offering employees a stake in the business, whether through share ownership or share options (which when exercised give the employee shares in the company) or through tax efficient profit-related pay schemes. Charities with trading companies may be encouraged to consider setting up similar schemes for employees of that company, but they should be very wary about doing so. Comparisons between commercial groups of companies and charities are very often misleading and overlook the fundamental objective of a charity, namely to act for the public benefit. Many charities share some of their staff and/or premises with their trading companies. If staff who are partly engaged on the trading company's business know that they may improve their personal financial position by increasing the profits of the trading company, they may well concentrate their efforts on boosting the trading company's activities, to the possible detriment of the charity. Their loyalties will be divided and they will be pulled towards the trading company.

7.223 Moreover, the trading company may need working capital to finance its activities. It may seek this from the charity. That capital may be vital to the company's success and, hence, to the remuneration of the employees. But who will write the report to the trustees requesting that this financial assistance be provided? It could well be employees of the charity who also work for the trading company, and who thus have a vested financial interest in the outcome of the application to the charity for working capital! What is more, the lower the rate of interest charged by the charity on a loan to the trading company, the higher the profits of the trading company might be, which may in turn result in an enhanced profit bonus for staff members! Such a conflict could lead the writer of the report to err on the side of recommending a low rate of interest, which would be a breach of the Charity Commission's guidelines. It may be difficult for volunteer trustees to spot all these ramifications in a short meeting in which they are, understandably, relying on a report prepared by the staff.

7.224 This is but one example of a commercial practice aimed at increasing motivation which could have serious knock-on effects in the very different world of charities. Consequently, charities should act with considerable caution in this area.

TAXATION

Taxation of profits

7.225 While charities enjoy a privileged position so far as direct tax is concerned, trading companies owned by charities will be subject to the normal rules of corporation tax and will pay tax on taxable profits as follows (2008/09 rates):

- 21% on the first £300,000;

- 28% on profits over £1,500,000;

- a marginal rate of between 21% and 28% on profits between £300,000 and £1,500,000.

Bear in mind that the above thresholds are per group of associated companies. In reality, in most charity and trading company situations, there are two associated members – the charity and the trading subsidiary – so, using the above rates, the trading company will pay tax at 21% on the first £150,000, and 28% tax on profits over £750,000, etc.

7.226 The corporation tax year starts on 1 April (and not 6 April, as for other taxes). Corporation tax is charged on the actual tax adjusted profits of each accounting period. This will usually coincide with the period for which the company prepares its annual accounts, but it cannot exceed 12 months. The accounting period may well span two corporation tax years, requiring apportionment of the profits between the two years. For example:

A trading company prepares its audited accounts for the year 1 July 2007 to 30 June 2008. Its profits were £100,000. (Corporation tax rates for 2007/08 were 20% on the first £300,000.) It pays Corporation Tax (CT) as follows.

CT year 1 from 1 April 2007 to 31 March 2008:
CT rate 20%

CT year 2 from 1 April 2008 to 31 March 2009:
CT rate 21%

CT payable for year 1: £100,000 × 275/366 × 20%	£15,027
CT payable for year 2: £100,000 × 91/366 × 21%	£5,221
TOTAL	£20,248

(Note that 2008 was a leap year – hence the use of 366 days in the example, rather than 365!)

7.227 Corporation tax has to be paid 9 months after the end of the accounting period. In this example, the accounting period ended on 30 June

2008. Tax must be paid by 1 April 2009 even if no tax assessment has been received. Corporation tax returns must be submitted within 12 months of the year end.

7.228 However, if the trading company can reduce its taxable profits by giving them away to the charity which controls the trading company, the position changes. There will be *less* or *no* corporation tax to be paid, depending on the level of taxable profits remaining in the trading company at its corporation tax date.

Shedding profits by management charges

7.229 It is standard practice in the commercial world for subsidiary companies to pay a management charge to the holding company in return for the provision of head office and other services. The charge has to be fair and reasonable – if it is excessive, the charge will not be treated as a tax deductible expense in the hands of the subsidiary company because it will be deemed not to have been paid for the purposes of the trade (see ICTA 1988, s 74). But, subject to that caveat, some charity finance directors, accustomed to the practices of the commercial world, may suggest that the simplest method of stripping out taxable profits from the trading company and putting them in the parent charity is for the charity to charge the trading company a management fee.

7.230 As explained at **7.191–7.197**, it is proper, and indeed necessary, for the trading company to reimburse the charity for its share of any facilities (such as office overheads and staff time) used by both organisations. This is generally achieved by the charity levying an appropriate management charge on the trading company. But the level of the charge should be fixed at a level which ensures that the charity is not subsidising the trading company in any way. Equally, the charity should not generally be making a profit on the management charge (see **7.194**).

7.231 To the extent that management charges are paid to the parent charity, the trading subsidiary's taxable profits will be reduced, so the mechanism is tax efficient.

Payment of profit by way of dividends

7.232 Payment of the profits of a wholly owned subsidiary to its parent charity by way of dividend is not tax efficient. Dividends are paid out of taxed profits. So the company will have paid corporation tax of at least 21% before the dividend is paid. To take account of this, the dividend is received by the payee with an attached tax credit. But this is only 10%, and it is no longer possible for charities to reclaim dividend tax credits from HMRC. This means that there is effectively no way of recovering the corporation tax paid by the trading company. For example:

– XYZ Trading Limited has taxable profits for the year ended 31 March 2008 of £90,000.

– Corporation tax of 20% (2007/08 rates) is payable on the profits, ie £18,000.

– The company's net profit after tax is £72,000.

– XYZ Trading Limited declares a 100% dividend and gives to XYZ Charity, its parent charity:
  • a cash dividend of £72,000;
  • a tax credit of £8,000.

– But the charity will be unable to take advantage of the tax credit, which is, in any event, less than the tax paid by the company.

– So the charity receives only £72,000.

If all the trading company's profits – £90,000 – had been paid up to the charity under gift aid, the charity would have received the entire £90,000.

Payment of profit using gift aid

7.233 The simplest, most tax-efficient way for a trading subsidiary to pay its profits to its parent charity (or charities in the case of a trading company set up as a joint venture by two or more charities) is by way of gift aid.

7.234 Gift aid was introduced in the 1990 Budget, as a tax-effective mechanism for making single payments to charity. The gift aid regime has been simplified and extended over the years. It now applies in the following way.

7.235 Where a company makes a payment to charity out of its profits, the level of profit which is chargeable to corporation tax is reduced by the amount of the payment. In technical terms, the payment is not treated as a distribution of profit, but as a 'qualifying donation' and charge on income under ICTA 1988, s 339. This means that if a trading company pays the whole of its taxable profits to charity, its taxable profits will be reduced to nil, and it will have no corporation tax to pay.

7.236 Depending on cash flow and many other factors, the trading company may choose to make the gift aid payment(s) in the accounting period concerned, or may choose to make the payments after the year end. Where the trading company is wholly owned by one or more charities (see **7.239–7.250** for more detail on joint ownership of a trading company) the gift aid payment may be made at any time within 9 months of the end of the relevant accounting period. This should allow the trading company sufficient time to work out what its taxable profits are, particularly since for accounting periods beginning on or after 1 April 2008 companies must file their accounts with Companies House within 9 months of the year end. The charity must make a claim to HMRC within 2 years of the end of the accounting period during which the donation is actually paid, to the effect that the donation should be treated as paid in the earlier accounting period. For example:

–   XYZ Trading Limited makes taxable profits of £100,000 in the financial year ended 31 December 2008.

–   On 30 August 2009 it makes a payment of £100,000 to XYZ Charity.

–   In December 2011 XYZ Trading makes a claim for the August 2009 donation to be treated as if it was paid during the tax year ended 31 December 2008.

–   This reduces the level of XYZ Trading Limited's taxable profits for the accounting period ended 31 December 2008 to nil.

7.237   There are certain restrictions on gift aid. A payment will not be a 'qualifying donation' if:

•   it is made subject to a condition as to repayment;

•   the company or a connected person (defined in the legislation) receives a benefit which exceeds a certain defined value in relation to the payment;

•   it is conditional on or part of an arrangement involving the charity acquiring property (other than as a gift) from the company or a connected person; or

•   it is made by a charity.

These are unlikely to cause problems in relation to straightforward payments of profits by a trading company, but charities should be aware of them.

7.238   Prior to the introduction of gift aid, trading companies donated their profits to charities via deeds of covenant. Where deeds of covenant remain in place, they are still legally binding, but the advantages associated with them no longer exist. Instead, payments made under deeds of covenant will be treated as donations to which the gift aid regime applies.

JOINT VENTURES

7.239   It is perfectly possible for a charity's trading operations to represent a joint venture between the charity and others. There are a myriad of ways of structuring third party involvement in a charity's trading activity.

Practical considerations

7.240 Whenever a charity is thinking of collaborating with a third party, certain safeguards should be observed. The greater the degree of involvement by the third party in the charity's activities, the more important it is that the charity spends time in ensuring that it is happy with the association. For instance, greater research and preparation will be needed before setting up a jointly owned trading subsidiary with another organisation than is necessary where a charity is simply accepting a small one-off grant in support of its trading enterprise.

7.241 The factors which should be taken into account include:

- Will the association with this person or organisation damage the charity's reputation? (See **5.90–5.92** for more on collaboration with commercial organisations.)

- What conditions are attached to the third party's support? Are they the best that can be obtained in the circumstances?

- Is the charity happy about the financial status of the third party? Have appropriate due diligence checks been carried out?

- Are the parties agreed on the level of their respective investment and involvement in the venture?

- Are non-competition provisions required?

- How will intellectual property be shared?

- How will the risks be shared between the parties?

- What provision will be made for agreeing the various stages of the project? Who will represent each party? Who will be the lead party or lead member of staff? How often will the respective parties meet?

- How will disagreements be resolved?

- How will the parties extricate themselves from the arrangement if problems arise?

- The details of the arrangement should be properly documented. It is particularly important that the objectives of the joint venture arrangement are agreed and written down in advance.

- If the partners are to co-own a trading subsidiary, how will the board of directors be made up and how will the shares be owned? How will the company and its shares be valued as and when the arrangement comes to an end?

7.242 Third party support may take any number of forms: from grant, to loan, to support in kind, such as secondment of staff, to full-blown equity investment. There are particular issues to bear in mind where a charity and a third party are to share ownership of a trading company. These are outlined below.

Gift aid

7.243 As explained at **7.233–7.238**, typically a charity will extract any profits from its trading subsidiary by way of gift aid payment from the trading subsidiary to the charity. Where the trading subsidiary is 100% owned by the charity, the payment may be made at any time within 9 months of the relevant accounting period.

7.244 Since April 2006 this method of extracting profits has also been available where a trading company is owned by more than one charity. Provided all shareholders are charities, payments can be made to shareholders under gift aid, and the payments may be made at any time within 9 months of the end of the accounting period. The payments may be made in proportion to the shareholdings. For example:

– The shares in XYZ Trading Limited are all owned by Charity A and Charity B. Charity A owns 75% of the shares and Charity B owns 25%.

– XYZ Trading Limited makes a taxable profit of £10,000 in the financial year ending on 31 December 2008.

– On 31 January 2009 XYZ Trading Limited makes a donation of £7,500 to Charity A and a donation of £2,500 to Charity B and makes a claim for these donations to be treated as if they had been paid during the year ended 31 December 2008.

– The donations qualify as gift aid payments, reducing XYZ Trading Limited's taxable profits to nil.

7.245 The position is different where the shares are owned by a charity and another person or organisation which is not a charity, for example an individual or a non-charitable company.

7.246 In these circumstances the trading company can, in principle, make gift aid payments to charities, including charities which own shares in the company. However, these must actually be made during the relevant financial year: the nine-month carry back period does not apply.

7.247 Most importantly, a payment by a trading company to a charity which owns shares in that company will not qualify for gift aid relief where the payment is a 'distribution in respect of shares in the company'. HMRC will argue that payment is akin to a dividend which (as we have seen at **7.232**) is not tax deductible. For example:

– The shares in XYZ Trading Limited are all owned by Charity A and B Limited, which is not a charity. Charity A owns 75% of the shares and B Limited owns 25%.

– XYZ Trading Limited makes a taxable profit of £10,000 in the financial year ending on 31 December 2008.

– On 31 January 2009 XYZ Trading Limited makes a payment of £7,500 to Charity A and a payment of £2,500 to B Limited.

– If, as is likely, HMRC argues that these payments are distributions in respect of the shareholdings of Charity A and B Limited, they will not qualify for gift aid relief.

7.248 Whether a payment by a trading company to a charity is regarded as a distribution in respect of shares is a question of fact. HMRC's 'Detailed guidance notes for charities' (ch 3, para 3.22.2) read as follows:

'Broadly, any payment made by a company to a charity in its capacity as a shareholder is regarded as a distribution in respect of shares in the company, and as such will not qualify as a Gift Aid donation (ie as a charge on income). Factors that HMRC would take into account in deciding whether a payment is a distribution, made to a charity in respect of its shareholding, would include evidence from underlying documents (eg the company's minutes of meetings; correspondence between the company and its shareholders; whether payments were made to the non-charity shareholders – and if so when and in what amounts).'

It is the authors' experience that a clear board minute agreeing a gift aid payment will decide the issue.

7.249 There is, however, a way of structuring a relationship between a charity and a non-charity in a more tax-efficient manner, through the use of a limited liability partnership, taking advantage of the fact that a limited liability partnership is transparent for tax purposes. For example:

– Charity A owns all the shares in a trading subsidiary, Charity A Trading Limited. Charity A Trading Limited and B Limited, which is not a charity, decide to enter into joint venture arrangements using a limited liability partnership, XYZ LLP.

- The arrangements are formalised in a partnership agreement. Charity A Trading Limited will receive 75% of the profits and B Limited will receive 25%. XYZ LLP is registered at Companies House.

- The profits of XYZ LLP during the year ended 31 December 2008 are £10,000. These are paid up to the partners in the appropriate proportions, namely £7,500 to Charity A Trading Limited and £2,500 to B Limited.

- For tax purposes, these are treated as belonging to the partners: the LLP does not itself pay tax.

- Charity A Trading Limited has received £7,500. This is taxable, as Charity A Trading Limited is not a charity, but tax can be avoided to the extent that Charity A Trading Limited pays its profits up to Charity A under gift aid!

- B Limited has received £2,500, on which it will pay tax.

Investment

7.250 A charity's duties as regards investment in a trading company and sharing resources with a trading company will be particularly important where the charity does not own all of the shares in the trading company. When committing any investment or resources, the charity must be alert to the fact that the company is partly owned by a third party, which makes consideration of these issues much less straightforward.

COMMUNITY INTEREST COMPANIES

7.251 The community interest company is a special type of company which has been available since 2005. A community interest company (or 'CIC') may be structured as a company limited by shares or a company limited by guarantee, and it may be a private or public limited company. A CIC must be registered with Companies House, and all the usual company law rules about accounts, filings, meetings and so on apply.

7.252 However, a separate layer of regulation also applies to CICs. The Companies (Audit, Investigations and Community Enterprise) Act 2004 and secondary legislation made under that Act impose restrictions on the activities of the CIC and a statutory 'asset lock' which cannot be removed. CICs are subject to the supervision of the Community Interest Company Regulator, an independent public office holder whose function is to encourage development of the CIC brand and provide assistance and guidance on CIC issues (see www.cicregulator.gov.uk).

Community interest test

7.253 In order to be registered as a CIC the company must satisfy a community interest test. The test is whether a reasonable person might consider that the company's activities are being carried on for the benefit of the community. The assessment is carried out on the basis of information provided in the application to register the company as a CIC, in which the directors are asked about the community the CIC seeks to serve, its activities and how those activities benefit the community.

7.254 The CIC must continue to meet the community interest test and provide evidence of this during the course of its existence, which it does by sending a community interest company report with its annual accounts to Companies House, both of which are placed on the public record.

Asset lock

7.255 The 'asset lock' means that the assets of the CIC, and the income and profits generated by it, must be applied for the benefit of the community. The asset lock imposes obligations that:

– restrict the transfer of assets at less than full market value (unless to another asset-locked body, ie another CIC or a charity, or applied in the community interest);

– cap the amount of dividends a CIC can pay to its shareholders (currently dividends must be no higher than 5% above the prevailing Bank of England base lending rate, by reference to the paid up nominal value of the share, with an aggregate dividend cap of 35% of the company's distributable profits in any year: these limits may be amended by the CIC Regulator);

– cap the amount of interest paid on performance-related loans (this is currently limited to 4% above the prevailing Bank of England base lending rate: again it may be amended by the CIC Regulator); and

– require that on dissolution any surplus assets must be paid to another asset-locked body (ie a charity or another CIC), which must be specified, or will be chosen by the CIC Regulator in consultation with the directors at the time.

Other features

7.256 There are no tax advantages to CIC status: CICs pay corporation tax on their profits like other companies. Directors of CICs may be paid, provided their pay is not so high that it calls the company's community interest focus into question.

7.257 The name of a community interest company must end with the words 'community interest company' or the initials 'c.i.c.'.

Establishing a trading subsidiary as a CIC

7.258 It is perfectly possible for the trading subsidiary of a charity to be established as a community interest company. However, it is not necessary, and the pros and cons need to be fully understood.

7.259 One of the main advantages to CIC status is that those who found and subsequently devote resources to the company can be confident that the company's assets must always be used to further the community interest, except to the limited extent allowed by the payment of dividends. There is no danger that the company's assets will, at the end of the day, simply be paid to the shareholders. However, this is much less of an issue where the company is wholly owned by a charity. The shares in the company represent assets of the charity, and the charity is, in any event, obliged to use all its assets in furtherance of its charitable purposes. If the trading company were wound up, all of its remaining assets would necessarily be used for charitable purposes.

7.260 The position would be different if the charity did not own all of the shares in the CIC. This might be the case if the company was only part-owned by the charity from the outset, or if some or all of the charity's shares were transferred to a third party at some stage in the future. The charity would know that, even if the company were wound up, its surplus assets would not be distributed to its shareholders, but must be used in the community interest. The CIC may be a way of ensuring that a joint venture with a commercial partner is not manipulated against the charity's interest.

7.261 On the other hand, the 'asset lock' will almost certainly make the CIC less attractive to other owners. Third parties will be interested in acquiring shares in the trading company for two reasons: either because they are interested in the trading subsidiary's work and wish to support it, or because they hope to make a financial return. Those who wish to support the work of the charity and its trading subsidiary may not be put off by community interest company status: they may be happy to accept that they will receive limited dividends, and no entitlement to share in the capital growth of the assets of the company on a winding up. But those who wish to make a commercial return from their interest in the company will undoubtedly be concerned about the negative impact which the asset lock has on their rights to dividend and capital returns. These concerns would not apply if the trading subsidiary had been established as a straightforward limited company.

7.262 Note where the CIC is owned by one or more charities the dividend cap will not be a concern, as in this case the charity or charities will not generally be paid by way of dividend, but under gift aid (see **7.233–7.238**).

7.263 Another main advantage of CIC status is branding: there is a certain amount of goodwill associated with the CIC brand, and the hope is that this will grow over time as the CIC becomes more well-known. Where the trading company has a name which clearly associates it with the parent charity, branding is unlikely to be a concern, since the trading company will be profiting from the charity's goodwill. Where the trading company has a name which does not automatically demonstrate its public interest nature, CIC status can be a useful reminder to the public of the non-profit and social aims of the business.

7.264 It is always possible to convert a straightforward company limited by shares, or by guarantee, into a CIC after it has been established. The memorandum and articles will need to be altered to include provision for the 'asset lock'. It is not possible for a CIC, once established, to lose CIC status, unless it converts to a charity.

CONSOLIDATION OF ACCOUNTS

7.265 While both charities and trading subsidiaries will need to prepare their own accounts, when should the accounts of the trading subsidiary be consolidated into those of the parent charity? The Statement of Recommended Practice 2005 (or 'SORP') contains a specific section on the consolidation of accounts. Subject to a few exceptions, consolidated accounts will be required if:

(1) The gross income of the group exceeds the threshold set out in regulations made under the Charities Act 1993. At the time of writing the threshold for charities in England and Wales, for financial years beginning from 1 April 2008, is £500,000, after consolidation adjustments.

(2) The parent charity is a company and company law requires consolidation. The rules on consolidation of company accounts are governed by the Companies Act 2006. The rules are detailed, and advice should be taken from an accountant, but broadly speaking if two of the following conditions are met in relation to the group, consolidated accounts will not be required under company law:
    •   Aggregate turnover of not more than £6.5 million net, or £7.8 million gross.
    •   Aggregate balance sheet total of not more than £3.26 million net, or £3.9 million gross.
    •   Not more than 50 employees.

It is always open to charity trustees which fall outside these limits to choose to consolidate the accounts. SORP sets out the method of consolidation.

CONCLUSION

7.266   Use of a trading subsidiary is a tried and tested way of dealing with the tax and charity law restrictions on a charity carrying out non-primary purpose trading. However, the establishment and running of a trading subsidiary have their own complications, relating to investment, administration, cost-sharing and finance. All of these need to be properly understood before setting up and funding a subsidiary trading company.

Chapter 8

CONTRACTS AND THE REGULATION OF TRADING

8.1 *This chapter, and the chapters which follow it, deal with the rules which apply to anyone carrying on a trade, be they a charity or not. This chapter covers broad principles of contract law and other relevant areas including consumer protection, internet and electronic trading, advertising and competition law. Chapter 9 covers intellectual property and Chapter 10 insurance, while Chapter 11 deals with the rules on insolvency.*

INTRODUCTION

8.2 Any trading activity, by its very nature, involves contractual relationships. Charities and their trading companies enter into contracts all the time: whether for the sale of goods in a charity shop or via a website, the supply of a service, the sale of tickets to a fundraising event, the grant of rights of entry to a historic property, or the licensing of a charity's name and logo to a commercial organisation. It is therefore essential to have some understanding of the general principles of contract law, including what terms may be implied into contracts and what terms may be excluded.

8.3 Organisations which trade are also subject to a host of regulations – from product safety to electronic commerce rules, from advertising standards to competition law. The amount of regulation is vast and increases almost daily. As earlier chapters show, the range of trading activity carried out by charities is enormously varied. We do not claim to provide a comprehensive guide to the regulations affecting all charity trading, but seek in this chapter to identify significant legislation and regulations that currently apply to broad areas of trading activity. We discuss the rules on product safety and consumer protection, special regulations which apply to business conducted electronically (including practical tips on running an online shop), legal restrictions on advertising and competition law.

8.4 Charities would be well advised to seek specific advice to ensure contracts are valid and that they are not inadvertently breaching the law.

CONTRACTS

General principles of contract law

8.5   Many people think that a contract has to be written. That is wrong. It does not. Only some contracts are required by law to be in writing, e g contracts for the sale of land, hire purchase agreements, guarantees, assignments of copyright, and some insurance contracts. Otherwise, an oral or verbal agreement is quite sufficient. Moreover, a contract may be part written, part oral. So, just because there is a written contract does not mean that statements made at the time of the contract are not part of the contract. They may be, depending on the nature of the statements and the terms of the contract.

8.6   In most cases, however, it is much more practical and sensible to try to record an agreement between parties in writing.

8.7   At **8.8–8.52** we explore the basic principles of contract law, implied contractual terms and standard terms of business.

Existence of a contract

8.8   When is a contract made? For a contract to exist there must be three elements:

- an offer to enter into a contract (e g 'I would like to buy your car.');

- an acceptance ('OK.'); and

- consideration has to pass, ie some value must be given or contemplated ('So we agree, I'll buy your car for £1,000.' 'Yes, it's a deal.').

Note that a contract is only complete when all these elements come together. There must be:

(a)   an offer: and

(b)   an acceptance of the offer (not a counter-offer, e g '£1,000 is not enough, but I'll take £1,100.').

8.9   Once the offer is accepted, the contract is made. With mail order the contract commences when the supplier posts an acceptance letter, a confirmation, or the goods (whichever comes first) to the customer. Offers and acceptances can be communicated by email, but the courts have not yet ruled when acceptance is deemed communicated. It seems likely that communication is effective when it is received (rather than when it is sent).

8.10   Usually the parties will agree the price before the offer is accepted.

Terms of the contract

8.11 Some terms are implied into a contract in order to reflect certain minimum standards imposed by law in relation to the supply of goods or services (see **8.18–8.19**). In addition to these minimum standards, businesses draw up their own terms and conditions of varying degrees of complexity. They are frequently compressed in small print on the back of invoices, order forms or business notepaper, or may appear on an organisation's website (see **8.96–8.98**). They may appear on notice boards. Some typical points to be included in such standard terms and conditions are considered at **8.52**.

8.12 But what is the status of such terms and conditions? Is the contract governed by them? The answer is that such conditions will usually govern the contract, subject to a few basic points.

(a) The conditions must be brought to the other party's attention before he (or she) makes the contract. Hence, it is no use for a charity's trading company to rely on a statement made in its terms and conditions which limits its liability when the terms and conditions are sent out after a customer has ordered goods from a catalogue. However, if the customer had seen the terms having previously received goods through the catalogue, he would almost certainly be considered to be aware of the statement by virtue of having seen it previously. This principle applies equally to trading over the internet (see **8.96–8.98**).

(b) The last terms and conditions specified before acceptance of an offer apply to the contract. In the legal world this is known as the 'battle of the forms'. What happens if XYZ orders goods from ABC and sends a purchase order to ABC? On the back of XYZ's purchase order are its standard terms and conditions and they state that XYZ's terms are to apply. On receipt of the order ABC sends a confirmation notice, including ABC's standard terms and conditions! ABC produces the goods and sends them off with a delivery note, again including ABC's terms. XYZ accepts the goods. ABC despatches an invoice, also incorporating ABC's terms and conditions.

   If there is a dispute over the contract (eg over the quality of ABC's goods), whose terms and conditions apply? This is a very real problem. The general rule is that the applicable terms are the last ones despatched before conclusion of the contract. Hence, in this illustration, ABC's terms would apply.

(c) If there is any ambiguity or uncertainty in the contract terms, these will be interpreted against the person who inserted them and now seeks to rely on them.

(d) Some terms may be unreasonable, unfair and/or unenforceable due to being in breach of various protective legislation (see **8.22–8.28**).

8.13 Not every charity or its associated trading company will need to draw up terms and conditions of business. It will depend on the nature and complexity of the business in which it is involved (see **8.47–8.52**).

Signing contracts

8.14 The conventional mode of establishing a contract is both parties signing a copy of the agreed terms and conditions. Sometimes contracts are signed in 'counterpart', ie each party signs one copy and exchanges it for the other. In addition, documents can be signed electronically.

8.15 Electronic signatures, including digital signatures, are the electronic equivalent of written signatures and the main issue, therefore, is to guarantee their authenticity and the security of the information communicated. There are a number of ways to do so, including encryption, where the content of the communication is encoded so that it can only be read by its intended recipient, or the use of digital certificates that are attached to an email account and authenticate communications and documents signed by the holder of the account. For encryption and digital certificates to be used, both the sender and the recipient of the information must have appropriate software and agree to these methods being used. See www.tscheme.org for details of approved suppliers of digital certificates.

8.16 In practice, emailed confirmation of agreement is, in many circumstances, sufficient.

Buying and selling goods and services

Types of contract

8.17 Where charities or their associated trading companies are involved in selling goods and/or services, it is important for them to distinguish between two types of contract:

(a) consumer contracts: the contract is made with the consumer (eg a charity shop in a museum sells a book to a customer); and

(b) non-consumer contracts: the contract is made with a business (eg a charitable consultancy undertakes work for a government department).

Implied terms

8.18 The Sale of Goods Act 1979 and the Supply of Goods and Services Act 1982 lay down certain fundamental terms about the sale of goods and contracts for the supply of goods and services. These are:

(a) That the seller has the right to sell the goods (ie if the goods turn out to be stolen, the purchaser can claim his money back).

(b)   That the goods are of satisfactory quality (ie fit for their normal expected use).

(c)   That if the purchaser makes known to the seller a particular purpose for which the purchaser wishes to use the goods, the goods must be fit to fulfil that particular purpose rather than being of general satisfactory quality.

(d)   That the goods are as described.

(e)   In a contract where goods are purchased following the inspection of a sample, the bulk of the goods will correspond with the sample in quality. The goods should be free from defects which would not be noticed on examining the sample.

8.19   The term 'satisfactory quality' is defined by reference to what a reasonable person would think is satisfactory quality in the circumstances, taking into account any description of the goods, price and other relevant circumstances. But the obligation to sell goods of satisfactory quality is not an obligation to sell perfect goods. Minor blemishes, scratches, etc are not usually considered to be a breach of the obligations. A lower standard is generally expected for second-hand goods than for new goods, but a seller can still be sued for breach of contract if it sells donated goods which are not of satisfactory quality.

Misrepresentation

8.20   A representation is a statement of fact made by one party to a contract to another which does not form part of the contract but is one of the reasons that the second party enters into the contract. A misrepresentation is a representation that is untrue. It is covered both by the general law and by the Misrepresentation Act 1967.

8.21   The law of misrepresentation is unfortunately extraordinarily complex for what should be a straightforward matter. A brief summary is:

(a)   Not all statements made by salespeople are representations. The law accepts that they use exaggerated language to sell their wares (eg 'great value', 'unbeatable'). These are known as 'puffs'; just because the item is not 'unbeatable' does not mean the customer can claim misrepresentation.

(b)   A statement of opinion is not a representation (ie 'That is a fantastically interesting book.'). So, if a consumer purchased a book on such recommendation in a charity shop and found it to be deeply boring, they could not claim that there had been a misrepresentation.

(c) Misrepresentation must relate to a fact (eg 'These bookshelves will last indefinitely.'). If the bookshelves collapse after 3 months, this would be a misrepresentation, even if the seller honestly believed the statement to be true. It is still a misrepresentation.

(d) The misrepresentation must have been relied on to the buyer's detriment.

(e) Misrepresentation can be written or oral.

Proving a misrepresentation has been made is often very difficult, as it will frequently be a case of the purchaser's word against that of the salesperson. If the purchaser has an independent witness, they will find it easier to prove their case.

Contracting out

8.22 It is possible, to some extent, to contract out of the terms set out in the Sale of Goods Act 1979, the Supply of Goods and Services Act 1982 and the Misrepresentation Act 1967 in business and consumer contracts. However, charities should seek legal advice before trying to contract out of these terms, as such restrictions may fall foul of the Unfair Contract Terms Act 1977 and the Unfair Terms in Consumer Contracts Regulations 1999 (SI 1999/2083). The rules for consumer and business contracts are given below.

8.23 For consumer contracts:

(1) The seller cannot avoid liability by any contract term or notice for death or personal injury arising from its negligence. For example, the Youth Hostels Association cannot avoid liability should a youth hosteller be injured or killed at a youth hostel because of its negligence.

(2) The seller cannot exclude its obligations under the Sale of Goods Act 1979 and the Supply of Goods and Services Act 1982 to sell only goods for which it has title. Hence, a charity shop cannot sell stolen goods without being in breach of the Acts.

(3) The seller cannot exclude its liability under the Sale of Goods Act 1979 and the Supply of Goods and Services Act 1982 to sell goods that are of satisfactory quality, fit for a particular purpose or as described. However, in the case of the sale of second-hand goods, the standard of care will be lower than for new goods.

(4) The seller can exclude liability for misrepresentation, if this is 'reasonable', as laid down in the Unfair Contract Terms Act 1977 (see the 'reasonableness' test at **8.26–8.27** below).

(5)   Under the Unfair Terms in Consumer Contracts Regulations 1999, any term which the consumer can show to be 'unfair' will not be legally binding on the consumer.

(6)   The Office of Fair Trading ('OFT') has issued guidance to suggest that a term using the expression 'consequential loss' may be unfair when attempting to limit or exclude liability. This is on the basis that consumers may be unclear about the meaning of 'consequential loss'. The OFT suggests that less ambiguous wording should be used instead, eg 'we will only pay costs which are incurred as a direct consequence of the event which leads to a claim by you under this policy'.

8.24   For business contracts:

(1)   The seller cannot avoid liability by any contract term or notice for death or personal injury arising from its negligence.

(2)   The seller cannot exclude the obligation under the Sale of Goods Act 1979 to sell goods for which it has title.

(3)   The seller can exclude its obligation under the Sale of Goods Act 1979 to sell goods that are as described or sampled or of satisfactory quality or fit for a particular purpose, provided that it is 'reasonable' to do so. The requirement that the exclusion be 'reasonable' only applies if the contract is made on standard written terms of business. If a charity or its trading company negotiates an individual contract with its business customer (or vice versa) the parties can contract out of these various obligations, even if that appears to be 'unreasonable'.

(4)   The seller can exclude liability for misrepresentation, again if this is 'reasonable'.

(5)   The seller can exclude any other liabilities arising from a breach of the contract, eg for delay, distress or economic loss, if this is 'reasonable'.

The reasonableness test and the fairness test

8.25   Clearly it is crucial to determine whether or not an exclusion of liability clause is 'reasonable' or 'fair' within the meaning of the relevant legislation. If it is 'reasonable' or 'fair', the trader can exclude or limit liability under the contract to a very considerable degree. If it is not 'reasonable' or 'fair' to exclude liability, then the trader will have much more extensive contractual obligations.

8.26   The test of what is or is not reasonable depends on the court's interpretation of s 11 of the Unfair Contract Terms Act 1977, which provides that the exclusion of liability clause shall be 'fair and reasonable ... having regard to the circumstances which were, or ought reasonably to have been, known or in the contemplation of the parties when the contract was made'. Section 11 gives a judge some guidelines to apply when considering whether or not a clause is 'reasonable'. These include the following:

(1)   The relative bargaining strength of the parties (eg can XYZ charity with annual turnover of £1 million really negotiate a contract on equal terms with the UK Department for International Development?).

(2)   Did one party receive an inducement to accept the terms (eg 'accept my terms, and I shall reduce the price by 10%')?

(3)   Were the terms widespread in the trade, and were they therefore well known (such that the customer ought reasonably to have known of their existence) or had there been any previous dealings?

(4)   Were the goods manufactured, processed or adapted to the special order of the purchaser?

(5)   Where liability is limited to a specific limit (eg 'maximum liability accepted £500'), could the supplier have covered the risk by insurance and, if so, at what cost?

8.27   As an illustration of how the reasonableness test works, in one case the defendants supplied £130 worth of cabbage seeds. The seeds were useless – they were not cabbage seeds. No cabbages grew. The plaintiff farmer sued for his loss of profit on the crop (£61,000). The defendants tried to rely on an exclusion clause which limited their liability to the cost of the seeds (£130), but it was held by the court that the exclusion clause was unreasonable, and damages were awarded to the farmer for the loss of his profit (£61,000).

8.28   Under reg 5(1) of the Unfair Terms in Consumer Contracts Regulations 1999 a term is 'unfair' if it causes a significant imbalance in the positions of the parties to the detriment of the consumer in a way which is contrary to the principles of good faith.

Breach of contract

8.29   A breach of contract occurs when one of the parties to the contract fails to fulfil one of the terms of the contract. What happens if there is a breach of contract?

Breach by the seller

8.30   Assuming there are no valid exclusion clauses in a consumer contract, a buyer has a right to reject goods up to the point that he, she or it has 'accepted' them, although this right is quite limited.

8.31 Acceptance is not the same as payment. The buyer is not treated as having accepted the goods until he, she or it has had a reasonable opportunity to inspect them to see whether they conform to the contract (although this right to inspect post payment can be excluded in business to business contracts).

8.32 As ever, the word 'reasonable' crops up! What is a 'reasonable' opportunity to inspect the goods? Again, the law is by no means clear. There have not been many cases concerning this section of the Sale of Goods Act 1979. In one case in 1987 involving a family Nissan car, the High Court said that keeping a brand new car for 3 weeks, despite many complaints, constituted 'acceptance'. So, a buyer wishing to reject goods needs to act quickly.

8.33 However, subsequent case law has indicated that what is a reasonable time must be flexible and should involve a balancing act between the interests of the buyer and seller.

8.34 It is sensible not to have faulty goods repaired by the supplier, because acceptance of the repair can be deemed to be acceptance of the goods. If a buyer properly rejects goods, he is entitled to have his money back.

8.35 If it is too late to reject the goods and thus cancel the contract, the buyer can still claim damages for all losses 'naturally and directly' flowing, in the ordinary course of events, from the breach of contract. The precise amount of damages to be claimed will depend on the circumstances.

Non-delivery by the seller

8.36 The buyer may buy similar replacement goods (if available) at the normal market price and claim the difference (if any) from the seller. If the buyer cannot buy alternative goods, then it can sue for the loss of profit it would have made on resale of the goods, but is unable to make because the goods were not available.

Delay in delivery

8.37 If a seller makes a late delivery of a profit-earning item (e g machinery), the buyer can recover damages for loss of use based on normal use made of that item. This sort of loss is described as 'consequential'.

Defective quality

8.38 If the goods are of defective quality, the measure of damages for the breach of contract will be that the seller should pay the buyer the sum necessary to put it in the position in which it would have been had the contract been performed. Any loss must have been reasonably within the contemplation of the parties. For example:

(a)   The difference between the actual value of the delivered goods and the value they would have had if they complied with the original contract.

(b)   Any fine the buyer has to pay because of the defects (eg caused by food being unfit for human consumption).

(c)   The buyer's loss of profit on a subsale (eg where the seller knows the buyer intends to re-sell the goods and it is 'reasonable' to expect that the seller knew the buyer would lose profits if the goods were defective).

(d)   Compensation for physical injury to the buyer because of the defects.

(e)   Compensation for damage to other property of the buyer (for example, in one case dairy farmers bought meal for feeding to their pheasants. Many chicks died and others grew up stunted, as the meal contained a toxic substance. It was held that the farmer could recover damages for the loss of the birds and the reduced value of the survivors).

Obligation to mitigate

8.39   The buyer's right to claim damages for breach is subject to a very important obligation. The buyer must take reasonable steps to reduce or 'mitigate' its loss. It cannot sit back, do nothing and let the damages mount up. It must, so far as is reasonable, try to limit the damage to its business. If it succeeds in avoiding its loss, then it can make no claim for damages. Any expenses or losses it incurs in carrying out its duty to mitigate its loss are recoverable from the seller, even if the attempts to mitigate fail.

Seller's remedies for buyer's breach of contract

8.40   The normal way in which a contract is broken by a buyer is by its failure to pay. Direct remedies include:

(a)   If the seller has control of the goods it can exercise a lien. A lien is the right to retain goods until they are paid for.

(b)   If the buyer becomes insolvent whilst the goods are in transit, the seller can tell the carrier to stop the goods and, if the seller wishes, to bring them back.

(c)   The seller can retain ownership or title of the goods, even after they have been delivered and accepted by the buyer. This requires a special clause in the seller's terms and conditions of business, known as a 'reservation of title' clause. If the seller's terms and conditions apply to the contract and contain such a clause, the seller can go into the buyer's premises and seize back its goods which have not been paid for.

It is essential to ensure that any reservation of title clause is well drafted, and legal advice should be taken on this. Such clauses can be very useful. Charities or their trading companies which sell wholesale goods or raw materials, or receive payments by instalments, should consider including such a clause in their terms and conditions of business.

(d) Sue for the price. If the seller cannot exercise any direct remedies, it can sue for the price of the goods delivered plus interest.

The supply of services – additional points

8.41 Under the Supply of Goods and Services Act 1982 suppliers of services (e g charities giving consultancy advice; housing associations repairing houses) have a duty to exercise reasonable care and skill in providing them. This applies only where the services are provided as part of a business. It does not apply to services given by a charity free of charge.

8.42 But what is 'reasonable care and skill'? This test leaves much room for interpretation and potentially for dispute, and it is not a standard of perfection. For example, it has been held that a solicitor is not bound to have a perfect knowledge of the law, but he or she should have a sound knowledge. The distinction between a 'perfect' and a 'sound' level of knowledge is a subtle matter to be decided on the facts of each individual case!

8.43 The implied term to the effect that the supplier will carry out the service with reasonable care and skill can be excluded from a non-consumer contract if the exclusion clause is 'reasonable'.

Suitable materials

8.44 The 1982 Act implies that the supplier will use suitable materials of proper quality. Again, this term can be excluded from a non-consumer contract if it is 'reasonable'.

Reasonable period

8.45 If the time for carrying out the service is not fixed by the contract, the 1982 Act implies that it will be carried out within a reasonable time.

Reasonable price

8.46 If the price for a service is not fixed by the contract, there is an implied term that the charge made will be 'reasonable'. This applies to all contracts, not just those where the supplier is in business. Note, too, that this implied term applies only if the parties have not agreed a price. If they have, that price is binding, however unreasonable it may be.

Standard terms of business

8.47 Does a charity or its trading company need to draw up standard terms of business to apply to its trading contracts? Or should it rely on oral contracts with the implied terms set out above? The answer will vary, depending on the type of the business involved, but as a general rule it is sensible to have written terms and conditions and to seek to impose these. It may be possible to use a standard set of terms and conditions which apply to a charity's particular area of activity (eg the supply of services to run a residential care home).

8.48 It is wise to instruct a solicitor to draw up your terms and conditions. Too many charities think they can cobble together a set of business conditions by taking what they regard as the choicest morsels from various documents and merging them together in what can be a real legal hotchpotch. Be warned. By all means take along examples of similar terms and conditions to your solicitor for him or her to be aware of the particular problems associated with your industry. He or she will know that slavishly copying them will be a breach of copyright.

8.49 Once you have settled on your standard terms, you must ensure that these are available to your customer. It is often sensible to include your standard terms with brochures, order forms and invoices where appropriate. Many commercial organisations present their standard terms in tiny print in faint grey on flimsy paper so that the terms are barely readable. This is not a good idea. If the conditions are too difficult to read, then a judge might rule that they do not apply. By all means print standard terms and conditions of business on the back of quotations or order forms or invoices, but do print them legibly! Note again that they must be provided to the buyer before the deal is done. So providing them for the first time in the first invoice would be too late.

8.50 It is also important to remember that any unusual terms must be brought fairly and reasonably to the other party's attention and must be clearly identified as contractual terms. For example, in one case a picture lending library imposed a heavy penalty if transparencies were returned late. This was an onerous term and it was held that it had not been brought fairly and reasonably to the customers' attention.

8.51 See **8.96–8.98** for guidance on terms and conditions when business is conducted via a website.

Checklist of standard terms and conditions

8.52 Set out below is a short checklist for a general set of terms and conditions of trading. It is not exhaustive, but merely highlights certain important issues. It is for a sale of goods, but suitably adapted could apply to a supply of services. Clearly, each individual case will demand its own particular type of terms and conditions.

(a) *Parties* – Who are the parties? Do make sure, for example, that if the contract is with the charity's trading company and not the charity itself, this is clear (see **7.220–7.221**).

(b) *Date* – What is the date of the agreement? It is amazing how many contracts are entered into without the date being specified.

(c) *Scope of contract* – What does the contract cover? What are the goods? What are the seller's obligations? Does the seller seek to limit its obligations as to satisfactory quality, fitness for purpose or correspondence with samples under the Sale of Goods Act or the equivalent obligations in respect of services?

(d) *Warranties and limitation of liability* – The seller may give express warranties regarding the goods or services it is providing. It will often seek to keep these to the minimum required by law and to exclude all other express and implied warranties. A seller may also seek to limit its liability for any losses arising out of the contract so that its liability for negligence, delay, consequential loss, etc is limited (eg to the value of goods sold). Warranties and limitations of liability must be drafted carefully and will be subject to the Unfair Contract Terms Act 1977 and the Unfair Terms in Consumer Contracts Regulations 1999.

(e) *Price* – What is the price? Can the seller increase the price, and if so, how? Is the price exclusive of VAT? Does it include carriage, insurance or freight?

(f) *Terms of payment* – What are the payment dates? What time is given to pay? If it is an export contract, in what currency is payment to be made? If a seller wants to be able to terminate the contract in the event of late payment, the contract must make time 'of the essence' in respect of payment.

(g) *Interest* – Is interest due on unpaid invoices? If so, at what rate? From when will interest be charged? Unless express provision is made for interest on late payment, the seller will need to rely on the Late Payment of Commercial Debts (Interest) Act 1998 (although this only applies to business to business contracts).

(h) *Delivery* – Who delivers? Are delivery dates estimates only? Are delivery dates 'of the essence', allowing termination of the contract if they are not met?

(i) *Risk and property* – When does the buyer take on the risk of damage to or loss of the goods (ie the need to insure), as opposed to taking physical delivery of the goods?

(j)   *Reservation of title* – Does the contract contain a reservation of title clause? If so, is the buyer obliged to store the seller's goods separately and mark them as being the property of the seller?

(k)   *Force majeure* – Is there a force majeure clause which allows the seller to avoid liability for any loss caused by failure to fulfil its obligations under the contract for reasons beyond its control (e g fire, bad weather, strikes or destruction of premises)?

(l)   *Arbitration or mediation* – Should disputes be referred to an expert arbitrator rather than being left to the courts? This option is generally only available in the case of business contracts. Arbitration clauses in consumer contracts which automatically refer disputes to arbitration rather than to the courts may be considered unfair under the Unfair Terms in Consumer Contracts Regulations 1999.

If arbitration is necessary, who is to appoint the arbitrator?

Mediation offers contracting parties an alternative means of dispute resolution which allows them to reach an agreement themselves without having to accept something imposed by a third party. If appropriate, it can offer a more flexible and conciliatory method of dispute resolution.

(m)   *Termination* – How is the contract to be ended if it is more than a one-off agreement? What notice should be given? What happens if there is a breach of contract by one party? Does that automatically give the other party the right to terminate? Is the defaulting party allowed a 'rectification period' within which to put things right?

(n)   *Governing law* – Does the contract stipulate which legal system is to regulate any disputes? This is very important, as otherwise legal costs may be incurred in deciding which legal system applies to the contract. This is relevant even for trading within the United Kingdom, as English, Scottish and Northern Irish law can differ. It is another example of why it can be very important to ensure that your trading conditions apply to the contract.

LIABILITIES TO THIRD PARTIES

8.53 So far in this chapter, we have considered contracts and the responsibilities and liabilities which exist between the various parties to a contract. To what extent is a trader vulnerable to claims from individuals or organisations with whom they do not have a contractual relationship?

Contracts (Rights of Third Parties) Act 1999

8.54 There is a legal principle, 'privity of contract', which means that, as a general rule, a contract cannot confer rights or impose obligations on any person other than the parties to that contract. However, the application of this principle was changed by the Contracts (Rights of Third Parties) Act 1999 which allows a third party to enforce a term of a contract to which it is not a party, in some circumstances, namely if:

(a) the third party is expressly identified in the contract by name, as a member of a class or answering to a particular description, even if the third party was not in existence when the contract was entered into; and

(b) the contract expressly provides that the third party may enforce a term of the contract; or

(c) the term purports to confer a benefit on the third party.

In such a case the third party will have all the contractual rights and remedies that it would have been entitled to, had it been a party to the contract. The Act only applies in these circumstances and it does not allow parties to a contract to impose obligations on a third party.

8.55 However, it is standard to exclude all third party rights under the Contracts (Rights of Third Parties) Act 1999 in order to avoid it having unintended effects.

Negligence

8.56 There is a general legal obligation to avoid causing loss, damage or injury to others through negligence. This principle can give rights to individuals or organisations which are not contractual parties. Consider the following example.

Example

8.57 A charity's trading company runs a restaurant open to the general public. It sells salmonella-infected chicken nuggets to Danny. Danny gives some to Smithy. Smithy falls ill. Danny has a contract with the trading company. Danny can sue the trading company for breach of its obligation to supply satisfactory chicken nuggets, but Smithy has no contract and will not be covered by the Contracts (Rights of Third Parties) Act. However, he has other legal rights against the trading company. He can sue, not in contract, but in a completely separate area of the law called 'tort' and claim damages on the grounds that the trading company has been negligent in selling salmonella-infected chicken nuggets. 'Tort' is the legal word for the law concerning wrongs done to a person for which compensation can be obtained, but where there may be no contract.

8.58   In contract, Danny would merely have to prove that the chicken nuggets were infected with salmonella (which should be quite straightforward), and therefore were not of satisfactory quality. However, as Smithy is suing in tort he would have to prove:

(a)   that the trading company had been negligent in allowing salmonella to get into the chicken (which might be much harder to prove than just establishing that the chicken contained the salmonella);

(b)   that he was owed a duty of care by the trading company not to be negligent;

(c)   that it was reasonably foreseeable that he would suffer loss or injury as a result of the negligence.

If he can establish that the company had been negligent and that it did owe him a duty of care and that it was reasonably foreseeable that he would suffer loss, then he will be able to recover damages in negligence. Note that the type of damages available in response to negligence claims are different from those which apply to contractual claims: for instance, 'pure economic loss' (ie loss which is not directly connected to physical injury or damage to property, usually in the form of wasted expenditure or loss of profits) is generally not recoverable in tort claims, although there are some exceptions.

8.59   Third parties also have rights under the consumer protection legislation (see **8.64–8.82**) and in many cases it may be easier for a consumer to rely on this legislation rather than on the law of negligence. However, negligence is still relevant:

(a)   for cases of defective non-consumer products;

(b)   if a consumer wishes to sue for consequential loss caused by a defective product, as this cannot be recovered under the Consumer Protection Act.

8.60   Negligence also remains relevant to the supply of services. For instance, a charity or its trading company may prepare a report which is then used, not by its client (with whom it has a contract), but by a third party. Assuming that the third party is not covered by the provisions of the Contracts (Rights of Third Parties) Act 1999, it will not have contractual rights against the charity or trading subsidiary. Nevertheless, the law of negligence may provide a remedy to the third party in certain circumstances, as in the case of *Smith v Eric Bush* [1989] 2 WLR 790. A surveyor prepared a report on a house for a building society. The report was negligently prepared. The report was passed on by the building society to the purchaser, who bought the house on the strength of it, only to find defects later. The purchaser sued the surveyor and received damages despite the fact that the survey had included a disclaimer of liability clause. The House of Lords held that the disclaimer was unreasonable under the Unfair Contract Terms Act 1977, and hence could not be relied upon by the surveyor.

8.61 In similar circumstances, a charity could prepare a report for a client which was then used by a third party. If that report had been negligently prepared, but it was held that the charity owed a duty of care to the third party and it was reasonably foreseeable that the third party would suffer loss, the charity could be made liable for these losses. For this reason it may be appropriate for a charity or its trading subsidiary to consider taking out professional indemnity insurance (see **10.49–10.50**), especially if it is involved in providing advice.

Limiting liability for negligence

8.62 Can a supplier avoid liabilities for negligence by a suitably worded notice? Back to the Unfair Contract Terms Act 1977 – it does not apply just to contracts, despite its name! The supplier cannot limit liability for death or personal injury arising from its own negligence. It can limit liability for other forms of damage if it is reasonable to do so – the question of reasonableness is determined by whether it is 'fair and reasonable' to allow reliance on it, having regard to all the circumstances when the liability arose.

8.63 Many suppliers attempt to use wide drafting to exclude or limit their liability under contracts. Such widely drafted clauses, especially in contracts with consumers, are more likely to fail the test of reasonableness than carefully drafted clauses which specify the types of liability which are being excluded. If suppliers wish to exclude liability, they should do so clearly and succinctly, making sure that separate exclusions are listed separately (or 'severally', as lawyers say) to avoid the risk that an unfair exclusion might invalidate a fair one.

CONSUMER PROTECTION AND RELATED REGULATION

Consumer Protection Act 1987 and the supply of goods

8.64 It is often very difficult for third parties to prove that manufacturers or suppliers have been negligent. To combat this, rules originally developed by the European Commission impose what is called 'strict liability' on producers or importers of defective products. Strict liability means that the producer of a product is liable for any damage which is caused by a defect in that product, whatever the cause. All the claimant has to do is to prove to the court that:

(a)   there was a defect; and

(b)   the defect caused damage.

This is set out in the Consumer Protection Act 1987.

8.65 It must be emphasised that the Consumer Protection Act does not only apply to third parties. The purchaser of the defective goods who has rights in contract (for breach of satisfactory quality) also has rights under the Consumer Protection Act.

8.66 In summary, the Act makes the producer of a product (and certain others) liable in damages for personal injury and some property damage caused by a defect in the product, without the claimant having to show fault, although certain defences may be used by the producer.

8.67 What is defective? A product is defective if the safety of the product is not such as persons are generally entitled to expect. In determining whether a product is defective, a number of factors will be taken into account, including how the product was marketed and any instructions or warnings issued in relation to that product. The persons who may be liable for supplying defective products are:

(a)   the producer;

(b)   any person who puts his name on the product;

(c)   any person who imports the item from outside the European Union.

8.68 The Act only applies to defective products which are ordinarily intended for private use, occupation or consumption and which were intended by the person suffering the loss or damage for his own private use, occupation or consumption. Hence, where business property is damaged, the Act does not apply, since it is designed to provide *consumer* protection.

8.69 Damages which can be recovered under the Consumer Protection Act are only in respect of death, personal injury or any loss of or damage to property. This does not cover loss of profits or consequential loss. Thus, if an engine component in a car exploded damaging the engine, the damages which could be claimed would be the costs of repairing the damage to the engine. No claim can be made for any loss of sales caused by the owner not having his car, ie consequential loss, as the Act is concerned with consumers only. There is also no liability for the loss of or damage to the defective product itself: it is the loss caused by the defect that is relevant.

8.70 Certain defences are available to a claim made under the Act:

(a)   The person did not supply the product.

(b)   The defect did not exist at the time of supply.

(c)   The stage of scientific and technical knowledge at the relevant time was not such that a producer of such products might be expected to have discovered the defect. This is called the 'development risk' defence. Reasonable though it may sound, it is highly controversial, as many consumer groups consider that it puts back on the victim the job of proving the producer was negligent, which is what the Consumer Protection Act was designed to stop.

8.71   A producer or supplier cannot 'contract out' of its obligations under the 1987 Act. Accordingly, the best protection a producer or supplier or importer of non-EU goods can secure is to make sure it has adequate insurance cover for product liability (see **10.45–10.48**).

Consumer safety

8.72   Other parts of the Consumer Protection Act 1987 and, more recently, the General Product Safety Regulations 2005 deal specifically with consumer safety. The Regulations are designed to establish consistently high levels of product safety throughout the European Union. All products supplied to consumers are covered by the Regulations, except where product safety is already regulated by other legislation (eg toys, cosmetics and medical devices).

8.73   The Regulations state that a producer should not supply a product or put it on the market unless it is a 'safe product'. A safe product is one which, under normal conditions of use, does not present any risk or only the absolute minimum risk, which is compatible with the safety of the user of the product.

8.74   In assessing the safety of a product, a number of factors will be taken into account, including:

- the characteristics of the product;

- its packaging;

- the labelling and other information provided for the consumers; and

- the categories of consumers at risk from using the product, particularly children and the elderly.

8.75   If a charity or its trading company is producing goods, it must put measures in place which inform customers of the risks the product might pose, using labels and instructions, eg 'this product may contain nuts'.

8.76   It is important to appreciate that these Regulations apply to any product intended for consumers or likely to be used by consumers, whether new, used or reconditioned. The Regulations apply to a sale 'in the course of commercial activity', which will include the sale of donated goods by a charity or its trading subsidiary.

8.77 Failure to comply with the Regulations can be a criminal offence.

8.78 Numerous other regulations deal with consumer safety in relation to particular products, eg electronic equipment and toys.

The Consumer Protection from Unfair Trading Regulations 2008

8.79 These new regulations represent a very significant development in consumer protection law. They have introduced a general prohibition on businesses treating consumers unfairly. They also prohibit businesses from misleading consumers through acts or omissions, or subjecting them to aggressive commercial practices, such as high pressure selling techniques.

8.80 In addition to these prohibitions, the Regulations also specify 31 commercial practices which will be deemed unfair in any circumstances. These include, but are not limited to:

(a) displaying a quality mark without authorisation;

(b) falsely claiming to be a signatory to a code of conduct;

(c) falsely claiming that a product will be available for a very limited time in order to obtain an immediate decision;

(d) falsely claiming that a product is able to cure illnesses.

The 31 unfair practices are strict liability offences and so it will not be necessary to show that the business intended to breach these prohibitions. Businesses may have a defence to these offences if they can show that the offence was due to a mistake, reliance on information provided by another person, or an accident.

8.81 Enforcement is undertaken by the Advertising Standards Authority for advertising (see **8.125–8.133**), and for other or more serious practices, by Trading Standards and the OFT, which may seek undertakings and injunctions, or prosecute traders. Individual consumers do not have a right of action against businesses themselves.

8.82 These Regulations came into force in the UK in May 2008, so it is likely to be some time before certainty is reached on the scope of their impact on commercial practices in the UK.

Description of goods and services

8.83 A range of primary and secondary legislation regulates the description of goods and services. The Trade Descriptions Act 1968, as its name suggests, makes it an offence for any person acting in the course of a trade or business to apply a false trade description to goods or to supply goods to which a false trade description applies. The Act also applies to services.

8.84 The Consumer Protection Act 1987 makes it an offence for a trader to give misleading price indications for goods, services and facilities to consumers, or to fail to correct a price indication that has become misleading.

8.85 Other regulations apply in specific areas such as price marking and weights and measures.

Other regulations

8.86 Other regulations which may affect particular types of trading include the following.

Contracts made away from business premises

8.87 The Cancellation of Contracts Made in a Consumers' Home or Place of Work etc Regulations 2008 (SI 2008/1816) apply to contracts made where a trade agrees to supply goods or services to a consumer during an unsolicited visit to the consumer's home or place or work. The consumer is entitled to a cooling-off period within which he may cancel the transaction. (See also the Consumer Protection (Distance Selling) Regulations 2000 (see **8.107–8.109**).)

Food

8.88 The Food Safety Act 1990 states that all food produced and/or sold within the United Kingdom should be fit for consumption and not detrimental to the health of the consumer. The Act also provides for the regulation of food composition by clear and legible labelling on all food produced within the UK.

8.89 There is a considerable amount of regulation relating to particular types of food and their method of production.

Consumer Credit Acts 1974 and 2006

8.90 This legislation applies to specialist credit businesses as well as to those who allow customers to buy on credit. A licence may be required, and the agreement with the consumer should be in writing and include certain prescribed information.

Financial services

8.91 The Financial Services and Markets Act 2000 imposes strict regulation on all financial services activity, including the sale of insurance and funeral plans.

Licensing

8.92 A large number of commercial activities can only legally be carried out if a licence is first obtained, usually from the local authority or specialised national agencies. A non-exhaustive list of activities for which a licence may be required is:

- the sale of alcohol;

- childminding and children's nurseries;

- consumer credit;

- dog breeders;

- public entertainments (e g music and dancing);

- film and video shows;

- market and street traders; and

- nursing and residential homes.

Company law

8.93 Under company law, a company must disclose its full name, its place of incorporation (e g England and Wales) and its company registration number, its limited liability status (if this is not clear from its name), and the address of its registered office on its business letters and order forms, business emails and website. This is additional to the requirement under the Charities Act 1993 for charities to disclose their registered charity status (see **2.75–2.77**).

INTERNET AND ELECTRONIC TRADING

8.94 The internet boom in recent years means that the internet is increasingly used by commercial entities and charities alike. E-commerce (ie electronic commerce) is a fantastic opportunity for charities to advertise their activities, raise funds, and sell their goods and services around the world.

8.95 Wise use of the internet can be instrumental in the development of a charity's business and it is essential to consider the legal issues underlying such use. Issues which charities and their trading companies will need to consider range from choosing a domain name (see **9.82–9.90**) to setting up a website providing secure payment facilities.

Website terms and conditions

8.96 If a charity or its trading company wants to sell goods or services via the internet, besides complying with the regulatory requirements outlined below, it needs to consider how contracts with customers will be entered into. It is essential that customers are provided with the terms of the contract, which will generally be standard terms and conditions, and that they accept them before the sale is concluded. This is often done in practice by the customer ticking and clicking on an 'I accept' box or merely clicking on an 'I accept' button.

8.97 Terms and conditions will need to cover all the activities that a user could do on the website, whether under one set of terms and conditions, or several. It should always be clear to the user what legal entity he is dealing with; so the terms and conditions of the sale of charity Christmas cards, for example, must, if appropriate, make it clear that the user is purchasing these items from the trading subsidiary and not from the charity (see **7.220–7.221**). This can be difficult in practice when using web-design tools or consultants which are primarily set up for the commercial sector.

8.98 It is a good idea to keep any 'Give Online' facility separate from the purchase of products or services, or at the very least include clear terms and conditions appropriate to each.

The Electronic Commerce (EC Directive) Regulations 2002

8.99 In August 2002, the Electronic Commerce (EC Directive) Regulations 2002 (SI 2002/2013) implemented into UK law most of the provisions of the Electronic Commerce Directive, which is aimed at encouraging greater use of e-commerce across the European Economic Area (European Union plus Iceland, Liechtenstein and Norway).

8.100 The Regulations apply to the following activities:

• advertising goods or services online (ie via the internet, mobile phones or interactive television), eg on a company website;

• selling goods or services to businesses or consumers online; and

• transmitting or storing electronic content or providing access to communications networks, eg providing web servers.

8.101 The main obligations are in terms of providing information to the end-users and can be divided into three categories according to the activities carried out:

• basic information requirements (advertisement of, or sale of, goods or services online);

- commercial communications (active promotion of goods/services through any form of electronic communication, eg email);

- electronic contracting (orders placed online and contracts entered into online).

8.102   The basic information requirements include providing end-users with:

- the full contact details of the business;

- details of any relevant professional body/trade organisation to which the business belongs;

- details of any authorisation scheme relevant to the online business;

- the charity/trading subsidiary's VAT number (if the online activities are subject to VAT);

- clear indications of prices, which, if relevant, should include any tax and/or delivery costs.

8.103   The commercial communication requirements include providing end-users with clear identification of:

- any electronic communications designed to promote (directly or indirectly) the charity or trading company's goods, services or images (eg an email advertising goods or services);

- the sender;

- any promotional offers (eg discounts, competitions) and a clear explanation of any qualifying conditions in relation to such offers;

- any unsolicited commercial communications as such, eg by using the words 'advertisement' or 'unsolicited email' in the subject of the email.

8.104   The electronic contracting requirements include providing end-users with:

- a description of the different technical steps to be taken to conclude a contract online;

- an indication of whether the contract will be kept by the business and whether it can be accessed;

- clear identification of the technical means to enable end-users to correct any inputting errors they make;

- an indication of the languages offered in which to conclude the contract;

- if applicable, details of codes of conduct applicable to the business, and how the customer can access them;

- if trading on one party's terms of business (eg standard terms and conditions), these must be available for customers to store, eg by downloading them and saving them or printing them.

It is important to note that the above contracting requirements are optional for business to business contracts, and will not apply at all where the parties actually conclude their agreement using email or other individual, 'one to one' communications.

8.105   Breach of the Regulations affecting the collective interest of consumers may lead to action by the OFT or another regulatory body designated by the Secretary of State for Business, Enterprise and Regulatory Reform. Their actions can take a variety of forms, ranging from requiring the business concerned to give undertakings to 'stop now' orders under Part 8 of the Enterprise Act 2002. 'Stop now' orders are enforcement orders granted by the courts on application by the OFT or other designated bodies. Companies that have been the subject of such orders are listed on the OFT website (www.oft.gov.uk). The courts can also order businesses to publish corrective statements. Failure to comply with an enforcement order is a contempt of court punishable by fines and/or imprisonment.

8.106   It is important to note that the Regulations limit the liability of internet service providers ('ISPs') which transmit the information as mere conduits, temporarily store it ('caching') or host the website through which the breach occurs.

The Consumer Protection (Distance Selling) Regulations 2000

8.107   These Regulations (SI 2000/2334) specify that goods or services sold at a distance or where there is no face-to-face contact, such as by phone, mail order or via the internet or digital TV, must not only comply with the normal buying and selling rules outlined in this chapter, but also with further requirements.

8.108   The Regulations require certain information to be provided to a consumer (ie a person not acting in the course of business) in good time prior to the conclusion of the contract. This includes the identity of the supplier, the description and price of the goods, details of any delivery costs and, in particular, the existence of a right to cancel the contract. The Regulations provide the consumer with a right to cancel the contract within 7 working days beginning on the day after which the contract is concluded or after which the required information has been provided. This can mean that if a business fails to provide the appropriate information to the consumer, the right to cancel can subsist for up to 3 months and 7 working days after the contract has been concluded.

8.109   A charity or its trading subsidiary using the internet or mobile phones to conduct business will need to consider compliance with these Regulations, as well as with the Privacy and Electronic Communications (EC Directive) Regulations 2003 (SI 2003/2426) and data protection legislation (see Chapter 9).

Other regulation

8.110   A charity or its trading subsidiary which provides or uses premium rate telephone services will need to ensure compliance with the code of practice issued by the premium rate services regulator, PayPhone Plus.

8.111   Advertisements in non-broadcast electronic media, such as commercial emails, may be caught under the Advertising Standards Authority (ASA) Code of Practice (see **8.128**).

Technical issues

8.112   A number of technical issues have to be considered in preparation for carrying out e-commerce.

Web-hosting

8.113   Depending on the size of the business and the technical capacity of the IT team, a charity or its trading subsidiary may choose to host its own website or contract with an independent provider to host it. There are four main factors that need to be considered:

- *Functionality* – relates to the content of the website, ie the information available and how it is presented, as well as other features of the site, such as the possibility for users to buy online or to post information or messages. Functionality will depend on the software being used, including web design software, the web server operating system and, if appropriate, e-commerce software.

- *Performance* – relates mainly to the speed of the site, which is itself dependent on the speed of the internet connection supporting the site.

- *Reliability* – is the accessibility of the site 24/7, which may depend on having a support team available round the clock.

- *Security* – it is essential to ensure the security of the information produced and used by a business, even more so where online transactions are conducted. The term 'security' encompasses:

- integrity of the information (ie that the content arrives as sent);
- authenticity (of the identity of the sender and receiver);
- non-repudiation (ie to avoid claims that messages were not sent/received); and
- confidentiality.

Failure to address those issues actively may cause serious risks and losses for the business as a result of industrial espionage, computer viruses or identity fraud, not to mention loss of customers.

8.114 Ensuring that information is secure is achieved through a number of measures, from identifying the information and assessing the risks, to training staff and ensuring that the business website complies technically with high security levels.

8.115 For practical advice, visit the Government's Business Link website (www.businesslink.gov.uk) and the Information Security section of the BERR website (www.berr.gov.uk/whatwedo/sectors/infosec/index.html).

8.116 Whilst most ISPs will be able to ensure the performance, reliability and security of the site, the main disadvantage to the business will be a loss of control of the site and the need to trust the ISP. Hosting a website in-house can be more expensive than using an ISP, as the business will need to purchase appropriate hardware and software, but it will allow the business to retain full control of the site. The charity or trading company will also need to consider the technical skills and availability of its IT team to develop and maintain the site at all times, and to keep it secure.

Setting up and running an online shop

8.117 The foundation on which a charity will build its online shop is its website and it is therefore important to consider the issues outlined at **8.113–8.116** above in relation to web-hosting. Providers of web-hosting services may also be able to host the online shop.

8.118 An online shop will be the public face of the charity's trading business and could have a significant impact on its development. It is essential to get it right, and to build and maintain customers' confidence so that they can safely and efficiently use the online shop. The following issues will be instrumental in the running and success of an online shop.

Secure payments

8.119 Ensuring that payments made by customers are secure is critical. It is advisable to have a secure area of the website dedicated to customers placing orders and giving their payment details. The business will need to make sure that it has adequate technology and systems in place to prevent access by unauthorised third parties to the payment information (such as credit card details) and to ensure the confidentiality of such information. To reassure customers that their payments are made in a secure way, it is a good idea to display statements detailing the security measures in place.

Delivery

8.120   It is essential to have appropriate delivery systems in place so that goods ordered online are delivered within a reasonable time.

Contents of the site

8.121   The actual design of the site and representation of the products sold will depend on the charity's specific requirements and the nature of the products and services. However, it is important to ensure that any information displayed on the website is up to date and, therefore, that there are resources in place regularly to monitor the contents of the website/online shop. It is also essential to comply with relevant regulatory requirements such as those set out in the Electronic Commerce Regulations 2002 and the Consumer Protection (Distance Selling) Regulations 2000 (see **8.99–8.109**).

Promotion

8.122   When setting up and running an online shop, the charity or trading company will also need to consider how to advertise it to existing and potential customers. This can be done by traditional advertising (newspapers, radio or television), by links on other businesses' websites or by notifying search engines that will direct internet users to the site. The business will need to make sure that any regulatory requirements for advertising are complied with (see **8.124–8.135**).

8.123   Addressing all of the above issues appropriately will help to build the reputation of an online shop and contribute to its success and that of the business. See also **9.35–9.56**, which outline points to consider when purchasing bespoke computer software, and **9.82–9.90** on domain names.

ADVERTISING

8.124   A host of different types of regulation affect advertising. Many statutory controls have been introduced to protect consumers in the context of specific goods or services. There are specific rules affecting consumer credit advertising and specific codes relating to broadcasting. When contemplating advertising, there are other areas of law that have a wider application to advertising and are dealt with in other sections of this book (eg copyright, trademarks and passing off – see Chapter 9).

Advertising Standards Authority (ASA)

8.125 The ASA is a not-for-profit organisation independent from the advertising industry. Its main aims are to be a best practice 'one-stop shop' for advertising regulation and to ensure that advertising is legal, decent, honest and truthful. One of the ASA's major roles is to investigate and adjudicate complaints from the public and industry about the content of advertisements.

8.126 The ASA's area of operation includes broadcast and non-broadcast advertisements, including direct marketing and certain internet activity such as 'paid for' spaces on the internet (ie pop-up and banner adverts and sponsored links). However, the ASA operates only for those advertising within the UK, and in relation to the internet the relevant geographical reach is sometimes hard to determine.

Broadcast advertising

8.127 The Office of Communications (Ofcom) has statutory responsibility for the regulation of broadcasting and media under the Communications Act 2003. However, in 2004 Ofcom contracted out the regulation of broadcast advertising (including television and radio advertising) to the newly established broadcast arm of the ASA, which is responsible for enforcing the relevant broadcast advertising codes. Television advertising must be cleared pre-broadcast by Clearcast, and radio advertising is cleared by the Radio Advertising Clearance Centre. Separate Ofcom rules govern product placement in and sponsorship of programmes.

Non-broadcast advertising

8.128 Press advertising, posters, direct mail, sales promotions, commercial email, online promotions and internet banner advertisements are regulated by the British Code of Advertising, Sales Promotion and Direct Marketing ('the CAP Code'), which is enforced by the ASA.

Misleading advertising

8.129 Any objective claims should be capable of substantiation if challenged. The ASA may refer cases to the OFT or Trading Standards under the Consumer Protection from Unfair Trading Regulations 2008 (see **8.79–8.82**) if the advertisement amounts to an unfair commercial practice. The OFT and Trading Standards have the power to apply to the courts for an injunction, or to prosecute the advertiser for a criminal offence.

Comparative advertising

8.130 Specific rules apply to broadcast and non-broadcast advertisements which seek to refer to competing products. UK legislation and codes relating to comparative advertising reflect EU legislation which permits a comparison when:

- it is not misleading;

- it compares like with like;

- it is objective and verifiable;

- it does not make unfair use of the goodwill attached to a trade mark or name;

- it does not discredit or denigrate the competitor/products;

- it does not create confusion with a competitor/its products.

Offensive advertising

8.131 The codes enforced by the ASA also have rules concerning offensive or harmful advertising. Particular attention is paid to advertisements likely to cause serious or widespread offence on grounds of race, religion, sex, sexual orientation or disability, and those likely to cause harm to children.

How does the ASA operate?

8.132 The ASA operates primarily by receiving complaints either from individual members of the public or from interested organisations. Only one complaint about an advertisement needs to be received to trigger an ASA investigation. The ASA has no power to force an advertiser to comply with its requests in relation to non-broadcast advertising, although it can refer cases to the OFT. ASA's broadcasting arm can give directions to advertisers and may refer cases to Ofcom. A charity should always consider the effect of an adverse ASA ruling on its reputation. All ASA adjudications are published on the ASA website. In addition, Charity Commission publication CC9 'Speaking Out – Campaigning and Political Activity by Charities' states that a serious breach or persistent breaches of the CAP Code might be an indicator of underlying mismanagement or maladministration of the charity's affairs, and therefore require regulatory action by the Charity Commission.

8.133 The ASA may require that advertisements are pre-vetted where advertisers have persistently breached the relevant codes.

Other codes and legislation

8.134   There are a number of self-regulating advertising codes; for example:

- The Direct Marketing Association has a code of practice with which its members must comply.

- There is a code of conduct for the advertising of interest bearing accounts drawn up by the Building Societies Association and the British Bankers' Association.

8.135   In addition:

- The Financial Services and Markets Act 2000 imposes strict regulation on the advertisement and promotion of investments.

- The Personal Pension Scheme (Advertisements) Regulations 1990 (as amended) apply to the content of advertisements for personal pension schemes.

- The Consumer Credit Act 1974 (as amended) applies to advertisements offering credit to customers.

There is also specific legislation applying (amongst others) to lotteries, betting and gaming, food and medicine, as well as additional code rules in these areas, and for alcohol.

COMPETITION LAW

Introduction

8.136   The laws relating to the control of restricted trade practices, monopolies and state aid may seem a far cry from the activities of charities and their trading companies. Of course, that is true for many charities which carry on trade at relatively modest levels. Nonetheless, these laws have a wider scope than many people appreciate, and charities (and/or their trading companies) could find that they have unwittingly broken the law or that they are required to repay funds which were granted to them in breach of competition law. This risk will increase as charities' trading activities increase and is of particular significance when charities contract with public authorities. Charities may wish to reach agreement about not competing with each other and then find they have acted in breach of competition law. This section is not a detailed study of competition law. Instead, it offers a very basic overview of competition law and seeks to identify where such laws could affect charities.

8.137   Charities and their trading subsidiaries should be alert both to the risk that they may be in breach of competition law and to the possibility that they may be victims of potential breaches. If a charity or trading subsidiary considers that it is being affected by competition law infringements, it should seek specialist legal advice.

Overview

8.138   The key types of practices which are caught under competition law are:

- anti-competitive agreements;

- abuses of a dominant position;

- state aid; and

- merger control.

Anti-competitive agreements

8.139   The Competition Act 1998 prohibits agreements which affect trade within the UK and which are designed to, or result in, the prevention, constriction or distortion of competition in the UK.

8.140   Anti-competitive agreements can relate to any type of product or service and at any level of the supply chain (including retail). Agreements between companies at the same level in the supply chain, ie between two retailers, are more likely to be considered anti-competitive than agreements at different levels of the supply chain, eg between a manufacturer and a distributor. Therefore, agreements between two stores agreeing to fix prices in particular products are more likely to be anti-competitive and fall foul of competition law.

8.141   A cartel is an agreement under which companies operating in a market agree not to compete with each other. This is a typical anti-competitive agreement. Organisations might enter into an agreement not to compete by fixing prices or quantities, or by dividing regional areas between each other. The prohibition on such agreements extends to include situations where there is no written evidence of the agreement, but simply collusion between companies.

8.142   There is a limited immunity for any 'small agreement', which is defined as an agreement between parties whose combined group turnovers in their last financial year prior to infringement do not exceed £20 million. This immunity does not apply to price-fixing agreements and will not be applicable to all practices. However, it is indicative of the fact that, for many charities, the prohibition on anti-competitive agreements will be of very limited relevance.

Abuse of a dominant position

8.143 The Competition Act 1998 also prohibits abuses of a dominant position. The prohibition applies to any conduct by one or more undertakings that amounts to the abuse of a dominant position in a market. It applies where the abuse might affect trade in the UK or any part of it. A company will be dominant if it has a large market share and abuses its position, eg by charging excessively high prices. A company does not need to be dominant across the UK in order to be caught under the Act for abuse of its position. The Act will apply if the company is dominant in relation to a specific product in a region, or even in a town. For instance, the OFT has investigated allegations of abuses of a dominant position in relation to the sale and distribution of free or paid-for newspapers in the Aberdeen area.

8.144 Again, there is a limited immunity from this prohibition in the case of 'conduct of minor significance', which is defined as conduct by a firm with a turnover in the previous financial year of no more than £50 million. Two or more firms which jointly or collectively hold a dominant position may, in some circumstances, amount to infringement of the dominant position prohibition.

State aid

8.145 State aid is the area of competition law which is most likely to be of relevance to charities. The European Treaty prohibits the supply of aid by EU member states to specific companies or in relation to certain goods or services where this may confer preferential advantage which would affect trade between member states of the EU.

8.146 The principal objective of the state aid rules is to prevent large national industries from being granted unfair competitive advantage through subsidy. The rules apply to charities where state subsidy, in the form of local authority grants or other preferential support, could have an effect on competition and impact trade between EU member states. The rules are widely drafted and a significant number of UK public authorities are interpreting their rules with caution. State aid is increasingly cited by public authorities as a potential obstacle to public authority grants, preferential loans and other funding.

8.147 The impact of the state aid rules is potentially very significant for charities, as many public authorities have responded to this issue by requiring charities to undertake to repay grant funds if the grant they receive is found to be unlawful under the state aid rules. This is particularly unfair and reverses the appropriate allocation of responsibility. Charities should be alert to the potential impact of such clauses and resist them where possible (see also **3.133–3.134**).

Merger control

8.148 Whilst a merger between two companies may bring substantial benefits to both consumers and the economy (eg by producing goods more efficiently and therefore lowering their prices), it may have the effect of strengthening a dominant company, eg by enabling it to increase prices unilaterally. It is worth noting, however, that in the UK the OFT will only be concerned with mergers where the turnover of the enterprise being taken over exceeds £70 million, or where the result of the merger is the establishment of one company having a market share of at least 25% in relation to the purchase or supply of goods or services in the UK market or a substantial part of it. Again, it is unlikely that merging charities or their trading companies will be affected by the anti-competitive restrictions imposed on mergers.

Chapter 9

INTELLECTUAL PROPERTY RIGHTS AND USE OF INFORMATION

9.1 *This chapter covers intellectual property, including copyright, computer software, names and logos, trade marks, domain names, patents, design rights, use of databases and confidential information.*

INTRODUCTION

9.2 Protection of intellectual property rights can be key to the success of a business. Commercial organisations protect their intellectual property rights assiduously, through the registration of trade marks and patents, for example, and through active enforcement of their rights. Similarly, charities and their associated trading companies should take steps to ensure that their intellectual property rights are properly protected. Intellectual property rights may be a means of generating significant income for charities and/or their trading companies, as well as having intangible value.

9.3 Intellectual property is an area which can be highly complex, and appropriate professional advice should be taken.

COPYRIGHT

9.4 Copyright is the right to prevent unauthorised copying of materials. Charities and their trading companies will frequently create or commission materials which are protected by copyright. In order to protect against unauthorised use by others, they need to ensure that they deal with copyright matters effectively. There is no system for registering copyright in the UK.

9.5 Copyright law has a wide application and covers publications, books, software, drawings (including logos in many cases), designs, sounds, images and databases, as well as art works, films, music and broadcasts. The main copyright legislation in the UK is the Copyright Designs and Patents Act 1988 which has been amended several times to take account of EU legislation. By s 1 of the 1988 Act, copyright exists in:

(a) original literary, dramatic, musical or artistic works;

(b)   sound recordings, films, broadcasts or cable programmes; and

(c)   the typographical arrangement of published editions.

9.6   For charities carrying out trading directly, copyright can be a significant consideration. For example, a research charity may be commissioned to write reports in connection with bespoke research; an educational charity may commission and publish a book from an author (eg the Oxford University Press or the Directory of Social Change); an art gallery may wish to use a picture from its collection on a postcard or greetings card; a charitable theatre may commission designs for a stage set; a religious charity may publish hymn books. Who owns the copyright in these items?

9.7   Charities trading through trading companies will similarly encounter copyright issues, eg in the design of Christmas cards, in commissioning market research, in designing a sales catalogue, in building up databases of customers, in commissioning advertisements. Again, who owns the copyright?

9.8   First, it is worth emphasising a few basic principles of copyright law.

9.9   There is no copyright in an idea. This is a simplification of a key legal principle in copyright, which is that ideas, opinions, information and facts should be freely available. Copyright law merely protects the way in which the author has expressed such ideas or information. However, there are some ways in which ideas can be protected. For example, an idea may be disclosed only after the recipient has signed an undertaking whereby he or she agrees to honour the confidentiality of the idea. The originator of the idea has a claim in law if the idea is then disclosed in breach of the undertaking.

9.10   There is no central registry of copyright. Copyright is not established by filing details with a government department. It comes into being simply by creating a work which contains a sufficient degree of intellectual innovation and originality to be protected by the law. The position is different in the USA, where there is a central registry and filing with the registry is necessary to enforce copyright.

9.11   In the UK there is not even any legal obligation to use the © symbol or put a copyright notice on copyright material, although it is sensible to do so, both as a sign of the owner's intention to enforce copyright and in case the work is used in overseas territories where enforcement requires the use of the symbol.

9.12   If an author is concerned that there could be a dispute over when a copyright work was created, he or she can send a copy of the work by recorded delivery post to an independent third party for safekeeping (eg a solicitor or a bank), so that there is separate independent evidence of when the copyright work was created.

9.13   There need be no literary or artistic merit in a copyright work. The creative input required in order to create copyright is not usually onerous, and varies with the medium concerned. For example, quite a low expectation of intellectual input is required to establish copyright in a database containing names and addresses of contacts or customers (see **9.108**). On the other hand, a higher degree may be required in connection with the writing of a book.

9.14   An employer owns the copyright in any material produced by an employee in the course of his employment. This can come as a considerable surprise to both employers and employees. If office work is done outside business hours, then it may still be treated as having been done in the course of employment. The other side of the coin is that copyright in materials produced by a *consultant* (or, indeed, anyone who is not an employee) will vest in the creator, even though the commissioned material has been paid for. This means that a charity (or its trading company) should, wherever possible when commissioning designs, reports or other copyright materials, seek to ensure that the copyright is assigned (ie transferred) to the charity or to the trading company, as the case may be (see **9.30–9.31**).

Example

9.15   One court case involved an action brought by Henry Moore's daughter against the Henry Moore Foundation (a registered charity). Henry Moore's daughter claimed that a large number of her father's sculptures did not belong to the charity but to Henry Moore personally and thus, on his death, passed to his successors under his will. But the court was satisfied that Mr Moore had been *employed* by the Henry Moore Foundation for many years prior to his death and thus all his works produced during the years of his employment belonged not to Mr Moore, and hence to his beneficiaries, but to the Henry Moore Foundation.

9.16   Copyright in literary, dramatic, musical or artistic works lasts for 70 years from the death of the creator. Even where copyright itself is owned by a company because the creator was employed by a company, the copyright period is based on the life of the creator who created it on behalf of the company. If two or more authors jointly own the copyright it will last until the end of the 70 years from the end of the calendar year in which the last of them died.

9.17   Copyright in sound recordings (other than film sound tracks) lasts 50 years. In film, the copyright in the different elements lasts 70 years from the death of the survivor of the principal director, the author of the screenplay, the author of the dialogue, or the composer of the music. Copyright in broadcasts and cable programmes usually lasts 50 years from first transmission. For computer-generated work, the period is 50 years from first transmission.

9.18   Copyright in the typographical arrangement (ie the layout) of published editions lasts 25 years from the end of the calendar year in which the edition was first published.

Copyright infringement remedies

9.19 There are two types of remedies for breach of copyright: criminal proceedings or civil remedies (damages, an injunction, an account of the profits, the return of infringing articles, etc). A civil action for copyright infringement may be brought by the owner of the copyright or by a person to whom an exclusive licence has been granted.

9.20 In order to succeed in an action for infringement of copyright, it is not necessary to prove damage. The claimant may be entitled to a share of profits which the infringer earned from breach of the copyright (known as an 'account of profits') or to a sum equivalent to the fee which could have been charged for the use of the work.

9.21 An injunction can be obtained to restrain a copyright infringement, although it will not be available if the court considers that damages would provide adequate relief in the circumstances. An interim injunction may be available to restrain an infringement pending trial, provided that the claimant is able to establish that he has a sufficiently serious claim which is not frivolous or vexatious, and that on the balance of convenience the likely damage from the claimed infringement will exceed the harm caused to the claimed infringer by the injunction.

9.22 If someone who infringes a work can show in the circumstances that he did not know (or have reason to know) that the work was protected by copyright, a claimant should not be entitled to damages for the infringement. This is an objective test: would a reasonable man with the knowledge of the infringer believe the work is protected by copyright? Under certain circumstances the court, in assessing damages for infringement, has power to award additional damages having regard to all the circumstances, in particular, to the flagrancy of the infringement and to the benefit which accrued to the infringer by reason of the infringement.

9.23 An account of profits is an 'equitable' remedy, only available if the claimant has himself acted equitably.

9.24 There is no fixed proportion of work that can be copied without infringement – copyright in a work is infringed if a 'substantial part' is taken. What amounts to a substantial part is a question of both quality and amount – it depends on the significance of the copied part. You can infringe: a drawing by doing another drawing that looks similar; a novel by writing another novel about very similar characters with the same plot-line; a computer program, not only by copying the entire source or object code, but also by copying the structure of the program. The question is whether the alleged infringer has made use of a substantial part of the skill and labour of the creator, in the making of the copy.

Examples

9.25   In the context of a literary work, four lines from Kipling's *If* used in a Sanatogen advertisement, were held to be a 'substantial part'.

9.26   In the context of a musical work, an extract of 60 seconds' duration from *Colonel Bogey* constituted a substantial part.

9.27   It is important to note, however, that coincidental creation of a similar work independently does not constitute infringement, even though it covers the same ideas.

Possession or legal ownership

9.28   It is necessary to distinguish between possession and legal ownership of a physical work on the one hand, and the intangible copyright in that work on the other. If, for example, a gallery has purchased a picture by, say, Francis Bacon, it will not own the copyright in the picture unless it has been assigned to it. The painter's heirs, as laid down in the painter's will, will be entitled to exploit the copyright in the picture, unless the painter assigned the copyright. Once the copyright period has expired, the owners of the picture can control copies of the picture by limiting access or charging fees for taking copies, etc. Copyright will also exist in any photographs of the original, and will belong to the photographer.

Flexibility of copyright

9.29   Copyright is flexible and attaches to each level of creative endeavour in a finished work. For example, a book may be adapted as a stage play and then into a television show with background music. There will be separate copyrights in the stage play, the television show, the composition of the background music, the recording of the background music, the performance of the background music, the master tape and the broadcast. If, for example, a charity is planning to commission a publicly performed work of music which is filmed, recorded and broadcast, it will need to deal with all the various copyrights which comprise the work as a whole. Equally, copyright in a work often consists of a number of different rights that can be separately exploited. For instance, the right to publish a book is considered distinct from the right to base a film or television programme on it.

Dealing with copyright: assignment and licences

9.30   To be valid in law, an assignment of copyright must be in writing and signed by the assignor. Once made, an assignment is permanent. Rights that have been assigned once can usually be assigned onwards without the consent of the original owner.

9.31   Grants of rights in copyright which are not assignments will be licences. Licences are more flexible and can be in whatever form is agreed by the parties. A licence can be terminated in accordance with contract law, including non-performance of any of the contract terms, such as non-payment of part of the remuneration. A licence can be exclusive or non-exclusive and this can be a key distinction, as exclusive licences are generally more valuable. Unless specifically permitted, there is generally no right to sublicence copyright. A licence of copyright does not need to be in writing, although oral licences can be difficult to prove. In many cases small scale use of a work is licensed through an umbrella licensing scheme, such as that run by the Newspaper Licensing Agency ('NLA'), which manages UK national newspaper copyright collection. The NLA works on behalf of the UK's newspapers and licenses organisations to make paper and digital copies of newspaper content, without each organisation having to negotiate a separate agreement with each newspaper.

Moral rights

9.32   Copyright legislation protects the 'moral rights' of authors, composers, artists and film directors. These are rights that creators retain, even after the copyright has been sold on. The rights are:

(1)   to be identified as the creator of a work by credit or acknowledgement. This is often called the right to 'paternity';

(2)   to object to derogatory treatment of the work (eg if a movie is edited in a way that damages its artistic integrity);

(3)   to protection against false attribution of the work (ie wrongly crediting someone as the author);

(4)   to privacy in certain private photographs and films.

9.33   Moral rights become important after copyright has been assigned, as the creator is then unable to control copying of the work by enforcing his or her copyright. Moral rights cannot be assigned, but they can be waived, and in many industries it is standard practice for a full waiver of moral rights to accompany a copyright assignment.

Rental and lending rights

9.34   The right to lend or rent a copyright work is also restricted under the Copyright Designs and Patents Act 1998 (as amended in 1996). Royalties are payable by the lender when a work such as a book is loaned (even if it is loaned for no charge by, for instance, a public library). These royalties are collected by a collecting society, which from time to time remunerates the owner of the lending rights – usually the author. The rental right is likely to be of greater value than the lending right – for instance, when DVDs are commercially rented. Both rental and lending rights are unlikely to be of significant relevance to most charities or their trading companies.

SOFTWARE AND COPYRIGHT

9.35 Almost all charities and their trading companies will use computer software, and in some cases will have expensive and sophisticated software packages. UK law explicitly recognises that computer software is protected by copyright. A charity or its trading company will deal with three main types of software: bespoke software which it has commissioned, customised software where the supplier has a standard package but adapts it to fit the requirements of the purchaser, and standard software programs it has bought from a supplier, such as Microsoft Outlook. A purchaser will not be able to negotiate the terms and conditions of the contract for a standard software program, but will have to take or leave those terms. These may include restrictions on the number of users, or the use to which the purchaser can put the software. Normally the purchaser can use the software only for its own internal purposes. The software supplier will generally own or have itself taken a licence of intellectual property rights in the relevant product, which it then licenses or sublicenses to the purchaser.

9.36 In relation to bespoke programs, the purchaser must consider the following questions.

What will the purchaser get?

9.37 The purchaser will need to specify what functions the software is to perform and how well it will perform them (eg speed of response). The purchaser will need to know with what hardware it is compatible and what capacity it has for expansion and improvement. There should be specifications dealing with these issues to ensure that the system is 'fit for the purpose' of the purchaser's requirements as explained by the purchaser to the supplier. Almost certainly the contract will contain a provision known as the 'entire agreement clause' under which the purchaser effectively surrenders his rights to rely on any assurances given about the product which are not incorporated or expressly referred to in the contract.

Who obtains copyright in the software?

9.38 Should it be the purchaser? This will not happen unless there is an express assignment of the copyright in the program contained in the contract with the software supplier. It may be in the purchaser's interest to allow the creator of the software to retain title in the program and to license it to others, so as to encourage the creator of the software to maintain it. In this way the software may acquire a larger number of users, which may assist in ensuring that faults are more quickly identified and remedied, which means that maintenance is quicker and cheaper. There is also a counter-argument that, as the purchaser is paying for the development of bespoke software, it should own the intellectual property rights. Where the purchaser owns the intellectual property in the software, it will want an undertaking from the supplier that it will not use the software except for the benefit of the purchaser.

9.39 If the purchaser obtains a licence to use, rather than ownership of the software, then sublicensing or transferring of rights under the licence will not normally be permitted. Where the purchaser is a company in a 'group' (for instance, a trading subsidiary and its parent charity) it may, therefore, need to negotiate the terms of the licence so that other companies in the group can use the software. It is also desirable to incorporate a provision under which the supplier permits the transfer of the rights if the business is sold.

9.40 Who has the copyright in a report which identifies the need for the bespoke program? The copyright will be owned by either the author (if an independent contractor) or his employer (if the author is an employee), unless it is assigned in writing. However, it will be hard to stop the creator of the software from using the ideas or concepts in the report, unless it has agreed not to do so by signing a confidentiality agreement.

Timetable and delivery

9.41 If nothing is specified, there is a legal implication that delivery of the completed product will take place within a reasonable time. In practice, there should be a timetable agreed in advance which sets out the various stages of the software development. Often, this is elaborated in a project initiation document which also specifies how the parties will liaise while the development is being carried out.

Price

9.42 The price is usually paid by instalments as each stage of the development is successfully completed. There is no general practice as to the amount and regularity of instalment payments, but there would normally be a substantial payment made on the signing of the agreement and the largest instalment on acceptance by the purchaser of the software. It is always desirable for the purchaser to retain 10%–20% of the total payment until the software has been running for a reasonable period (ie between 30 and 90 days).

Warranties

9.43 The purchaser should seek assurances in the contract on such matters as the fact that the software will comply with the specification, will be or has been written with due skill and care and as to the hardware on which it will run and its interoperability with other software. Software suppliers should also be asked to specify in the contract any particular technical requirements needed to maximise efficient operation. Some warranties will be limited to claims made within a certain period of delivery and acceptance. This can vary, but would not normally exceed 12 months. Correction of any errors in the software within that period should not be charged under any maintenance contract, although often the maintenance contract will be timed to commence once the warranty period expires.

Additional work and charges

9.44 During the course of development of substantial software the purchaser may well find that it needs to alter or expand the specification. Such changes may need to go through a formal 'change control' procedure, with the supplier specifying the alterations to price and delivery times which the alterations would entail. The supplier will normally quote for carrying out changes on the basis of the number of hours to be worked by and seniority of the programmers and system designers involved. Although the rates per hour can be controlled, the purchaser will have difficulty disputing the number of hours involved and, hence, the overall charge. This emphasises the importance, so far as possible, of encapsulating all the purchaser's needs in the original specification.

Acceptance

9.45 The purchaser should not accept the system until it has passed the agreed 'acceptance tests'. If the software fails the tests initially, the supplier is normally given a relatively short period (often 2 or 3 weeks) to correct the faults revealed and have the system retested. This process may be repeated more than once, but the purchaser needs to set a limit so that after a certain period of delay the purchaser has the right to withdraw from the contract and claim back what it has paid, although often in these circumstances it will not be able to claim further damages such as the cost of the losses it will have suffered by not implementing the system.

Installation

9.46 This process needs to be part of the timetable and to be completed before the final acceptance of the software.

Indemnity

9.47 The software provided by the supplier will often have features belonging to other software providers or freely available on certain terms. The supplier will be licensed to use these features and to sublicense their use to the purchaser. It will need to reflect the terms of its own licence to exploit these features in the contract with the purchaser. Use of software belonging to a third party should be at the supplier's risk, and the purchaser should have an indemnity from the supplier against any breaches of the intellectual property rights of third parties involved in operating the software. The purchaser should have the right, if the supplier cannot amend or obtain a licence for the infringing software, to return the software, require that an adequate replacement is provided at no extra charge and in good time, or back out of the contract.

Limits on liability

9.48 Standard industry practice is for suppliers to try to exclude liability for financial losses caused by breach of the contract, to place a financial limit on claims and to put a limit on the damage to property for which the supplier is liable. Invariably the supplier's standard form contract will exclude, so far as permitted, all rights which the purchaser may have under statute or common law, so that the purchaser can rely on only the express terms of the contract and statutory warranties which it is unlawful to exclude; one of these is the statutory provision that if a business purchaser is dealing on the standard terms of a supplier (whether for goods or services), the exclusions from, and limitations on, liability are only enforceable to the extent that they are reasonable (see **8.24**).

Insurance

9.49 The purchaser may require the supplier to effect insurance up to a specified level against negligence in developing, adapting or advising in relation to the software. The purchaser needs to have the right to inspect the relevant policy and premium receipts to check that the proper cover is being maintained.

Purchaser remedies

9.50 Subject to the enforceability of limitations of liability, the purchaser will have the normal contractual remedies if the supplier is in breach of contract, such as damages and (if the breach is sufficiently serious) the right to terminate the contract. It is possible for the parties to agree in the contract what the amount of damages will be in respect of certain breaches. Typically damages would be fixed at a certain level for each day for which delivery of the software is delayed beyond an agreed date. These are known as 'liquidated damages'. Such liquidated damages must be a reasonable pre-estimate of loss, otherwise they may be treated as a penalty and not enforceable. Where the purchaser has the right of termination for a serious breach, normally the supplier is allowed some time to remedy the defective performance (if it is remediable), often set at anywhere between 14 and 30 days.

Escrow

9.51 The purchaser will often be reliant on the software for the running of its business. Where the software code is not assigned to the purchaser, the wrongful termination of the agreement by the supplier or the supplier's failure or inability to correct faults can produce very serious consequences for the purchaser. To protect themselves in these circumstances purchasers often require that the source code and other materials which would be required by a competent programmer to maintain the software are placed in 'escrow' (ie deposited with a third party, normally a specialist escrow agent). The supplier and the purchaser enter into an agreement with the escrow agent under which, if specific events take place, the purchaser will have access to the source code and other materials. The events need to be carefully considered. The purchaser will want to have access to the software, not only because of the supplier's insolvency. The escrow agent will not itself determine whether a release event has occurred and, in the case of a dispute, the matter may have to be referred to the courts or arbitration, depending on the terms of the contract. Often escrow costs are shared. The supplier should be obliged to deposit changes to the source code, etc with the escrow agent.

Maintenance contracts

9.52 Programs are not warranted to be error free. Although the supplier normally undertakes to correct errors (free of charge) that appear during the (often very limited) period of the warranty, once that period has expired the purchaser usually needs an ongoing commitment to correct errors, and often to provide upgrades to the software. These issues are dealt with in a maintenance agreement between the supplier and the purchaser. With some standard software this service is provided by the supplier as part of the cost of the annual licence fee. In other cases, though, it is paid for separately.

9.53 Maintenance contracts provide for some or all of a variety of services, e g error correction when required (paid for on a time basis at fixed hourly rates or for a fixed annual charge), or enhancements and upgrades (but not a replacement system) provided within the annual charge. The purchaser will need to be reassured that the supplier will offer to maintain, and preferably provide upgrades for the system, for a certain length of time in the future (e g 3 or 5 years).

9.54 If the supplier is to commit itself to long-term maintenance, the price for this should be fixed for the commitment period. Commonly the supplier will have the right to increase its charges each year by an agreed amount (such as the same rate as inflation). If the amount is not agreed, then the purchaser may have the right to terminate the contract if it is not willing to pay the increase. Rather than a simple obligation to maintain the system, maintenance agreements usually include specific requirements for the service levels which the supplier is expected to achieve. Of prime concern to the purchaser is the time within which a fault will be corrected. Obviously the greater the severity of the fault and the longer the delay in fixing a fault, the greater the compensation that the purchaser should receive.

9.55 Commonly the contracts for initial supply and for the maintenance of the software need to be considered together. Where maintenance is provided by a third party, the position is less satisfactory. When faults are discovered it may be difficult for the purchaser to establish whether the initial supplier or the maintenance company is at fault.

Software leasing contracts

9.56 Purchasers can finance the purchase of software systems through leasing. The supplier grants the licence to use the software to a bank or other finance house, which in turn sublicenses it to the purchaser. The supplier has to agree the arrangement, as sublicensing is otherwise normally prohibited. The financier may also have other requirements it will need to agree with the supplier. As the financier and not the purchaser will enter into the licence contract for the software, the purchaser needs to ensure that it has direct rights to ensure the supplier complies with the warranties etc. Normally there should be a separate 'collateral' contract between the supplier and the purchaser covering this. The purchaser will not be able to make any deductions for faults, etc from the fees it pays to the financier for its sublicence or the right to use the software.

NAMES AND LOGOS

9.57 One of a charity's most precious assets is its reputation or goodwill. Some charities have very powerful brand names. In the UK 95% of people have heard of the Citizens Advice Bureau. Charities recognise the need for good names, such as 'Greenpeace', as well as distinctive logos, such as the Red Cross.

9.58 Names, and logos with no design element, are not usually protected by copyright, but instead are protected under English law (and the law in many other territories) as trade marks. However, if a charity or its trading company commissions a distinctive logo design, there will be copyright in the logo and the charity or company should make sure that all rights are transferred to it. As outlined at **9.14**, the mere act of payment for the design of a logo does not mean that the rights in it transfer to the purchaser. The omission to obtain a transfer of such rights can give rise to problems.

Example

9.59 In one case a charity commissioned a distinctive artistic logo from a designer, but the charity failed to take an assignment of the rights in the logo. The logo became well known and, hence, valuable. As a result the designer had the charity over a barrel. Whenever the charity had to prove it had ownership of the logo (eg if it wanted to enter into an arrangement whereby it allowed a third party to use it), it had to obtain a licence (for a fee!) from the owner.

9.60 These problems would have been avoided if the charity had taken a written transfer of all rights in the logo when it placed the order for its design with the designer – when the designer's negotiating position was much weaker than it subsequently became.

9.61 A trade mark can be registered or unregistered. Registered marks are dealt with at **9.68–9.81**. Even if a name is not registered as a trade mark, a charity or its trading company can still protect their names by bringing a 'passing off' action in the court, if required. Passing off occurs if there is evidence of the public being confused as to the owner of a mark. If two organisations with similar marks operate in completely different markets, there can be no confusion, and the law will not intervene. The claimant must also usually show damage. This could be loss of income or sales. Less tangible damage to reputation is also a ground for a claim.

9.62 Historically it was claimed that the remedy of passing off was not available to charities, as they had no commercial reputation to protect. This is not correct. In a number of cases charities have obtained injunctions to protect their names and reputations.

Examples

9.63 Dr Barnardo's Homes (now Barnardo's) was able to restrain the publication of novelettes as a Barnardo publication (*Dr Barnardo's Homes v Barnardo Amalgamated Industries Limited* (1949) 66 RPC 103).

9.64 The British Legion was entitled to restrain a non-political social club from the use of 'British Legion' in its name (*British Legion v British Legion Club (Street) Limited* (1931) 48 RPC 555).

9.65 In the *British Diabetic Association v The Diabetic Society Limited* [1995] 4 All ER 812, [1996] FSR 1 the British Diabetic Association, a registered charity, obtained an injunction to stop the defendant (which was in the process of being registered as a charity) from using its confusingly similar name.

9.66 In 2002 the World Wildlife Fund (now the Worldwide Fund for Nature) succeeded in obtaining an injunction against the US World Wrestling Federation restricting its use of the acronym WWF (*World Wide Fund for Nature (formerly World Wildlife Fund) (WWF) v World Wrestling Federation Entertainment Inc* (2002) *The Times*, 8 May).

The commercial exploitation of names

9.67 Partnerships with commercial organisations are dealt with in Chapter 5. These will often include a right for a commercial partner to use a charity's name and/or logo. Often the logo itself will be referred to by a trade mark registration number, or if the mark is not registered then the image will be annexed to the agreement. It is important that the agreement with the commercial partner sets out clearly the parameters under which the commercial partner will be entitled to use the name. This should cover the territories and the media in which the partner can use the name. It should also require the partner to notify the charity if it becomes aware of any unauthorised use of the name, or if any other person claims that the name or logo infringes a third party's rights. The agreement should also provide that any goodwill and rights which are built up in the name by the commercial partner belong to the charity and are transferred to the charity in the agreement itself.

TRADE MARKS

What is a trade mark?

9.68 In the UK trade marks are protected under the Trade Marks Act 1994 and European Council Regulation 40/94/EEC.

9.69 A 'trade mark' is defined as any sign capable of being represented graphically which is capable of distinguishing goods or services of one undertaking from those of other undertakings.

9.70 A trade mark may, in particular, consist of:

(a)   words (including personal names);

(b)   designs;

(c)   letters;

(d)   numerals;

(e)   the shape of goods or their packaging.

9.71 Under the legislation existing before the 1994 Act, in order to register a trade mark it was necessary for the mark to be used in connection with the supply of services in consideration for money or money's worth. This made it difficult for a charity which was not receiving direct financial reward for its activities (such as Samaritans) to register a mark. Since 1994 such organisations have been able to register trade marks.

What cannot be registered as a trade mark?

9.72 Certain items cannot be registered as trade marks, namely:

(a)   Those which are devoid of distinctive character.

(b)   Those which consist *exclusively* of signs or indications which may serve to designate the kind, quality, quantity, intended purpose, value or geographical origin at the time of production of goods, or the rendering of services or other characteristics of goods or services, unless they have acquired distinctiveness through use. For example, the word 'soup' cannot be registered in relation to washing powder.

(c)   Signs that are not capable of being registered graphically.

Why have a trade mark?

9.73   The advantage of registering a trade mark is that it gives the owner of the mark a monopoly in using the mark in relation to the types of goods or services for which it is registered. If someone is making unauthorised use of a registered trade mark in relation to the same goods or services, it is a relatively simple matter for the trade mark owner to obtain an injunction to restrain the unauthorised use and claim damages. The trade mark owner merely has to show that the defendant is using the registered mark, or one that is confusingly similar to it, in relation to the same or similar goods or services. This is easier to establish than a passing off claim, where the claimant has to start by establishing that it has a sufficient reputation in the mark in order to bring an infringement claim. This can be difficult and expensive to prove.

9.74   Section 59(3) of the Charities Act 1992 provides further assistance for a charity seeking to obtain an injunction in such circumstances. This provides that if, on the application of a charity, the court is satisfied that any person is acting as a professional fundraiser or a commercial participator in relation to that charity without there being a s 59(1) or (2) agreement in force (see **5.81** and **5.139**), the court will grant an injunction restraining the professional fundraiser or commercial participator. It will not be necessary to show confusion in these circumstances, but merely the act of seeking to raise funds by using the name of the charitable institution without an agreement in the prescribed form. Since the introduction of the 1992 Act, however, this right has not been widely used in the courts – perhaps because of the general aversion that most charities have to initiate court proceedings.

9.75   It should be emphasised that this right to seek an injunction under s 59(3) only applies to a 'charitable institution'. The definition of a charitable institution does not extend to a trading company owned by a charity. Hence, in the absence of a registered trade mark, a trading company in these circumstances will have to rely upon its common law rights in passing off.

How do you register a trade mark?

9.76   Detailing the process for registering a trade mark is beyond the scope of this book. In the UK an application has to be made to the UK Intellectual Property Office ('UKIPO'). Alternatively, an application for a trade mark covering the entire European Union including the UK can be made at the European trade marks registry. This is good value if protection is sought in more than two EU member countries.

9.77 There are 45 different classes of goods and services in which a mark can be registered. Registration can take from 6 months to several years to achieve. The protection offered by registration of a UK trade mark is deemed to run from the date upon which the application was originally filed, provided the mark is ultimately successfully registered. Registration will last for 10 years and is then renewable for further 10-year periods.

Can registration of a trade mark be revoked?

9.78 Registration of a trade mark can be revoked:

(a) if within 5 years following the completion of the registration it has not been put to genuine use in the United Kingdom; or

(b) if such use has been suspended for an uninterrupted period of 5 years and there are no proper reasons for the non-use; or

(c) if in consequence of acts or inactivity of the owner it has become the common name in the trade for a product or service for which it is registered; or

(d) if the trade mark was registered invalidly.

Licensing of trade marks by a charity to its trading company

9.79 A charity may wish to authorise its trading company to utilise the trade mark. Normally the charity will grant the trading company a non-exclusive licence to utilise the mark, since by s 28 of the Trade Marks Act 1994 an 'exclusive licence' means that only the licensee has the right to use the trade mark. That would mean that if a subsidiary holds an exclusive licence, even the charity, as the owner of the registered trade mark, could not use it. It is recommended that the trading company registers the grant of the licence with UKIPO within 6 months of the date of the licence. If this is not done, then the trading company, as licensee, is not directly entitled to damages or to sue for profits in respect of any infringement of the trade mark. The charity could still seek an injunction to restrain unlawful use, but may face difficulties claiming loss of profits if it has now been conducting the relevant business via the trading company. The trading company will be able to register the licence of mark in its name for those classes of activities which *it* determines.

Trade marks outside the United Kingdom?

European Community

9.80

The Community Trade Mark ('CTM') gives its owner the exclusive right to use that mark throughout the member countries of the European

Union. The existence of an earlier conflicting trade mark in any country in the EU gives the owner of the earlier mark the right to prevent registration of a CTM.

The Madrid Protocol

9.81   The Madrid Protocol 1989 allows marks to be registered in any other country which is a signatory to the protocol. This is not a method of obtaining a single worldwide individual trade mark registration, but allows the owner of a mark in the UK to apply to register the mark in any designated territory via the offices of the World Intellectual Property Organisation ('WIPO') in Geneva.

DOMAIN NAMES

9.82   Domain names are the entry point to a charity's online presence and an important part of its IP. The name itself is a trade mark, which in many cases can be registered using the procedure described above. However, there are some additional legal issues which affect domain names and do not apply to other types of trade marks. In particular, it should be noted that a domain name registration applies to the internet and therefore transcends national boundaries, unlike trade marks, which have to be registered in each territory for which protection is sought.

9.83   Registration of a domain name is an entirely separate procedure to the registration of a trade mark, and many names are registered under both procedures by their owner. There are a large number of companies which provide domain name registration services and, in selecting one, you should pay attention to its track record, eg how long it has been in business? Companies established in the UK and which can easily be contacted by telephone will be easier to approach in the event of any problems arising.

Costs in relation to domain names

9.84   The cost of registering a domain name can vary from £20 to £100 or more for a 2-year registration. A domain name is not 'owned' in the way that a trade mark is. The holder of a registered domain name obtains only a right to use the domain name for a period.

9.85   Registrations can be extended or renewed at any time up to a 10-year maximum. So, on 1 January 2009, a domain name can be registered (or a registration extended) up to 31 December 2018 and in 2019 will have to be renewed. Charities should make sure that the registration is recorded in their name, not in the name of the individual who makes the registration. It is also important to have systems in place so as not to miss the date when the registration is due to expire, as the registrar will remove from the register domains that are not renewed between 30 and 45 days after the renewal date, following which the name is released back to the marketplace, potentially for someone else to register. Some companies specialise in purchasing such names and they can then be very hard to recover.

Issues to consider when registering a domain name

9.86 Domain name owners should check (eg on www.betterwhois.com) that the domain name registration company has actually paid the registrar for the full term of years that has been paid for by the owner. Some companies charge clients for up to 10 years' registration, but only pay the registrar for the first year! They may claim that they will pay annually. However, if the registration company should go out of business, the domain name will be valid only until the end of the current year, following which the registration will lapse, unless further fees are paid.

Searches

9.87 Before applying for the registration of a domain name as a trade mark, checks should be made to determine whether any other business owns or is using the same or a similar name. This will also minimise the risk of the domain name owner being accused of trade mark infringement or 'passing off', which could result in the domain name being compulsorily transferred to the trade mark's owner. Checks can be made by looking informally at the trade press, searching through directories such as the Yellow Pages, using search engines and checking trade mark registries.

Domain names and trade marks – a comparison

9.88 Domains are cheap to purchase and quick to register, and it is advisable to purchase as many variants on a name as finances allow. For instance, consider registering key acronyms as domain names and as individual words separated by hyphens. Consider not only .org or .org.uk, but also .com, .co.uk, .info, .biz and .eu.

9.89 Trade marks take longer to register and are more expensive. However, a domain name alone offers little protection from others using the same or a similar name in relation to their products or services (eg by registering one of the variants discussed in the paragraph above or by using the name in branding products or services). It is therefore strongly recommended that before a website is publicly launched, especially where a significant investment is involved in a new brand name, trade mark applications for the name(s) are made in all key territories (eg the UK, Europe and the USA). Trade mark registries do not regard domain name suffixes (such as .com or .co.uk) as adding anything to the distinctiveness of the mark, and so the mark should be registered without a suffix.

Trade mark infringement and domain name disputes

9.90   Unintentional use of a domain name which incorporates a trade mark, such as bt.org or marksandspencer.co.uk, has been held to be unlawful, because such use takes advantage of the distinctive character and reputation of the part of the domain name which precedes the suffix marks, and this is 'unfair' and 'detrimental'. There are formal dispute resolution procedures in place for dealing with domain name disputes.

PATENTS

9.91   'Patent' derives from the Latin word meaning 'an open letter'. In the seventeenth century the Crown started to grant patents as a method of giving an inventor a monopoly, and the essential purpose of a patent remains the same – namely, to give the inventor of a new idea, which has a practical application in a product or process, a monopoly for a period of 20 years. Charities and their trading companies will come across questions of patents from time to time. For instance, charities which undertake research, such as those involved with developing new drugs or universities studying industrial processes. Patents are a highly specialised area. This book does not give a detailed explanation of the law relating to patents. If readers require detailed advice, they should seek it from an expert patent agent or solicitor specialising in this field.

What is a patent?

9.92   The following are key points to note in relation to patents:

(a)   The first person to apply for a patent will be the person who is granted it. The first in time gets the patent. This is the case even if the person who applies for the patent is not the first person to have invented the new idea.

(b)   Patents cannot protect ideas alone. The ideas have to have a practical application (eg the zip fastener or velcro). There must be a demonstrable new technological process or step in a process.

(c)   A patent will not protect:
   (i)   A discovery (this will have no use until a practical application has been found for the discovery).
   (ii)   A scientific theory (for the same reasons as a discovery).
   (iii)   A literary, dramatic, musical or artistic work (this is protected by copyright).
   (iv)   A mathematical method.
   (v)   A scheme, rule or method for performing a mental act, playing a game or doing a business (eg 'Monopoly').
   (vi)   A computer program (protected by copyright).
   (vii)   The presentation of information.

(viii) The invention of a method of treatment of the human or animal body, or surgery, or therapy, or of diagnosis.

(ix) Any variety of animal/plant.

How should a patent be applied for?

9.93 A patent should be investigated at an early stage in the research and development process, not least because a search of the patent register will reveal whether anyone else has already applied for a patent. This will help to avoid the costly and frustrating process of undertaking a large amount of research and development only to discover that someone else has got there first. The following persons may apply for a patent.

An employer

9.94 Under s 39 of the Patents Act 1977, employers own the rights in patentable discoveries/inventions created by an employee, if carried out in the course of the employee's normal duties or in connection with duties that have been specifically assigned to the employee.

Independent consultants

9.95 Consultants will own the patent rights in respect of inventions that they have created, even if this work is done under contract, unless the contract specifically deals with the question of patent rights. Hence, if a team of experts is being built up (as is frequently the case) which may lead to the discovery of a patentable invention, the organisers of the team should ensure that all independent consultants and contractors (as opposed to employees) sign appropriate contracts assigning all intellectual property rights (including the right to apply for patents) to the organiser.

International aspects

9.96 It is possible to apply under the European Patent Convention to the European Patent Office in Munich to register a patent there. A single application is filed, but is then split into separate national patent applications in each country which is a party to the Convention. There are proposals for one common patent which will be applicable in all Member States of the European Union, but so far discussions on this have stalled.

Charities and patents

9.97 It may seem inconsistent that a charity, which is for the public benefit and operates in the public domain, should be able to own a private monopoly such as a patent. Nonetheless, this may be justified on two grounds:

(a)   it puts the knowledge in the public domain (the patent register), albeit on terms that only the charity or its licensees can deal with it; and

(b) it allows the charity to benefit from the fruits of its research and prevents that valuable (and often expensive) asset from being stolen by commercial or other competitors.

(See **3.83–3.84** in relation to charities involved in research.)

9.98 There is, of course, nothing to stop a charity which holds a patent of, for example, a life-preserving drug, from procuring that it is sold cheaper than the normal commercial price. In reality what would happen is that the charity would grant a licence, either to a commercial operator or to its own trading company, to exploit the patent. The charity would need to ensure that the payments under the patent licence are received in the most tax-effective manner (see Chapter 2). Such a licence might stipulate the terms upon which the drug was to be sold (eg that it was not to exceed a certain price).

9.99 If a charity grants a licence to its trading company to exploit a patent, it should ensure that this is done in line with the principles set out in Chapter 7. The licence must be granted at arm's length and conform to normal commercial terms. The charity should not favour its own trading company, unless it can justify doing so as being in furtherance of its charitable purposes. If a trading company owned by a charity is the owner or licensee of a patent, it will be able to exploit the patent (including appointing a licensee or sublicensees) in a normal commercial manner, depending on the terms of the licence (if any) (see **3.87**).

REGISTERED DESIGNS AND DESIGN RIGHTS

9.100 Design protection covers the external appearance of a product, including shape, contours, texture, colours and decoration. Designs may be protected under registered design or design right both at the UK and EU level.

Design right and copyright

9.101 Design right applies to original designs of the shape or configuration of products, but does not apply to two-dimensional designs, which may be protected by copyright or registered design.

9.102 Design right lasts until the expiry of the earlier of 10 years after the date of first marketing of the products made to the design, or 15 years after creation. Copyright for artistic works manufactured by an industrial process is 25 years from the date of marketing of those articles.

9.103 Whereas there is no need for specific action (such as registration) on the part of the designer/author for design right or copyright to arise, the protection is limited to preventing actual copying, which can be difficult to prove. Furthermore, with design rights, it is only possible to stop someone from copying the design for the first 5 years. For the rest of the protection period, anyone is entitled to a licence to make and sell products to the design. Greater protection can be achieved by registering the design.

Registered design

9.104 The protection granted is a monopoly, ie an exclusive right to make, import, export, use or stock any product to which the design has been applied or in which it is incorporated, in the UK. It differs from design rights or copyright, as there is no need to prove copying in relation to infringement of the right. Only designs that are new and of individual character can be registered. Protection can last for up to 25 years. Registered designs cover not only the shape of the product, but also its two-dimensional aspects, such as any ornamentation, lines and colours. However, a new design may not be registered in respect of an article if the appearance of the article is not material, ie if aesthetic considerations are not normally relevant to persons acquiring or using articles of that description. Protection can last for up to 25 years.

DATABASES

9.105 Databases are becoming ever more important for charities and their associated trading companies. In 2005 *The Guardian* newspaper published figures indicating that, using 'face to face' recruitment, it costs between £50 and £100 to recruit each donor, though if a donor remains on a charity's database and continues to give support over a number of years, then this will significantly outweigh the recruitment costs. The average amount donated per adult in the year to 2006 was £183.36.

9.106 Whilst it is hard to put figures on the value of a charity's database, figures from NCVO (Natural Council for Voluntary Organisations) show that up to 70% of the voluntary income of large charities is specifically derived from direct marketing and related activities (including trading catalogues). In direct marketing, charities may use their own in-house database, or they may use lists owned and rented out or operated by commercial agencies.

Storage and use of data

9.107 The law concerning storage and use of data covers two distinct but interlinked areas:

(a) intellectual property law (ie copyright and database rights), which operates to protect the rights of the owner to prevent unauthorised copying and misuse; and

(b) the law on protection of personal data, which is designed to give rights to individuals to prevent misuse of personal information, and which is covered by the Data Protection Act 1998, and other legislation such as the Privacy and Electronic Commerce Regulations 1993.

Databases and copyright

9.108   Section 3A(1) of the Copyright Designs and Patents Act 1988 defines a database as:

'a collection of independent works, data or other materials which—

(a)   are arranged in a systematic or methodical way, and
(b)   are individually accessible by electronic or other means.

In other words, a database is a collection of information arranged in a structured manner. It can be anything from a mailing list, a register of those attending a course or the details of participants in an event, through to a detailed table of supporters containing information about their personal history, their lifestyle preferences and their past relationship with the charity. Copyright in a database arises by the creator inputting a sufficient degree of intellectual innovation and inventiveness (originality) into his or her work. The intellectual input required is not usually onerous and quite a low expectation of intellectual merit is required to establish copyright in a database. There is no requirement for a new innovative step – the mere compiling of information will suffice. Most databases will qualify under the CDPA 1988 as original literary works.

The database right

9.109   In addition to benefiting from copyright protection, a database may have further protection which is set out in the Copyright and Rights in Databases Regulations 1997 (SI 1997/3032). This separate 'database right' arises if there has been a substantial investment in obtaining, verifying or presenting the contents of the database. Database right is an automatic right like design right or copyright, in that there is no registration requirement.

9.110   Database right gives its owner the right to prevent extraction and re-utilisation of the contents of the database. This additional protection is necessary because such acts do not necessarily involve copying, so copyright would not protect against them. Protection is for 15 years from the making of the database or, if published within that period, 15 years from publication.

Ownership of rights in a database

9.111   If a database is built up 'in house' by an organisation (whether a charity or its trading company) using external consultants, the organisation should ensure that the consultant agrees to assign by contract all intellectual property in the database to the organisation. Otherwise the charity or the trading company may find that technically the part of the database created by the consultant is owned by the consultant! (See **9.14**.) If a charity or trading subsidiary obtains the right to use a database from a third party, such as a list rental agent, the licensor (ie the third party) should warrant that it owns the copyright in the database and should agree to indemnify the licensee (ie the charity or trading subsidiary) for any liabilities it may incur if the charity's or trading subsidiary's use of the database infringes another person's rights.

Checklist for those using a database

Complete copies

9.112   If you wish to use an entire database you must ensure authorisation is obtained from the owner of the database.

Public domain

9.113   Some data which is already in the public domain may be incorporated into your database without formal permission. Examples of such data include the Register of Companies, available from Companies House, and public records within the meaning of the Public Records Act 1958.

9.114   For the purposes of the relevant section of the Public Records Act, a privately published directory (eg of grant-making trusts or charity advisors) is not a public record.

Extracts

9.115   Where extracts from a database (or, indeed, from any copyright material) are used, or taken and stored in a database, there is infringement only where the whole of the work or any substantial part of it is affected: s 16(3)(a) of the CDPA 1988 and reg 16 of the 1997 Regulations. In this context 'substantial' means a part of the database which has been created by a significant investment of activity.

Damages

9.116   Damages for breach of copyright and database rights under CDPA 1988 and the 1997 Regulations are compensatory (ie the wronged party should be put in the same position as if the breach had not occurred).

Data protection

9.117   The law in this area tries to address the challenges of balancing an individual's rights of privacy and the user's legitimate use of information.

9.118   The Data Protection Act 1998 gives protection to the individual from misuse of information about him or her. This includes rights such as:

(a)   the right to be given a copy of most information which relates to him/her;

(b)   the right to correct such information if it is inaccurate or misleading;

(c)   the right to prevent processing for marketing purposes or which causes substantial damage or distress; and

(d)   the right to seek compensation if the information is being or has been misused.

It also imposes obligations on those who hold such information (other than individuals using it for private domestic purposes). The legislation protects 'Personal Data' (ie information from which a living individual is identifiable). Unless an organisation falls within one of the exemptions, it is an offence to process personal data without having notified (ie registered with) the Information Commissioner.

9.119   Schedule 1 to the DPA 1998 sets out the 'Data Protection Principles'. These are as follows:

(1)   The information to be contained in personal data shall be obtained, and personal data shall be processed, fairly and lawfully.

(2)   Personal data shall be held only for one or more specified and lawful purposes.

(3)   Personal data held for any purpose or purposes shall be adequate, relevant and not excessive in relation to that purpose or those purposes.

(4)   Personal data shall be accurate and, where necessary, kept up to date.

(5)   Personal data held for any purpose or purposes shall not be kept for any longer than is necessary for that purpose or those purposes.

(6)   Personal data shall be processed in accordance with the rights of data subjects under the Act (see **9.118**(a) to (d)).

(7)   Appropriate measures shall be taken against unauthorised or unlawful processing of personal data and against accidental loss or destruction of, or damage to, personal data.

(8)   Personal data shall not be transferred outside of the European Economic Area unless it is transferred to a territory where there is adequate protection for personal data.

Lists

9.120   An organisation can only lawfully supply to, or acquire marketing or other lists from, another organisation if the names and addresses on the list have been obtained fairly and lawfully (under the first data protection principle), and if the type of body or person to whom the disclosure is made is set out in the notification (ie the registration with the Information

Commissioner's office), eg an environmental charity's entry on notification may state that it can transfer the data to any other charitable/voluntary organisation.

9.121 In considering whether information has been fairly obtained, the Information Commissioner will also consider, inter alia, whether or not the person supplying the information could reasonably be expected to understand the purposes for which the information would be used or disclosed. The Commissioner will be particularly concerned where the data user is falsely given the impression that information will be kept confidential.

9.122 In addition, in order to comply with the first data protection principle, an organisation wishing to use a database for marketing purposes must normally either have consent from each person it wishes to contact, or must make contact in a way that is non-intrusive (eg not making calls to the individual late at night). Where an organisation wishes to send direct marketing by electronic means (such as email or SMS) the Privacy and Electronic Communications Regulations 2003 require that consent *must* be obtained from the recipient.

Electronic direct marketing

9.123 The Privacy and Electronic Communications (EC Directive) Regulations 2003 (SI 2003/2426) apply to marketing electronic communications, ie marketing by phone, fax or electronic mail. 'Electronic mail' includes text, voice, sound or image messages sent over a public electronic communications network, and therefore covers emails and texts. Different rules apply to each means of communication.

9.124 Automated calls, ie pre-recorded marketing messages can be only be made if the prior consent of the recipient has been obtained. The situation is different for telesales, ie direct 'live' marketing calls, which are allowed unless the recipient has expressly notified the company that he or she does not consent.

9.125 However, in relation to both telesales or marketing faxes, the first step, before sending unsolicited marketing material, is to make sure that the recipients (whether individuals or businesses) are not on the Fax Preference Service, Telephone Preference Service or the Corporate Telephone Preference Service. Further information can be found on www.tpsonline.org.uk. If you contact individuals or organisations who are on one of the lists, they can complain to the Information Commissioner, who may take enforcement action.

9.126 With faxes and electronic mail, the situation differs in relation to individuals and organisations. Marketing material can only be sent by fax or electronic mail to individuals who have expressly given consent to the sender. An exception to this applies when an individual has bought a product or service (or was in negotiation to buy a product or service) from the sender. This applies if the communication relates to similar products and the recipient was given an opportunity to refuse to be sent such communications. This exception is known as the 'soft opt-in'. It is not expressed to apply to donors, but the Information Commissioner is unlikely to take enforcement action against charities which rely on the soft opt-in to send direct marketing by email without consent to people who have contacted the charity about a potential donation.

9.127 In the case of businesses, they can be sent marketing material by fax unless they have notified the sender they do not consent to it. The Regulations do not cover marketing electronic mail messages sent to businesses.

9.128 Businesses using the above marketing methods also have an obligation to identify themselves and give their contact details.

Conclusion

9.129 Charities and their trading companies compiling or using databases must ensure that:

(a) they either have or obtain copyright in the database, or

(b) they have notified the Information Commissioner about their processing and comply with data protection laws, including the data protection principles; and

(c) they have consent for direct marketing by email, unless the 'soft opt-in' applies.

CONFIDENTIAL INFORMATION

9.130 There are several types of information that a charity or trading subsidiary may need to keep confidential, such as new campaign ideas, trade secrets or lists of customers. The issue of confidentiality should be considered in relation to third parties with whom the charity or trading subsidiary may share its information, and in relation to its own employees who will have access to the information.

9.131 With confidential information the starting point should be to seek to limit the number of people who will have access to the information, both employees and third parties.

9.132 If it is absolutely necessary to disclose the information, the charity or trading subsidiary should also ensure that there are sufficient contractual safeguards in place. This will be done through confidentiality and non-disclosure clauses, which may be included in contracts of employment or, in relation to third parties, in contracts with them or in separate non-disclosure agreements. If it is necessary to disclose sensitive information, the charity or trading subsidiary should make sure before, or at the time of disclosure, that the parties it is disclosing it to have undertaken in writing to keep the information confidential. Failing to do so may not be crucial, as common law does give some protection for confidential information, even in the absence of contractual safeguards, but relying on this is less certain and may lead to the charity's or trading subsidiary's sensitive information being used without its consent.

Chapter 10

INSURANCE

10.1 *In this chapter we look at the range of insurance cover which a charity or trading subsidiary involved in trading activity would be well advised to consider. We explain where insurance is compulsory, when it is recommended, and what practical issues should be addressed when obtaining or renewing cover.*

INTRODUCTION

10.2 Any charity or trading subsidiary which is engaged in trading activities needs to be aware of what risks it should be covering by insurance. Business carries many risks, and insurance is designed to cover some of those risks. As for individuals in everyday life, carrying adequate insurance is a matter of striking a balance between expenditure and protection in order to achieve relative peace of mind. Some insurance is compulsory. In some cases lenders and investors will insist that appropriate cover is in place and will want evidence that their money is as safe as is reasonably possible.

10.3 Law affects all aspects of insurance: be it the relationship between insurer and insured, the meaning of the risks or perils insured against, or the legal liabilities which insurance is designed to cover. The law relating to insurance is complex and this chapter does not attempt to cover all issues relating to insurance. It deals primarily with:

- insurance contracts;

- compulsory insurance – employers' liability and motor insurance;

- insurance cover which a business should take out – buildings, contents, business interruption (which covers consequential loss/loss of profits), public and product liability, and professional indemnity;

- insurance cover which a business might consider – trustee indemnity or directors' and officers' liability, legal expenses, key man, libel, goods in transit and cyberliability insurance.

10.4 On finding premises, kitting them out, purchasing stock (if appropriate) and engaging staff, a charity or its trading subsidiary must think immediately about insurance. It must distinguish between the many varieties of insurance cover available. It must take out employers' liability insurance and motor insurance – this is compulsory. If a property is purchased, the mortgagee(s) will require that the property is insured against damage by fire, water, wind, storm and other risks. If a property is leased, the lease will stipulate whether the tenant or the landlord should insure against various risks. It is essential that the charity or trading subsidiary's stock and assets are insured against physical damage and that the business is insured against public liability risks.

10.5 It is always prudent to have business interruption insurance (see **10.35–10.37**). Beyond that, a business' choice of insurance depends on what it is doing in the course of operating. If it is providing a service (eg a telephone counselling service), it may need professional indemnity insurance. If it is manufacturing goods, it will need product liability insurance.

AN INTRODUCTION TO THE WORLD OF INSURANCE

10.6 You can arrange most insurance policies either:

- by going straight to an insurance company; or

- by doing it via an insurance broker or, in relation to life assurance and health insurance, independent financial advisers.

Most of the major insurance companies cover the normal range of risks which most businesses will insure against, but you cannot be certain that the terms that company offers on each category of insurance are the best, and for this reason you may prefer to employ an insurance broker. A broker has access to a wider choice of insurers or underwriters (they mean the same thing) than if you go to one insurance company. You pay a broker, although he does not invoice for his service. He gets his fee from his 'brokerage', ie a form of commission paid to him by the insurer to whom he introduces the business, but calculated on the value of the business. Nowadays, for personal insurance, it is often possible to obtain much cheaper deals by going direct to an insurance company rather than using a broker. However, for business purposes, brokers still form a very useful function, as they provide a tailor-made service. The broker is *your* agent. If he fills in the proposal form incorrectly you may be uninsured, but if the error was due to his fault, he may be liable to you for breach of contract and fiduciary duty.

10.7 There are specialist insurers and insurance brokers which specialise in the charity, church and non-profit sector. You may want to consider if these specialists could provide a more appropriate service.

Jargon

10.8 The law and practice relating to insurance contracts is full of jargon that may be intimidating when first encountered. Below is a useful table of common words and their meanings.

Terms		Meaning
All risks	–	all risks insurance against most forms of physical risk (except wear and tear).
Excess (or deductible)	–	the initial part of each claim on your insurance policy which you agree to pay.
Insured	–	the person covered by the insurance.
Insurer	–	the person who provides the insurance cover.
Limit of indemnity	–	the maximum you can recover under the policy.
Premium	–	the price for insurance.
Risk (or peril)	–	what you insure against, eg fire.
Sum insured	–	the amount for which the insured property is insured.

Utmost good faith

10.9 Insurance contracts are different from normal contracts in that the insured has a duty to act with the 'utmost good faith' towards the insurer. Sometimes the latin term 'uberrimae fidei' is used. This means that you must advise the insurer of all material facts relevant to your application for insurance. You must reveal anything that may influence a prudent insurer either in deciding to take on the risk or in the level of premium. If you fail to disclose all material facts, the insurer can escape all liability. It does not matter that you thought a fact was irrelevant if it might have affected the mythical prudent insurer to whom you have broken your duty. So beware. Proposal forms (or telephone proposals) must be addressed with care.

Average

10.10 Most insurance policies which cover property (eg contents) contain an 'average' clause. This means that if you underinsure, the insurers will only be liable for a proportion of your loss.

10.11 Suppose your office contents are insured for £20,000. Their value is £30,000. Someone steals £10,000 worth of contents. Applying averaging you recover £6,666. Because you had only insured for two-thirds of the value of your contents, you are only able to recover two-thirds of your loss.

10.12 It is therefore highly advisable to check your level of insurance cover each year and make sure you increase the sums insured to reflect new purchases and inflation in values.

Indemnity calculation

10.13 Insurance covers you for your actual loss at the date of the accident or loss. Hence, you only recover the value of the goods at that date, ie their second-hand value. You do not get full replacement value unless you have specifically arranged a 'new for old' or 'replacement value' policy. Of course, nothing comes free and you have to pay a higher premium for the extra cover.

Excesses

10.14   Many policies are subject to a compulsory excess so as to discourage minor claims. It is usually possible to reduce the premium by taking a higher voluntary excess, thus balancing the perceived level of risk against cost.

COMPULSORY INSURANCE

10.15   Employers' liability insurance and motor insurance are compulsory.

Employers' liability compulsory insurance

10.16   The Employer's Liability (Compulsory Insurance) Act 1969 requires that every employer carrying on a business, trade or profession in Great Britain (separate legislation applies for Northern Ireland) takes out and maintains insurance with an authorised insurer against liability for bodily injury or disease sustained by its employees arising out of their employment. (There are some exceptions, for instance for some family owned businesses, but they are unlikely to affect charities.) The insurance covers the employer against claims from employees for accidents or sickness they may suffer as a result of working for the employer. Employers must have cover for at least £5 million.

10.17   It is worth noting that:

(a)   The indemnity is usually unlimited.

(b)   A certificate of insurance has to be displayed at the employer's premises and copies of expired certificates have to be retained for 40 years.

(c)   The premium is based on the estimated amount of annual wages and salaries.

(d)   The insurance only applies to employees but not to independent contractors.

10.18   Just because employers' liability insurance is compulsory does not mean that the employer is automatically liable for any injury that an employee sustains as a result of his employment. The employee still has to prove that the injury was a result of:

(a)   negligence by his or her employer; or

(b)   breach of statutory duty (eg breach of the Health and Safety at Work Act 1974); or

(c)   personal negligence of fellow employees.

10.19   A charity is considered to carry on a business or trade for the purposes of the legislation. So far as volunteers are concerned, it is best to treat them as employees and include them on any declaration to the insurer.

Motor insurance

10.20   Section 143(1) of the Road Traffic Act 1988 requires every person who uses, or causes or permits another person to use, a motor vehicle on a road to have a policy of insurance to cover any liability which may be incurred as a result of the death of, or bodily injury to, any person or damage to property caused by, or arising out of, the use of the vehicle on a road in Great Britain.

10.21   Note that insurance is not required by law against the following risks which arise from using a motor vehicle on a road in Great Britain:

(a)   Liability for death or bodily injury or property damage arising out of and in the course of employment of an employee of the person insured. The reason for this exception is that employers have to insure against their liability for death or bodily injury of employees under the Employer's Liability (Compulsory Insurance) Act 1969 (see **10.16–10.19**). Strangely enough, employers are not compelled to insure against their liability for damage to their employees' property either under the 1969 Act or the Road Traffic Act 1988, but it might be worth considering extending insurances to cover this risk.

(b)   More than £250,000 in respect of liability for damage to property (but not death or bodily injury) arising out of any one accident.

(c)   Damage to the owner's vehicle – in other words, only third party insurance is compulsory.

(d)   Liability for damage to goods carried for hire by the vehicle or any trader (such goods would normally be insured separately).

10.22   Therefore a charity or trading company should:

•   buy at least third party motor insurance for all motor vehicles it uses on the road and in other public places – this covers the charity or trading company's liability for personal injury to someone else or damage to property, but does not cover any damage to or theft of its own vehicles which, as for individuals, can be covered through a comprehensive insurance policy (which is generally to be recommended);

•   make sure that employees who use their own cars for business are adequately insured under their own private policies – the charity or trading company's liability for any damage caused by an employee's private car while on business will usually be covered under public liability insurance;

- check that the cover provided by the policy is appropriate, as there are different classes of business use – for example, a travelling circus or commercial representatives are considered differently from those who only make occasional business trips;

- consider that, if several vehicles are owned, fleet cover might offer better terms – a broker will be able to advise on this;

- check the licences of all drivers and advise the insurers of any accidents and motor convictions during the period requested by them, as well as accidents or convictions that occur after insurance is in place – otherwise the charity or trading subsidiary will not be covered.

10.23 A policy is of no effect under the Road Traffic Act 1988 Act unless and until the insurer delivers to the insured 'a certificate in the prescribed form'. The certificate is different from the policy: the policy sets out the terms and conditions of the insurance cover, whereas the certificate provides legal evidence of the cover and contains details of the vehicle, driver(s) and use covered under the insurance, as well as dates of validity of the cover. The schedule gives details specific to the particular policy, such as excesses, no claims discount and which parts of the policy apply (eg whether cover is comprehensive).

RECOMMENDED INSURANCE COVER

10.24 The following cover is usually recommended.

Damage to buildings insurance

10.25 This is optional. It is not normal for the tenant of a building to have to arrange insurance for damage to the building. It is normal for the landlord to insure. However, this is not always the case.

10.26 The normal risks or perils to insure against are destruction or damage by fire, lightning, explosion, storm, tempest and flood.

10.27 If a charity or its trading company owns a building freehold it should insure it – if it is mortgaged the mortgagee will require that it is insured.

10.28 When insuring a building or checking that a landlord's insurance cover is sufficient under a lease, it is wise to check that:

(a)   the sum insured to cover the cost of rebuilding is adequate, bearing in mind the length of time it can take to get planning permission and rebuild, and the nasty habit of building costs to escalate;

(b)   the perils insured against are wide enough to cover all possible risks – many policies, for example, do not cover subsidence;

(c)   the policy covers not merely building costs, but also professional fees (eg architects, surveyors, etc).

10.29   If a charity or trading subsidiary is letting out its building or is a tenant, it should make sure that:

(a)   The policy covers a reasonable period, eg two years' loss of rent.

(b)   The tenant's interest is noted on the policy.

(c)   The proceeds of the insurances are divided between the landlord and the tenant in accordance with their respective interests in the premises – this means that if the tenant has carried out extensive improvements and these are destroyed, it will be reimbursed for the value of those improvements from the landlord's insurance policy. If the landlord's insurance policy does not cover this, the tenant should insure its own improvements separately – this can be very important in retail outlets, where considerable sums can be spent in refitting.

Insurance against loss and damage to contents

10.30   It is wise to insure the contents of business premises against loss or damage. This covers stock, machinery, computers, office equipment, furnishings and employees' personal belongings. Insurance should be taken out against:

(a)   physical damage (eg fire, explosion, flood, etc);

(b)   theft.

10.31   A business may want to consider 'all risks' insurance in respect of valuable machinery or equipment. 'All risks' is a misnomer: it covers most forms of physical loss or damage and may include accidental damage or loss, but normally excludes wear and tear, electrical or mechanical breakdown and gradual deterioration, specifically stated in the policy document.

10.32   Under an 'all risks' policy, each item insured must be specified and a separate sum insured must be allocated to it. The geographical ambit of the policy will normally be the UK, but extensions can be obtained to cover movements of items abroad.

10.33 As ever, an adequate sum insured should be chosen, otherwise 'averaging' will strike.

10.34 Note that household buildings and contents policies do cover acts of terrorism. However, this is not the case for commercial premises, and if a business wants terrorist risks to be covered it will need to obtain these as an add-on to its cover or on a stand-alone basis.

Business interruption insurance

10.35 If business premises are destroyed, be it partially or totally, the business will suffer. Not only will it have to replace its damaged premises, but trading revenues will be lost too. So as to cover this potential loss, most businesses take out consequential loss or business interruption insurance (they mean the same thing). To add to the confusion, some insurers call such policies 'loss of profits' insurance.

10.36 Such policies generally cover not only loss of revenue, but also additional expenditure which a business may have to incur in consequence of loss, damage or destruction of premises. It will include the cost of fitting out replacement premises, increased rent, charges, rates, lighting, heating, moving costs, etc.

10.37 The premiums for this type of insurance vary according to the risks insured against, the level of indemnity and the length of cover. It would be normal to insure against the same risks as are covered by the buildings insurance policy. The length of cover after the loss is known as the indemnity period and is a matter of individual choice. It should not be less than 12 months.

Public liability insurance

10.38 The purpose of taking out public liability insurance is to cover the business against its liabilities to third parties for causing death, personal injury or damage to their property. The two broad fields covered by a public liability policy are as follows.

Risks arising from the ownership, occupation or management of premises

10.39 Broadly speaking, premises risks include:

- escape of dangerous substances from land/buildings;

- dangerous premises – under the Occupiers' Liability Act 1957, the occupier of any premises owes a duty of care to his visitors to see that they are reasonably safe in using the premises for the purpose for which they are invited; occupiers also owe a duty to those who are not visitors (eg trespassers) in relation to specific dangers, as provided under the Occupiers Liability Act 1984.

Hence, by taking on a lease or buying a freehold, a charity or trading company is under a duty to ensure that its premises are reasonably safe. If they are not and someone is injured, or their property is damaged, the charity or trading subsidiary can be sued.

10.40 A business may also be liable to visitors (as opposed to employees) under the Health and Safety at Work etc Act 1974, breach of which is also covered by public liability insurance.

Employees' activities

10.41 The risks arising from the activities of employees and agents arise from what lawyers call 'vicarious liability'.

10.42 An employer is liable for the negligent acts or omissions of its employees causing death, bodily injury or damage to property during the course of employment. Beware, as for these purposes 'an employee' has a very wide meaning. For the purpose of vicarious liability, a person is treated as an employee if the insured has the right to control the way in which the negligent deed was done. Hence, for example, a volunteer will be covered by the doctrine of vicarious liability.

Exclusions

10.43 The public liability policy is not all-embracing. It excludes many forms of liability which are covered by other insurance policies, such as:

(a)   Employer's liability.

(b)   Motor vehicles.

(c)   Liability arising under contract.

(d)   Product liability.

10.44 It is best to select a decent level of indemnity for the public liability policy. This type of insurance is quite cheap, so £1 million of cover should not cost too much and is well worth effecting. Many organisations which undertake contractual work (eg under contracts for the delivery of care in the community services) are obligated under contract to effect public liability insurance.

Product liability insurance

10.45 Mention was made in Chapter 8 of the obligations imposed on producers or importers of certain types of goods under the Consumer Protection Act 1987, the Sale of Goods Act 1979, or under the common law rules of negligence. Claims for breach of these obligations could render a business insolvent.

Example

10.46 A trading company owned by a charity produces or imports a defective product. A consumer sustains serious long-term injuries from using the product and sues the trading company. The costs of defending the action and of meeting any court award or out-of-court settlement could run into hundreds of thousands of pounds. Such costs could well force the trading company into insolvency, and would also mean that the trustees of the charity which owns the trading company would be forced to write-off the charity's investment in it. The position would be even worse if the item concerned was sold by an unincorporated charity, in which case the action would be brought against the trustees of the charity personally, and the claim could result in their personal bankruptcy. If a claim were to be brought in the United States, where juries have a tendency to award enormous damages for the most trifling injury, the potential liabilities could be huge.

10.47 To cover this risk, a business can take out product liability insurance. Such insurance is not cheap. Premiums depend on such obvious factors as amount of turnover, the nature of the business, where goods are exported to, the manufacturing process, etc. If a charity or trading company is manufacturing goods, the insurers will almost certainly want to inspect the premises.

10.48 This insurance will cover product liability, ie liability for loss, damage or bodily injury arising from defective products. It will not cover any costs of replacing a defective product. Such insurance can be obtained (at a price) – it is called product guarantee insurance.

Professional indemnity insurance

10.49 Suppliers of services are under a legal obligation to use reasonable skill and care in carrying out their duties, and professionals are under a higher duty.

10.50 The title 'professional indemnity' insurance is a misnomer. This type of cover is not only available for what are usually termed 'professionals'. Insurance can be obtained for those who provide a whole range of services as well as for professionals (eg plumbers, carpenters, etc).

OTHER INSURANCE

10.51 The following types of insurance should be considered.

Legal expenses insurance

10.52 Taking or defending legal proceedings is expensive. Even if at the end of the day the claimant wins and recovers some of his (her or its) costs, he will still have a major financial commitment whilst fighting the case, and until the judge or arbitrator gives his or her decision, the claimant will not know for certain if he will win. The fear of legal costs puts many people off taking or defending legal proceedings. To plug this particular hole it is possible to take out legal expenses insurance. As charities become more and more involved in delivering public services, either through primary purpose trading or through trading companies, it is wise for them to consider whether or not they need to take out legal expenses insurance so as to give them the backing of an insurance policy to fight legal battles.

10.53 There are various types of legal expenses insurance. Some are very specialised and give cover solely in respect of specific matters. For example, in relation to employment claims, insurers arrange telephone advice on handling complaints, disciplinary procedure, etc, as well as actually providing lawyers to contest tribunal or court proceedings. Others are more general, and give an indemnity for a wide range of legal costs within a limit of expenses that can be claimed in any year. The cover may be subject to certain exclusions, eg conveyancing, defamation, disputes with HMRC. This form of insurance is not very expensive and is well worth considering.

10.54 Whereas most legal expenses insurance policies are sold 'before the event' (ie to cover the legal costs of an event potentially occurring), it is also possible to take out 'after the event' insurance once that event has occurred.

Libel insurance

10.55 If a charity or its trading company is involved in printing or publishing books, magazines or journals, it should certainly consider effecting libel insurance.

Fidelity insurance

10.56 This insures a business against employees stealing the firm's money. There have been some spectacular cases of such thefts (involving charities), and charities should consider taking out such insurance. Charities involved in trading may be exposed to a greater risk in this area than a conventional grant-making trust. Be aware that if an organisation has this form of cover, it almost invariably has to take up a written reference on each new member of staff who handles money.

Trustee indemnity (or directors' and officers' liability) insurance

10.57 Section 73F of the Charities Act 1993 (as amended by the Charities Act 2006) provides a statutory power for charity trustees to purchase trustee indemnity insurance. This type of insurance is also known as directors' and officers' liability insurance, and is put in place by both charitable and commercial organisations to insure against claims arising from the insured person's acts or omissions in carrying out his or her duties as a director or officer of a company, and legal costs in defending such claims. Typical examples of risks include:

- negligent performance of duties;

- liability for torts of the company;

- breach of the Companies Acts;

- 'wrongful trading' – under the Insolvency Act 1986, if a limited company goes into insolvent liquidation, the directors can be made personally liable to creditors in certain circumstances (see **11.93–11.98**).

10.58 There are a number of exclusions from the typical policy, including liabilities arising from fraud or under guarantees or warranties given by the director, and often liabilities arising out of an action brought on the part of anyone who is insured under the policy.

10.59 Note that this type of insurance will not cover the potential unlimited liability of the trustees of unincorporated charities to third parties (see **11.15–11.34** and **11.115**).

Internet and cyberliability insurance

10.60 If a charity or trading company carries out e-commerce, it is important to obtain appropriate insurance cover. Internet and cyberliability insurance usually covers e-commerce, damage to data or to a website caused by unauthorised access, as well as internet fraud and transmission of a computer virus.

Goods in transit

10.61 This covers goods against damage or loss that may occur whilst the goods are en route from, for example, a seller to a purchaser, or to be delivered to the custody of a third party. If a carrier is engaged to deliver goods, it is likely that it will take out insurance, either in its own name or as agent to the business. It is important to ensure that there is an insurance policy in place to cover goods whilst in transit.

INSURANCE POLICIES AND OTHERS

10.62 A number of different people may be interested in the insurance policies entered into by a business:

(a) The landlord – the business may have to insure leased premises.

(b) Mortgagee/lender – if a charity or its trading company mortgages property (eg to a bank), the mortgage lender or 'mortgagee' will wish to make sure it is adequately insured. Depending on what property is mortgaged, this can cover buildings, stock, plant and machinery, goods in transit and consequential loss. The mortgagee may also want 'key man' cover, which is an insurance policy on the life and health of a 'key' or important employee whose death or incapacity would cause damage to the business. They may also want their interest as mortgagees noted on the insurance policies.

(c) Finance companies – if a business hires or leases equipment, or takes it on hire purchase, in the small print of the contract there is invariably an obligation on the hiree or lessee (not the owner) to insure the equipment against 'all risks' and to note the interest of the owner on the policy.

(d) Employees – they may demand pensions or medical expenses insurance or permanent health insurance.

PRACTICAL CONSIDERATIONS

When is it worthwhile taking out insurance?

10.63 It is easy to imagine that all types of disaster may strike a charity or its trading company and that therefore it should take out extensive insurance against the widest range of risks for the maximum sum insured. If this is done, the charity/trading company will probably have spent most of its working capital! So before deciding whether to take out insurance and the amount of such cover that is appropriate, try to answer the following questions first:

(a) Is this insurance obligatory?

(b) Is this insurance necessary?

(c) Is it prudent to take it out?

(d) Does the person recommending it understand the particular business?

(e) What is the premium?

(f)   Is there an alternative quotation? Remember there are numerous insurance companies – all (in theory) competing.

(g)   Has the proposal form been completed in full? Remember that insurance policies are contracts of utmost good faith, which obliges the insured to disclose all material facts to the insurer.

(h)   What risks are covered by the policy?

(i)   What risks are excluded?

(j)   What are the conditions of the policy (eg about storage of stock, etc)?

Negotiating cover

10.64   The following points will also be helpful when negotiating insurance cover.

Package cover

10.65   Insurance for small and medium-sized businesses is often sold in packages that group together the most common requirements, such as employers' liability, buildings and contents and business interruption.

10.66   Buying insurance as a package can save time for small businesses, as you only source and negotiate your insurance needs once. Each insurer or broker offers packages comprising different core elements. It is advisable to check the cover you require against the package contents and add other elements as needed. Some packages are tailored to cover specialist sectors (eg retail, construction and manufacturing). Note that motor insurance should be bought separately.

10.67   It is wise to make sure that you receive copies of the individual policy documents so you can check the cover provided and make a note of the warranties to be complied with. On a practical note, make a record of everything your insurer says is covered and confirm this in writing. This will help in the event of a dispute later between you and the insurer.

How to buy effectively

10.68   Calculate how much cover you need. Insufficient cover is one of the main reasons insurance claims are not paid in full. Always insure your assets for their cost price. Your policy should protect against inflation and increases in the value of your stock, equipment or liabilities.

10.69   Most policies require a minimum level of security and, for example, you may have to install a burglar alarm system or sprinklers according to your insurer's specifications. Your insurer may send an insurance surveyor to assess the risks and recommend improvements before granting cover.

Renewal

10.70 Each year, about 2 months before the insurance policies are due for renewal, it is sensible to review them with the insurer or insurance broker to make sure that the business is adequately insured both as regards:

(a) level of cover; and

(b) risks covered.

Ongoing obligations

10.71 During the year remember to:

(a) promptly notify insurers of all claims under any insurance policy; and

(b) promptly advise them of any significant change in the risk (eg has the business started to store high explosives?).

RISK MANAGEMENT

10.72 Whilst, as has been seen, some insurances are compulsory and many are advisable, insurance cannot be the only way that a charity manages its own or its trading subsidiary's risk. Sensible risk management precautions are necessary for charity trustees to discharge their fiduciary duties, and may also help to keep premiums to a reasonable level for those insurance policies that are taken out.

10.73 In addition, the Charities (Accounts and Reports) Regulations 2008 (SI 2008/629) place a legal requirement on charities whose accounts are required by law to be audited for the trustees' annual report to contain 'a statement as to whether the charity trustees have given consideration to the major risks to which the charity is exposed and satisfied themselves that systems or procedures are established in order to manage those risks'. The Charity Commission encourages the trustees of smaller charities to make such a statement as a matter of best practice.

10.74 What risk management steps need to be taken will depend upon the nature of the business, but should, as a matter of course, include establishing a risk policy, carrying out a comprehensive risk identification and assessment, evaluating what action needs to be taken in respect of risks, and periodic monitoring and assessment. It is also a good idea to maintain a risk log or risk register, which identifies the residual level of risk where steps to manage risk have been taken, or the 'net risk level'. See Charity Commission publication

Charities and Risk Management, available on its website at http://www.charity-commission.gov.uk/investigations/charrisk.asp.

10.75 As mentioned at **7.13–7.24**, charities may wish to 'ring-fence' risky activity so that it is undertaken solely by one or more trading subsidiaries.

Chapter 11

INSOLVENCY

11.1 *Charities which engage in trading, whether directly or through a trading company, may well need to consider questions of solvency or insolvency. This chapter covers the definition of insolvency, the insolvency of limited companies and unincorporated organisations, the consequences of insolvency, how to limit liability, and the relationship between charities and their trading companies with regard to payment of debts.*

INTRODUCTION

11.2 Charities which engage in trading inevitably take greater risks than grant-giving charities. Some of the risks which charities face when involved in trading are beyond their control: eg a charity involved in delivering public services may experience a very sudden reduction in fee income as a result of changes in government policy. A charitable, fee-paying school may decide to invest in building expensive new facilities but then fail to attract additional pupils; a charity running workshops for people with disabilities may take on extra staff in order to manufacture and build up additional stocks which do not sell; a charitable consultancy might experience a drop in orders for one reason or another; and, of course, there can be a simple downturn in the economy which affects all businesses, including charities carrying on trading directly, or charities' trading companies. Such events can affect a charity or a trading company's solvency.

WHAT IS INSOLVENCY?

11.3 Charities operate under a number of varying constitutional forms: companies limited by guarantee or (rarely) by shares, societies incorporated by Royal Charter, industrial and provident societies, unincorporated associations, or trusts. A new legal form for charities – the charitable incorporated organisation (or 'CIO') – is expected to become available by the end of 2009 or early 2010. As will be seen, the law relating to insolvency has a different impact depending on how a charity is constituted. Emphasis is placed in this chapter on company law, for the good reason that company law relating to insolvency is much more sophisticated and complex than the bankruptcy laws (which apply to individuals), that many charities carrying on trading activity directly will be incorporated, and subsidiary trading companies are always so established. But it must be remembered that a minority of registered charities are set up as limited companies.

11.4   The Insolvency Act 1986 is the main statute dealing with insolvency and has been updated several times in recent years to promote the 'rescue culture'. The Act applies, with modifications, to industrial and provident societies, including its provisions on fraudulent and wrongful trading (see **11.88–11.98**). The Insolvency Act is also expected to apply to CIOs.

11.5   In company law (which applies to all companies, whether limited by guarantee or by shares), the terms 'insolvency' and 'insolvent' are used in a number of ways. Broadly speaking, there are two separate tests to determine if a company is insolvent. These two tests are also used in relation to individual insolvency, and it is therefore important to understand them.

The going concern test

11.6   The basis of the going concern test is whether a company can pay its debts as they fall due. This is also known as the 'cash flow test'. This test is applied in various cases:

(1)   For the purposes of a declaration of solvency (a prerequisite for the solvent winding up of a company), the directors have to confirm that the company will be able to pay its debts in full plus interest within a 12-month period.

(2)   Sections 122(1)(f) and 123(1)(e) of the Insolvency Act 1986 provide that a company may be wound up by order of the court as insolvent if it is unable to pay its debts as they fall due.

Obviously, this test can be used by the directors of a company or the trustees of an unincorporated organisation who are concerned about solvency, in order to check on the financial health of the company or organisation.

The balance sheet test

11.7   Under the balance sheet test, insolvency denotes the actual or anticipated deficiency of assets to meet a company's liabilities. This is reflected in the Insolvency Act 1986, which provides that a company may also be wound up on the basis that it is unable to pay its debts if the value of its assets is less than the amount of its liabilities, taking into account its contingent and prospective liabilities (ss 122(1)(f) and 123(2)). Again, the directors may use this test to check on the company's financial health.

11.8   Section 41(2)(b) of the Charities Act 1993 provides that the accounting records of a registered charity which is not a company must contain 'a record of the assets and liabilities of the charity'. The Companies Act 2006, s 386(3)(b) imposes an identical requirement on charitable companies. Exempt charities which are not companies are simply required by CA 1993, s 46(1) to keep proper books of account, although some types of exempt charity may have more specific accounting requirements imposed by other regulators.

11.9 Under the company accounting regulations the accounts should include details of any liability the nature of which is clearly defined, and which is either likely to be incurred, or certain to be incurred but uncertain as to the date on which it will arise.

Interrelationship of the cash flow and balance sheet tests

11.10 The interrelationship between the balance sheet test and its requirement that full account be taken of contingent and prospective liabilities, and the going concern test of calculating liabilities causes difficulties. Under the going concern test it is assumed that a company will continue to trade and therefore that liabilities which would crystallise should the company cease to trade are not taken into account in assessing the company's actual or contingent liabilities. The going concern test is rather like a bicycle. So long as the cyclist maintains forward momentum, all is well. But if the rider loses impetus, the bicycle wobbles and falls over. Crash. So, too, with a company.

11.11 If a calculation of the value of assets and liabilities is made on the basis of the company ceasing to trade, as compared with the going concern test, the effect on the company's balance sheet may well be enormous. This is called the 'break up basis of valuation'. First, the value of the assets may be written down greatly – second-hand goods will almost certainly command a much lower price on the open market than their book value as stated in the company's accounts. Secondly, stopping trading will cause a number of major liabilities to crystallise and thus increase the company's indebtedness. For example:

(1) Staff will be made redundant, thus triggering compensation payments.

(2) Leasing companies who have hired out photocopiers or computers or cars (etc) will terminate the contracts and demand payment of all the future instalments due under the terms of the lease, less a small discount to reflect early repayment.

(3) The landlord of leasehold premises will demand any unpaid rent and may make a claim for damages for breach of a covenant in the lease (eg to repair).

(4) Claims may arise for breach of a contract to deliver services.

(5) Bank borrowings which were used to fund the ongoing operation will have to be repaid.

11.12   If the test is not calculated on a going concern but on a break up basis, the results will almost inevitably be much worse, and the prospects of insolvency much greater. It is thus very important for directors to know whether a valuation is to be done on the going concern or the break up basis, as the results will be very different. Directors may have a valuation prepared on the going concern basis, provided that they have *reasonable grounds* to consider that the company will be able to continue to trade. If, on the other hand, they conclude that it is not reasonable to assume that the company will be able to continue to trade, they *must* take that into account when the valuation is being prepared, which may mean considering preparation of the valuation on a break up basis.

11.13   The cash flow (or going concern) and balance sheet tests cannot be seen as a strictly either/or test. The two may well impact on each other. Hence, a deficiency of assets may eventually result in a cash flow crisis. Equally, an adverse cash flow may force a company to sell off assets cheaply, thereby causing it to fail the balance sheet test.

11.14   The consequences of insolvency will depend on the form of the organisation, and are explored below.

THE INSOLVENCY OF TRUSTS AND UNINCORPORATED ASSOCIATIONS

11.15   The debts of a limited company are its and its alone. If a company is insolvent, it may be forced into insolvent liquidation. The directors of that company will not incur any personal liability for the debts of the company, except in limited circumstances (see **11.87–11.98** below).

11.16   The position is very different for an unincorporated association or a trust. In either case there is no separate entity with limited liability. The debts of a charitable organisation without limited liability are ultimately the personal responsibility of the charity trustees.

Charitable trust

11.17   If a charitable trust is sued for a debt, then it is the charity trustees' names which will appear in the legal proceedings. If a trust incurs an obligation (eg it enters into a lease or contract), it is the charity trustees' names which appear on the lease or contract. A trust or an unincorporated association has no legal personality of its own. Well-advised trustees can seek to limit their liabilities under any contract or lease to the assets of the trust (see **11.17–11.18** for more detail).

11.18   Sections 50–62 of the Charities Act 1993 do contain a mechanism allowing charity trustees to incorporate their trust, but incorporation of this nature does not reduce the charity trustees' personal liabilities.

11.19   Many trust deeds contain an indemnity from the trust to the charity trustees for any liability properly incurred by them in the course of fulfilling their duties as trustees, such that the charity's funds can be used to pay these liabilities. However, this indemnity is useless if the trust lacks the financial resources to honour it.

Example

11.20   A charitable school, which had been carrying on primary purpose trading, closed down. The school was run by an unincorporated trust. The trust had insufficient reserves to meet its redundancy liabilities to the staff. The charity trustees were sued personally by the staff and each trustee had to pay £5,000 to meet the redundancy costs. The indemnity in the trust deed was useless.

11.21   If the trustees are held personally liable, the liability of the trustees is 'joint and several'. This means that all the trustees could be held equally liable or that the whole or a large part of the claim could be pursued against any one of the trustees. A creditor can sue only one of a group of trustees if he wishes. He can 'pick off' the one most likely to pay or to be able to pay.

11.22   The charity trustee who is forced to pay up has a right to petition the court for a contribution from each of the other trustees for a proportionate part of the debt due. Under the Civil Liability (Contribution) Act 1978, the court has the power to award in favour of one trustee against another a contribution of such amount as the court considers to be just and equitable, having regard to the extent of the responsibility of that other trustee for any loss. The court may exempt any person from liability to make a contribution.

Example

11.23   A charitable trust incurs trading debts to a third party and has insufficient resources to meet the debt. Trustee A is sued and pays £10,000 damages. The claimant does not sue the other trustees.

11.24   There are four other trustees. Trustee A may seek an order from the court to force the other trustees to contribute to the amount Trustee A has had to pay out.

11.25   If one of the trustees is unable to meet any contributions ordered by the court (eg because he is insolvent), the other trustees will have to meet the liability of the bankrupt trustee equally amongst themselves.

11.26   It is also open to the trustee being sued to join her or her co-trustees as party to the action.

11.27   If the liabilities of the trust exceed the trustees' personal wealth, the charity trustees could themselves be forced into personal bankruptcy (see **11.31–11.33**).

Unincorporated association

11.28   The members of the management committee of an unincorporated association are in the same position as the charity trustees of a trust – they, too, are charity trustees – except for one difference. Under the rules of an unincorporated association, the members of the association, who elect the management committee, may agree to indemnify the management committee members for liabilities properly incurred by them in serving on the management committee. It must be emphasised that the committee can only make the general members of the association personally liable if the association's constitution clearly provides for this, or if the members sanction the liability within the constitution.

11.29   In such circumstances, if an unincorporated association is unable to pay its debts as they fall due or if its liabilities exceed its assets, ultimately the members of the association may be liable equally for the association's debts. However, a creditor will be entitled to sue the members of the management committee who will have been responsible for running the association. The members of the management committee will then have to seek indemnity from the members, if this is appropriate.

Process

11.30   In terms of legal process, although an unincorporated organisation can become insolvent, there is no legal mechanism for the organisation itself to be put into liquidation or administration. If the unincorporated organisation lacks the resources to meet its liabilities, the burden will fall on the trustees or members of the management committee *personally*. If they fail to meet those obligations, the creditor can sue them (or any of them).

11.31   If the trustees are successfully sued, the creditor can ultimately petition to have them made bankrupt. A creditor may petition for the bankruptcy of an individual if the debtor owes a debt above a minimum of £750 and the debtor appears to be unable to pay, or appears to have no reasonable prospect of being able to pay that debt. A debtor appears to be unable to pay a debt if he has been served with a statutory demand and more than 3 weeks have elapsed since the demand was served upon him and he has neither complied with the demand nor applied to have it set aside. If the petition is successful, the trustee's assets become vested in an individual appointed by the court, bearing the somewhat confusing title of 'trustee in bankruptcy'.

11.32   The trustee in bankruptcy can be either a government official (the Official Receiver) or a private insolvency practitioner. The trustee in bankruptcy is responsible for gathering in the bankrupt's assets and paying off the creditors. If an individual is made bankrupt, he loses all his assets: he cannot obtain credit or serve as a director of a company. If he is a professional (eg a solicitor or a Member of Parliament), he will lose his ability to practise his profession. He is automatically discharged from the bankruptcy after one year, in normal circumstances.

11.33 So as to avoid bankruptcy, an individual debtor can try to strike a voluntary arrangement (known as an individual voluntary arrangement, or 'IVA') with his creditors. This can be achieved by getting 75% of the creditors (calculated by value) to vote to accept a compromise plan whereby the debtor agrees to pay a limited amount (eg 50p in the pound) to each creditor over an agreed period in return for the creditors not making him bankrupt. This compromise binds all creditors (even if they voted against the plan), so that they cannot seek to bankrupt him in respect of the debts which are subject to the voluntary arrangement.

Incorporation

11.34 As the world becomes more litigious, and individuals become more aware – and wary – of the risk of legal action, more and more charitable organisations (particularly those involved in trading activity) are choosing to move from unincorporated status to incorporated status. The risks to the charity trustees if an incorporated organisation becomes insolvent are much lower (see **11.87–11.98** below).

THE INSOLVENCY OF INCORPORATED ORGANISATIONS

11.35 There are various forms of insolvency which apply to companies, namely:

(1) Administration.

(2) Company voluntary arrangement.

(3) Administrative receivership.

(4) Scheme of arrangement.

(5) Compulsory liquidation.

(6) Creditors' voluntary liquidation.

(7) Members' voluntary liquidation (although strictly speaking this is not insolvency).

All of these are explored in more detail below.

Administration

11.36 The mechanism of company administration was initially aimed at rescuing financially distressed companies, but is also intended to provide a mechanism to facilitate the implementation of a plan for the maximisation of a company's assets in the event that a liquidation is unavoidable. In reality, the majority of companies that go into administration do so to obtain protection from creditors for a temporary period, whilst assets are realised to prevent a free-for-all attack by creditors.

11.37 Under the relevant legislation, any administrator appointed to a company must carry out his functions with the objectives of:

- rescuing the company as a going concern; or

- achieving a better result for the company's creditors as a whole than would be likely if the company were wound up (without first being in administration); or

- realising property in order to make a distribution to one or more secured or preferential creditors.

11.38 The rescue of the company as a going concern is the primary objective and the administrator must perform his functions accordingly, unless he thinks either that it is not reasonably practicable to achieve this or that the secondary objective listed above will achieve a better result for the company's creditors as a whole. Only in those circumstances can the administrator move to the second objective. He may only perform his functions in accordance with the third objective if he thinks that it is not reasonably practicable to achieve either the primary or secondary objectives, and if this does not unnecessarily harm the interests of the creditors of the company as a whole.

11.39 An application for an administration order in respect of the company can be made by way of an application to the court, or administration can be achieved outside of that process.

11.40 It is a prerequisite to administration that the company is or is likely to become unable to pay its debts and that administration is likely to achieve the purpose of the administration. The only exception to these preconditions is where the applicant is a qualified floating charge holder (see **11.64**), when there is no need to satisfy the court that the company is or is likely to become unable to pay its debts.

11.41 In all other cases the court will still have discretion whether to make an order or not. The court will compare the advantages to the creditors of an administration with those of a liquidation.

11.42 The company or its directors, or one or more of the creditors can apply for an administration order, as can the holder of a qualifying floating charge. There are others that may have standing to apply to the court.

11.43 If the court route to administration is followed, an administration application must be made to the court. If the out of court route is followed, it is sufficient simply for a notice of appointment to be filed at court in the appropriate form.

11.44 Where a company or the directors intend to appoint an administrator, they must give 5 business days' written notice to any person who is or may be entitled to appoint an administrative receiver, or any qualified floating charge holder who is or may be entitled to appoint an administrator using the out of court procedure. As time passes, this will become more infrequent as, since 2003, this power to appoint has been removed in respect of new security created, although there are sufficient older charges in existence containing this power for this still to be a consideration (see **11.64**).

11.45 An administrator is obliged, as soon as possible after his appointment, to obtain a list of all the company's creditors and to send a notice of his appointment to each creditor of whose claim he is aware.

11.46 In the short period until an administrator is formally appointed, there is an interim moratorium to protect the company and its assets from creditor action. Following the making of an administration order, a moratorium is immediately put in place and no resolution may be passed for the winding up of the company, and (most importantly) no step may be taken to enforce security over the company's property except with the consent of the administrator or with the permission of the court. The moratorium includes a prohibition on repossession of goods in the company's possession under a hire purchase agreement, the exercise by a landlord of a right to forfeit a lease, and the institution or continuation of legal process in each case without the consent of the administrator or the permission of the court. Furthermore, in respect of post-2003 security, no administrative receiver may be appointed.

11.47 However, it is important to note that the moratorium does not stop time running under the Limitation Act 1980, and a creditor with claims against the company will need to consider the position carefully and, if necessary, seek the permission of the court to issue protective proceedings, if the administrator's consent to do so is refused. It is clear that the court will expect the administrator's consent to be sought prior to the making of any application to the court. The court has set out guidelines to assist administrators in reaching a decision.

11.48 Once appointed, an administrator needs to obtain full details of and establish the company's up-to-date financial position as soon as possible, which will include requiring the directors to provide him with a statement of the company's affairs. Thereafter, he will provide proposals to creditors to be considered at an initial meeting of creditors to be held within 10 weeks of his appointment. In certain circumstances the administrator does not need to call such a meeting, but he can be required to do so by creditors whose debts amount to at least 10% of the total debts of the company.

11.49 In general terms, the administrator has all the directors' powers to do anything necessary or expedient for the proper management of the affairs, business and property of the company. He has control of the company's property and also has a duty to manage the company's affairs, business and property. He owes a duty of care to the company, its creditors and its shareholders.

11.50 The administrator acts as the company's agent and will not incur personal liability in respect of any contract or other obligation he enters into on behalf of the company. Liability incurred under a contract entered into while the company is in administration will be payable as an expense of the administration in priority to the administrator's remuneration. The reality is that, unless an administrator is confident that there are sufficient funds available to the company to meet any post-administration contractual liability, he will not enter into any contract on behalf of the company.

11.51 An administrator's appointment automatically terminates after one year, but that period can be extended by court order or by consent of the company's creditors for a further period of up to 6 months.

11.52 A termination of the administration may occur by court order or on the application of the administrator or a creditor. The most common exit from administration is a move to a creditors' voluntary liquidation or a company voluntary arrangement.

Company voluntary arrangement

11.53 A company voluntary arrangement ('CVA') is an agreement voluntarily entered into by a company with its creditors, by which the creditors accept, or are required to accept, payment of less than the sum due to them, in return for the creditors not suing for the full amount due to them. There are many similarities with an IVA (see **11.33**).

11.54 A nominee is appointed to act in relation to the implementation of the CVA.

11.55 A CVA can be proposed by an administrator as an exit from administration, or by the directors of the company. The procedures vary depending on whether the administrator is to be the nominee, whether the proposal is made by the directors and where the administrator is not the intended nominee, but in all cases a proposal is provided to creditors and the shareholders of the company.

11.56 There is no automatic moratorium on debts in a CVA, and so it is often the case that, before a CVA is proposed, an administration order is first applied for to give that protection to the company.

11.57 Whether or not a debt is released under a CVA will depend on the true construction of the arrangement documentation, as will all other matters in respect of the CVA.

11.58 Once a proposal for a CVA has been put forward, meetings of both the creditors and the members of the company are held, usually on the same day. These meetings are to decide whether to approve the proposed voluntary arrangement (with or without modifications).

11.59 The majority of *creditors* required to approve the proposal is in excess of 75% of the value of creditors present in person or by proxy and voting. If more than one half in value of the creditors voting against a resolution are creditors to whom notice was given, whose votes are to be counted and who are not connected with the company (as defined in s 249 of the Insolvency Act 1986) the resolution will fail.

11.60 The majority of *members* required is more than 50% in value of members present and voting.

11.61 If the creditors approve the proposal but the members do not, subject to the right of a member to apply to the court, the wishes of the creditors will prevail. It will be a rare case where the court will reject the wishes of the creditors.

11.62 When a decision approving the voluntary arrangement is made, it binds every person entitled to vote (whether or not represented), or who would have been entitled to vote if given notice of the meeting.

11.63 The supervisor of the arrangement (usually the nominee who has assisted in putting together the proposed CVA) is required to do all that is required to implement the CVA.

Administrative receivership

11.64 The holders of certain types of security (generally banks with a debenture and/or floating charge) may have the power to appoint an administrative receiver to a company. The administrative receiver will run the company and have control over all its assets and seek to realise them primarily for the party who appointed him. This process is becoming rarer since the Enterprise Act 2002, which effectively stopped administrative receivers being appointed in most situations, except under debentures or floating charges granted before 15 September 2003.

Scheme of arrangement

11.65 It has always been possible for a company in financial difficulties to agree some informal compromise or arrangement with its creditors, if those creditors unanimously agree to vary their entitlements. This avoids more formal procedures and the cost, delay and often (fatal) publicity that go with such procedures.

11.66 Speed is usually of vital importance. The difficulty is obtaining the unanimity of creditors who may have different interests and agendas. If one creditor 'breaks ranks', it is likely to ruin the prospects of such an arrangement succeeding. The greater the number of individual creditors, the less likely the prospect of success.

11.67 With the advent of administration and CVAs, such schemes are far less common than previously.

Liquidation

11.68 There are three forms of liquidation:

- compulsory;

- creditors' voluntary; and

- members' voluntary.

The first involves a court process, by which the company is compelled to go into liquidation, usually by a creditor. The other two do not involve the court.

Compulsory liquidation

11.69 There are various grounds on which a company may be wound up by the court, the most prominent of which is if the company is unable to pay its debts. There is also a general sweep-up provision which entitles the court to order the winding up of the company if it considers it just and equitable to do so.

11.70 In a similar way to bankruptcy, there is a procedure by which a company is deemed to be unable to pay its debts, namely if a 'statutory demand' has been served on the company and the company has not paid, secured or compounded the debt in question to the reasonable satisfaction of the creditor, or disputed the debt (see further **11.82–11.84** below) within 3 weeks of service. A statutory demand is a demand in a prescribed form, requiring the company to pay a sum due. The minimum debt in respect of which a petition can be demanded is £750.

11.71 A company will also be deemed to be unable to pay its debts if execution or other process issued on a judgment, decree or order of any court in favour of a creditor is returned unsatisfied in whole or in part, or if it can otherwise be shown that a company's assets are less than its liabilities, taking into account contingent and prospective liabilities (see **11.7**).

11.72 It is not always necessary to pursue the statutory demand route, but this is the most common means of ensuring that any petition subsequently presented for the winding up of the company cannot be challenged. If the statutory demand is not met within 3 weeks, the creditor is free to issue a petition for the winding up of the company. Issuing a statutory demand is often used by a creditor as a means of forcing payment by the company, but the debt claimed must not be in dispute (see **11.82–11.84** below).

11.73 On the hearing of the petition the court may dismiss it, adjourn it conditionally or unconditionally, or make an interim order or any other order it thinks fit. At any time after the presentation of a winding-up petition, the court may order a stay on any existing proceedings or prohibit the issue of any further proceedings.

11.74 Any disposition of the company's property after the commencement of winding up is, unless the court otherwise orders, void.

Creditors' voluntary liquidation

11.75 In the case of a creditors' voluntary liquidation, it is the obligation of the company to arrange a meeting of creditors not later than 14 days after the meeting at which the resolution for voluntary winding up is to be proposed. In that case the directors are required to lay a statement of affairs before the creditors. At the meeting of creditors, the appointment of the liquidator will be made and the liquidator will usually be the person nominated by the creditors, unless no such nomination is made. Any dispute regarding the identity of the liquidator will be resolved by the court.

The liquidator

11.76 It is the liquidator's job to gather in the company's property and apply it towards the creditors in the following order of priority.

11.77 To the extent that there are secured creditors, then their rights in their security remain. That security is not available to unsecured creditors. Preferential creditors are entitled to payment ahead of unsecured creditors: preferential debts consist of occupational pension scheme contributions, and amounts due to employees for unpaid remuneration (which includes wages or salary (which could include commission payments), guarantee payments, payments due in respect of time taken to look for work or training, time off for ante-natal care, time off for carrying out trade union activities, remuneration or suspension on medical or maternity grounds, remuneration under a protective award under s 189 of the Trade Union and Labour Relations (Consolidation) Act 1992) referable to the 4 months prior to the making of the winding-up order or resolution to wind up, but not exceeding £800 per employee, together with all arrears of holiday pay. After the non-preferred unsecured creditors have been paid back (which is highly unlikely), any surplus is paid to the shareholders.

11.78 There is no prohibition on a creditor continuing action against a company in a creditors' voluntary liquidation: the likely benefit of any such action would need to be considered.

11.79 The liquidator has a wide range of powers to compel compliance with his investigations into the company's affairs by any officer of the company, or any person who is or has been concerned or taken part in the promotion, formation or management of the company. If there is any lack of co-operation, the liquidator can apply to the court for an order compelling the person concerned to co-operate.

11.80 The liquidator will consider the conduct of the directors in the running of the company and, in particular, will consider whether there has been any malpractice, including fraud and wrongful trading (see **11.88–11.98**). The liquidator will also consider whether there have been any transactions at an undervalue or any preferences as defined in the Insolvency Act 1986.

Members' voluntary liquidation

11.81 As members' voluntary liquidations are done when the company is solvent, they are outside the scope of this chapter.

Disputed debts

11.82 It is quite common for creditors to threaten a company with winding-up proceedings or to serve a statutory demand upon a company. The courts have held that use of the winding-up procedures is not appropriate and is an abuse of its process where the debt in question is genuinely disputed. In the event that a company receives a statutory demand and/or is served with a winding-up petition based on a genuinely disputed debt, then it should immediately notify the creditor, providing full details, if not already provided, of the reasons for the dispute. The company should give the creditor an opportunity of withdrawing the statutory demand and/or the winding-up petition, failing which an application ought to be made to the court promptly to restrain presentation of a winding-up petition or, if already issued, to restrain advertisement of the petition until such time as the court is able to consider whether or not there is a genuinely disputed debt.

11.83 The court will not carry out a detailed investigation or carry out a mini-trial on the issue, but if there appear to be substantive grounds for disputing the debt (ie grounds which are not illusory or fanciful), then the court is likely to dismiss the petition or restrain the issue of a petition and to make an order for the costs incurred to be paid by the creditor.

11.84 It is vital, in such circumstances, that early action is taken. Once advertised, a winding-up petition becomes knowledge to the world and, in particular, to banks, who carry out a monitoring exercise on the issuing of petitions and will immediately freeze any bank account held in the company's name upon receiving notice of the issue of a winding-up petition. This can often have fatal consequences for the company, even where the debt in question is genuinely disputed.

Companies limited by guarantee

11.85 If the company is limited by guarantee, the members will have guaranteed to pay a certain amount to the company in the event of its winding up, which includes insolvency – this is usually a nominal amount such as £1: if it is that low, in practice it is unlikely to be collected from members. The level of guarantee is stated in the company's memorandum of association. The guarantee is only given by the members. It is not given by the directors (unless they are members).

11.86 In the unlikely event that funds remain after the creditors of a company limited by guarantee have been paid off, they will be distributed in accordance with the constitution: if the company is a charity, this will mean that the funds must be used for charitable purposes.

LOSS OF LIMITED LIABILITY PROTECTION

11.87 The protections of limited liability are not absolute. The directors of a limited company may lose the protections of limited liability and be made to contribute from their own personal assets towards the debts of an insolvent company in certain circumstances.

Fraudulent trading

11.88 By s 213 of the Insolvency Act 1986, on the application of the liquidator of a company, the court may order that any persons who were knowingly party to carrying on the business of the company with intent to defraud creditors, or for any fraudulent purpose, must make a contribution to the company's assets.

11.89 Intent to defraud creditors must be proved, and the onus of proof is on the liquidator. There must be evidence of actual dishonesty.

11.90 It has been held that in order to establish dishonesty under the Insolvency Act 1986, the court must find (1) that according to the ordinary standards of reasonable and honest people what was done was dishonest, and

(2) that the actor himself must have realised that the act was by those standards dishonest (*Morphites v Bernasconi* [2001] 2 BCLC 1). It is not necessary to prove knowledge that there would be no reasonable prospect of debts ever being paid: in *R v Grantham* [1984] 3 All ER 166 it was held that an intent to defraud might be inferred if the person concerned obtained credit when he knew there was no good reason for thinking that funds would be available to pay the debt when it became due or shortly afterwards.

Example

11.91   In *Re a Company (No 001418 of 1988)* [1990] BCC 526, a company went into insolvent liquidation owing £212,681. The court held on the facts that there had been fraudulent trading. It ruled that a person was knowingly party to the business of the company having been carried on with intent to defraud creditors if:

(a)   at the time when debts were incurred by the company, he had no good reason for thinking that funds would be available to pay those debts when they became due or shortly afterwards; and

(b)   there was dishonesty involving real moral blame according to current notions of fair trading.

The chairman, managing director and major shareholders had to pay £156,000 to the creditors.

11.92   It should be noted that it is not only directors who can be made liable for fraudulent trading. In the case of a charity or trading company, in addition to the charity trustees or directors of the trading company, the employees of an insolvent charitable company or trading company could be liable for fraudulent trading (if proven).

Wrongful trading

11.93   The liquidator of an insolvent company can also seek a contribution to the company's assets from a person who is or has been a director of the company, if it can be established that at some time before the commencement of the winding up of the company, that person knew or ought to have known that there was no reasonable prospect that the company would avoid going into insolvent liquidation, but the company traded on for a period of time after that conclusion was reached or ought to have been reached (IA 1986, s 214). The court will not make an order requiring such a contribution if it is satisfied that, subsequent to reaching that conclusion (provided it was reached at the proper time), the person concerned took every such step with a view to minimising the potential loss to the company's creditors as he ought to have done (s 214(3)).

11.94   The test is an objective one. The director must act as a reasonably diligent person having both the director's own knowledge, skill and experience and the general knowledge, skill and experience that may reasonably be expected of a person carrying out the same functions as the director. The standard expected will vary from one case to another. In *Re Produce Marketing Consortium Limited* [1989] 3 All ER 1, the court held that the expertise expected of a director is much less extensive in a small company in a modest way of business with simple accounting procedures and equipment than in a large company with sophisticated procedures.

11.95 This point is of particular relevance to charity trustees. Charity trustees are almost invariably non-executive directors of charitable companies. They may meet rarely (say 4 or 6 times a year) and are self-evidently very dependent on the professional full-time staff. They have to trust their staff. This is entirely fair, and the case of *Norman v Theodore Goddard* [1991] BCLC 1028 has shown that a director is entitled to trust persons in a position of responsibility until there is reason to distrust them.

11.96 What standard of duty will the court expect of charity trustees in a wrongful trading case? Will it be a lower standard than that of a full-time employee who is also a director (which is almost invariably the case in the private sector)? So far (to the authors' knowledge) no case of wrongful trading has been brought against the volunteer directors of a charitable company or a trading company, but whilst it would be reasonable to argue for a lower standard than for a full-time employee/director, non-executive directors of charitable companies should not rely on this being accepted and should operate to the standard of non-charitable directors so far as possible. It should be emphasised that a person with financial or legal skills, or a financial function (eg the Treasurer) would not be judged on this basis of a lower standard of duty, and thus will be at greater risk.

11.97 Wrongful trading applies to directors and to shadow directors. For the purposes of the Companies Acts a director is anyone who occupies the position of a director, by whatever name called. It is not necessary, in order to be treated as a director, for the director to have been registered as such at Companies House. This could include, for example, a chief executive. A 'shadow director' is a person in accordance with whose directions or instructions the directors of the company have been accustomed to act. This does not apply where the directors act on advice given to them by that person in a professional capacity. In the case of a charitable company or a trading company, it is possible that a charismatic and powerful chief executive (who almost invariably will not be a trustee and may not be a director of the trading company) could be treated as a shadow director.

11.98 Various provisions of the Charities Act 1993, the Companies Act 2006 and the Trustee Act 1925 allow the court, or the Charity Commission, to relieve an individual company director or charity trustee from liability if they have acted honestly and reasonably and ought fairly to be excused. These provisions will, however, apply neither to wrongful trading, nor to the liability of a charity trustee of an unincorporated charity to creditors of that charity.

LOOMING INSOLVENCY – THE PRACTICAL IMPLICATIONS

11.99   If insolvency looms for a charity or its trading company, the advice to give the charity trustees will vary according to the form of the charity's constitutional structure.

The implications for unincorporated organisations

11.100   As the debts and obligations of an unincorporated organisation are the personal liability and responsibility of the charity trustees (if the charity has insufficient assets to meet the debts and obligations), the primary aim of the trustees will be to minimise the build-up of debts and liabilities and to increase the assets by raising cash. But if attempts to generate income or cash fail, then in view of their personal risk, charity trustees may be keen to run down the organisation so as to minimise the chance of incurring personal debts, or even bankruptcy, or of being accused of breach of trust.

11.101   On the other hand, by closing down, new liabilities will crystallise. Moreover, closing down is easier said than done. Many charities will have long-term liabilities (eg a lease of a building or obligations under a contract), which it may prove impossible to assign. Hence, the trustees may find themselves obliged to continue to pay rent and service charges even after the charity has ceased to operate. If the charity lacks the means to pay these costs, the trustees will have to meet them personally. The advice about monitoring the charity's financial position and meeting regularly given for companies (see **11.103** below) applies equally to unincorporated organisations.

The implications for companies

11.102   In the case of a limited company, the charity trustees or the directors of a trading company will be anxious to ensure that the protections of limited liability are not lost. That means avoiding any allegation that the charity trustees or the directors have been guilty of wrongful trading or breach of trust.

11.103   Charity trustees and directors must be able to show that they took all reasonable steps to minimise the loss to the company's creditors. This means in practical terms that, once they know or ought to know that there is no reasonable prospect of avoiding insolvent liquidation, the charity trustees/ directors must:

(1)   Recognise that their primary duty is no longer to fulfil the objects of the charity or the trading company, but to act in the best interests of the creditors. Hence, they should not incur further liabilities (in the case of a charity) on charitable purposes, but rather should endeavour to pay off the creditors. The dilemma which the charity trustees/directors face in such circumstances is difficult. They must be neither cowardly nor rash.

They must not rush into liquidation (which might damage the interests of the creditors), nor must they plough on with insouciant disregard for the potential damage to creditors. They must not be carried away by the idea that because the charity fulfils a noble cause, and the trading company helps it, that this allows them to ignore their legal obligations to creditors. Nor should trustees or directors succumb to the inherent optimism of many that, in the words of Mr Micawber, 'something will turn up'. To protect the charity trustees and directors from a claim of wrongful trading, their actions must have been reasonable as viewed from the standpoint of the reasonable director. Belief in a possibility or trust in providence (cynical though this may sound) is not regarded by sceptical British judges as being reasonable.

(2) Hold regular meetings to show that they took matters seriously and acted with the interests of the creditors in mind. This may require meeting at very short notice.

(3) Ensure that they have appropriate written legal advice – again, so that they can show that they have acted responsibly. Such advice should be given to all the trustees and directors. It is not sufficient for it to be given to the chairman or chief executive – they should ensure that it is passed on, so that all the trustees and directors can make an informed decision. Equally, the organisation's legal advisor should seek to ensure that this is done.

(4) Ensure that proper and detailed minutes are kept of all meetings so that there is an adequate 'paper trail' to show how decisions were reached. Provided decisions are made carefully and with the benefit of professional advice (assuming, of course, that the charity or trading company has the financial resources to pay for such advice), a court will be reluctant to substitute with the benefit of hindsight its own commercial judgment for that of the charity trustees and directors, unless it considers that no reasonable director could have concluded that the action taken was in the interest of the creditors.

The concerns of the Charity Commission

11.104 If a charity or its trading company becomes insolvent and creditors are unpaid, there is a good chance of adverse press publicity or a complaint being made to a Member of Parliament or to the Charity Commission. In either case, this could trigger an investigation by the Charity Commission into the conduct of the charity's affairs.

11.105 The Charity Commission acts to protect the interests of the beneficiaries and potential beneficiaries of the charity. If the inquiry concludes that the charity trustees have been negligent in their conduct of the charity's affairs, the Charity Commission can petition the court for an order that the trustees make a contribution from their own assets to the charity to compensate it for loss suffered as a result of the breach of trust by the trustees. Negligence can constitute a breach of trust. This can apply to any charity howsoever constituted, whether incorporated or unincorporated. Limited liability gives the charity trustees no protection in this context.

Example

11.106 For example, a charity lends £250,000 to its trading company. The trading company becomes insolvent. The charity is forced to write off the loan. As a result, it fails the balance sheet test and the loss of the cash means it also fails the cash flow test.

11.107 The charity ceases its activities as it is insolvent. The Charity Commission concludes that the investment by the charity in the company was negligent and seeks to recover the monies lost from the charity trustees personally.

11.108 Although this train of events has not yet happened (to the writer's knowledge), such a scenario is perfectly possible.

11.109 This example illustrates again the need for the charity trustees to have proper minutes of all meetings and decisions so that, if investigated, they can show that, for example, the decision to invest charity monies in a trading company was fair and reasonable at the time (see Chapter 7).

Personal guarantees

11.110 A director of a limited company may agree to give a personal guarantee for the obligations of the company (e g under a lease). In such a case, that director will be personally liable under the guarantee.

PERSONAL LIABILITIES OF CHARITY TRUSTEES – WHAT CAN BE DONE?

Limiting liability by insurance

11.111 Some of the risks which are faced by charities carrying on trade themselves or through their trading companies, and which may force them into insolvency, can be reduced by effecting appropriate insurance cover (see Chapter 10). All charities (but especially unincorporated charities, in view of the potential personal liability of the trustees) should consider the relevance of:

(1)   public liability insurance;

(2)   product liability insurance (if selling/manufacturing products);

(3)   professional indemnity insurance (if supplying services);

(4) libel insurance (if publishing material);

(5) fidelity insurance (to protect the charity/trading company if an employee or trustee runs off with the charity's money);

(6) contents insurance (to protect the charity/trading company from loss or damage to its property, bearing in mind that if it leases equipment, the lease will almost certainly oblige the tenant to insure the property).

11.112 Failing to have adequate insurance could mean claims being made against the trustees personally (in the case of an unincorporated charity), if the charity does not have the assets to meet an uninsured claim. Moreover, failure to insure might be held to constitute a breach of duty by the trustees, exposing them (however the charity is constituted) to personal liability.

11.113 One form of insurance policy – trustee indemnity insurance – covers particular risks to which charity trustees are exposed (see **10.57–10.59**). Under a trustee indemnity policy, a charity trustee (and this can also be used for employees such as the chief executive) will have cover against personal liability arising from his or her breach of duty, breach of trust, negligence, error or omission or wrongful trading. The insurance cover will not protect the insured trustee if he has been guilty of a criminal act or has acted deliberately or recklessly. But it may well cover liability for wrongful trading, and associated legal costs, depending on the terms of the policy.

11.114 Since February 2007, it has been possible for trustee indemnity insurance to be purchased by the charity for the benefit of its trustees, provided the charity's constitution does not expressly prohibit such a purchase (Charities Act 1993, s 73F).

11.115 Trustee indemnity insurance is not a form of financial guarantee. It does not underwrite charity trustees' liabilities for the debts of a charity due to a third party if the charity is insolvent. It does not remove the trading risks to which the charity trustees of an unincorporated charity, in particular, are exposed.

11.116 A similar form of insurance – directors' liability insurance – can be taken out to protect the directors of a trading company.

Limiting liability by contract

11.117 As has been seen, charity trustees of an unincorporated charity do not enjoy the benefits of limited liability (although these protections are not absolute). But it is perfectly legitimate and effective for the charity trustees of an unincorporated charity to seek to have written into any contract to which the charity is party that the liability of the charity trustees shall be limited to the assets of the charity, so that the charity trustees shall incur no personal liability whatsoever. When it is explained that charity trustees are volunteers who perform their task for free, it is often possible to negotiate such a clause (eg on a contract for the delivery of services). It is more difficult to do this when acquiring something on a standard form contract (eg the purchase of goods or the hire of a photocopier), but may be simpler when the charity is issuing its own contracts, at least where the charity is in a position to dictate the terms. Note, however, that it is not always possible for the other party to validly 'contract out' of legal rights they may have against the charity trustees (eg employees generally cannot waive their employment law rights without entering into a written agreement on which they have received advice from a suitably qualified adviser or via an ACAS conciliator, and any attempt to do so which does not comply with statutory requirements will be void).

11.118 This is only useful in the case of contracts. It does not limit the charity trustees' liability in relation to third parties not party to a contract (see **11.15–11.29**). To cover some of these other risks, it is necessary to have proper insurance cover. However, for unincorporated charities which are carrying on a trade, clauses to limit trustees' personal liability written into contracts could be vital.

Limiting liability by incorporation

11.119 The trustees of an unincorporated charity labour under greater risks if the charity is insolvent as compared with the trustees of a charity which is a limited company. Hence, it makes good sense for any unincorporated charity which is carrying on any serious trading activities or employing staff, leasing buildings or equipment or engaging in any form of service provision, to consider transforming the charity into a limited company.

11.120 This process involves establishing a new charitable company, with the same objects as the unincorporated organisation, which must be registered with the Charity Commission. The assets and liabilities of the unincorporated organisation should then be transferred to the 'new' incorporated charity.

11.121 Once the charitable incorporated organisation (or 'CIO') becomes available as a legal form, a similar process will be possible should an unincorporated charity wish to become a CIO.

THE CONSEQUENCES OF INSOLVENCY

11.122 The consequences of insolvency have already been discussed at various points, but the following examples further illustrate the points discussed.

Uncompleted contracts

11.123 The other party to the contract will have a claim for breach of contract if a charity or a trading company ceases to deliver its contractual obligations due to insolvency. In the case of a limited company this claim will be made against the liquidator. The claimant will be one of the unsecured creditors of the company. Hence, the chance of the claimant recovering much by way of damages is remote.

11.124 In the case of an unincorporated charity, the position is different. If the contract did not contain a clause limiting the trustees' liability, the claimant will be able to sue the trustees personally (or any one or more of them) if the charity has insufficient resources to meet the liability.

Employment rights of employees

11.125 Certain sums due to employees (see **11.77**) are preferential, so that if the charity (being a limited company) or a trading company becomes insolvent, the employees' claim in the liquidation for these sums will rank in priority to the ordinary creditors. If the charity is unincorporated and action is brought against the trustees personally, forcing any of them into personal bankruptcy, the same rules concerning preference apply. However, it should be noted that an employee's entitlement to pay for the notice period and/or to a redundancy payment on termination of his employment is not a preferential debt. Employees rank as normal, unsecured creditors in so far as their claims for redundancy payments are concerned.

11.126 The Insolvency Service's Redundancy Payments Office covers various liabilities of insolvent employers from the National Insurance Fund, namely:

(1)   Arrears of pay (in respect of up to 8 weeks).

(2)   Notice pay, where notice was either not given by the employer or given but not paid, subject to a maximum of 1 week per completed year of service, up to a maximum of 12 weeks, and provided the employee in question has a minimum of 1 month's continuous service.

(3)   Holiday pay, provided it relates to the period of 12 months immediately prior to the insolvency and subject to a maximum of 6 weeks.

(4)   A basic award of compensation for unfair dismissal made by an employment tribunal.

(5)   Reasonable repayments of any premium or fee paid by an articled clerk or apprentice.

(6)   Statutory redundancy payments.

All of these entitlements are restricted to a maximum weekly pay rate of £350 (for insolvencies after 1 February 2009).

The interrelationship between an insolvent trading company and its parent charity

11.127 As discussed at **7.190–7.224**, the relationship between a charity and its trading company has to be kept at arm's length. The two are distinct legal entities and although the same, or many of the same, people may serve on the board of the trading company and as trustees of the charity, those individuals have different duties and responsibilities, depending upon which particular role they are fulfilling at any one time (see **7.167–7.176**). Provided all is well financially, these distinctions should not cause any problems. But if the trading company's financial position weakens and questions arise about its solvency, then the distinctions between the two organisations become more stark, and the differing duties of the directors and trustees become more obvious.

11.128 The relationship between a charity and its insolvent trading company will vary as to whether or not the trading company is fulfilling one of the primary purposes of the charity. Some charities, so as to lessen risk, put some of their primary purpose trading activities through a trading company (see **7.13–7.24** and **7.142–7.148**). For example, an educational charity might put its book publishing activities through a separate trading company. In this case, the relationship between the charity and the trading company will be different from that where the charity's trading company is undertaking a pure trading activity which does not fulfil one of the charity's primary purposes.

11.129 In the case of a trading company which is fulfilling the charity's primary purposes, the charity could, for example, take the activities of the trading company back into the charity or support it financially more readily than if the trading company were purely undertaking general trading.

11.130 Mention has already been made (see **11.6–11.13** above) of the balance sheet and cash flow tests which are used to assess whether or not a limited company is solvent. The trading company might be insolvent on the balance sheet test because its liabilities outstrip its assets. At that point, the directors of the trading company may request the charity (which may have lent monies to the trading company) to convert the loan into share capital in the trading company. This will have the effect of improving the trading company's balance sheet. But it might well damage the charity, because it will forgo its position as a secured creditor (see Chapter 7, which recommends that loans from a charity to its trading company should be secured), and become instead, as a shareholder, deferred to all other creditors. This may be in the best interests of the trading company so as to allow it to meet the balance sheet test, but it may not be in the best interests of the charity – which will lose its security.

11.131 Alternatively, the trading company may fail the cash flow test and need funds in order to meet its obligations as they fall due. It may ask the charity to lend it the necessary working capital. But should the charity agree?

11.132 These questions raise the issues of conflict of interest which can confront persons who are both directors of the trading company and trustees of the charity when the trading company faces issues of insolvency. The trustees have to act in the best interests of the charity in order to preserve its reputation and assets and to be able to continue its activities, but as directors of the trading company, those same individuals will need to take all necessary steps to act in the best interests of the creditors. Hence, directors of a trading company who are also trustees of the parent charity face a conflict of interests in such circumstances. They may also be concerned about their potential personal liabilities in the event of it being held that as directors of the trading company they had engaged in wrongful trading and therefore have a personal interest in ensuring that the trading company continues to trade, even if this means relying on the charity's support. This provides an additional dimension for conflict of interest. Trustees who find themselves in such a position of conflict should not vote on any resolution of the charity which considers giving financial support to the trading company, and should declare their interest at all meetings considering such matters. (See **7.167–7.176** and **7.182–7.187** for more on conflicts of interest.)

11.133 But, leaving aside questions of conflict of interest, can a charity give financial support to its trading company when the trading company is facing insolvency? Inevitably, such a decision will depend on the facts of each individual case. No generalised answer can be given. However, a number of issues should be taken into account:

(1) Does the trading company share the same name as the charity? If so, will the charity's reputation be damaged if the trading company is allowed to go into insolvent liquidation? It is likely that the trading company will share the charity's name, and that if the trading company goes into insolvent liquidation leaving creditors unpaid, this will damage the charity's reputation. However, just because this is the likely outcome of the trading company's insolvency, it should not in itself permit the charity trustees to expend the charity's monies in supporting the trading company. It is just one factor that can be taken into account, but should not be an overwhelming one.

(2) As explored in Chapter 7 (see **7.94**), the Charity Commission makes it clear in its guidance that:

> 'Investing in a company which is not economically viable, and has no real prospect of becoming so, involves a failure on the part of the trustees to discharge their duties with regard to investment. This applies more strongly where the only object in making the investment is to prevent the company from going into insolvent liquidation.'

The fact that the trading company is facing an emergency should not allow the trustees of the charity to suspend their normal obligations in relation to any proposed investment (see Chapter 7).

(3)   The trustees should also remember that, although claims may be made by aggrieved creditors of the trading company that the charity is a de facto guarantor of the trading company's debts, this will not, in fact, be the case. The charity does not have the legal capacity to enter into gratuitous guarantees in respect of the debts of its trading company (see **7.155–7.164**).

CONCLUSION

11.134   If a charity or its trading company appears to be potentially insolvent, the trustees of the charity or the directors of the trading company should assess as quickly as possible the organisation's true financial picture. Such an assessment should be based upon sober realism and not optimism. Any evaluation of the charity's or trading company's liabilities should at least consider the break-up basis of valuation (ie should take into account those liabilities which will arise if the organisation goes into insolvent liquidation or ceases to trade, such as redundancy payments, termination payments under lease agreements and any financial penalties for breach of contract).

11.135   It is wise to take early professional advice, so as to have an objective assessment of the figures presented, bearing in mind that in some cases the very financial crisis may be the result of ill-considered actions by the self-same people who are now producing the financial information for the trustees/directors to evaluate! Clearly, when an organisation is considering questions of solvency, it may be very strapped for cash and time, but nonetheless it is worthwhile for it to take professional advice in such circumstances if it possibly can. The trustees and directors should ensure that such advice is confirmed in writing and circulated to all members of the governing body or board of directors, so that all the relevant persons are informed.

11.136   It is also worth emphasising that there can be considerable personal tensions when questions of insolvency arise. The trustees may feel very nervous about their own personal position (especially if the charity is unincorporated) and their resulting potential personal liabilities. The staff, who the trustees may feel are responsible for having put the charity or the trading company into the insolvent position that it is in, are unlikely to risk personal liabilities in the same way as the trustees, but may face a loss of employment. Such tensions should, so far as possible, be confronted and understood early on in the process of evaluating the financial position of the insolvent organisation, so that all parties involved understand the various concerns, and matters can be discussed in an open and thorough manner.

Appendix 1

USEFUL ADDRESSES

Advertising Standards Authority
Mid City Place
71 High Holborn
London WC1V 6QT
Tel: 020 7492 2222
Fax: 020 7242 3696
Website: www.asa.org.uk

Association of Charity Shops
Central House
14 Upper Woburn Place
London WC1H 0AE
Tel: 020 7255 4470
Fax: 020 7255 4475
Website: www.charityshops.org.uk

Association of Medical Research Charities
61 Gray's Inn Road
London WC1X 8TL
Tel: 020 7269 8820
Fax: 020 7269 8821
Website: www.amrc.org.uk

Charities Advisory Trust
Radius Works
Back Lane
Hampstead
London NW3 1HL
Tel: 020 7794 9835
Fax: 020 7431 3739
Website: www.charitiesadvisorytrust.co.uk

Charity Commission
PO Box 1227
Liverpool L69 3UG
Tel: 0845 3000 218
Fax: 0151 7031 555
Website: www.charity-commission.gov.uk

Commission for the Compact
77 Paradise Circus
Queensway
Birmingham B1 2DT
Tel: 0121 237 5900
Fax: 0121 233 2120
Website: www.thecompact.org.uk

Community Interest Company Regulator
CIC Team
Room 3.68
Companies House
Crown Way
Maindy
Cardiff CF14 3UZ
Tel: 029 2034 6228
Fax: 029 2034 6229
Website: www.cicregulator.gov.uk

Companies House
Crown Way
Maindy
Cardiff CF14 3UZ
Tel: 0303 1234 500
Website: www.companieshouse.gov.uk

Directory of Social Change
24 Stephenson Way
London NW1 2DP
Tel: 020 7391 4800
Fax: 020 7391 4808
Website: www.dsc.org.uk

Gambling Commission
Victoria Square House
Victoria Square
Birmingham B2 4BP
Tel: 0121 230 6666
Fax: 0121 230 6720
Website: www.gamblingcommission.gov.uk

HM Revenue and Customs Charities
St John's House
Merton Road
Bootle
Merseyside L69 9BB
Tel: 0845 3020 203
Website: www.hmrc.gov.uk/charities

Institute of Fundraising
Park Place
12 Lawn Lane
London SW8 1UD
Tel: 020 7840 1000
Fax: 020 7840 1001
Website: www.institute-of-fundraising.org.uk

National Council for Voluntary Organisations (NCVO)
Regent's Wharf
8 All Saints Street
London N1 9RL
Tel: 020 7713 6161
Fax: 020 7713 6300
Website: www.ncvo-vol.org.uk

Office of Fair Trading
Fleetbank House
2–6 Salisbury Square
London EC4Y 8JX
Tel: 0845 722 4499
Website www.oft.gov.uk

Office of the Third Sector
Second Floor
Admiralty Arch
South Side
The Mall
London SW1A 2WH
Tel: 020 7276 6400
Website: www.cabinetoffice.gov.uk/third_sector

Social Enterprise Coalition
Southbank House
Black Prince Road
London SE1 7SJ
Tel: 020 7793 2323
Fax: 020 7793 2326
Website: www.socialenterprise.org.uk

INDEX

References are to paragraph numbers.